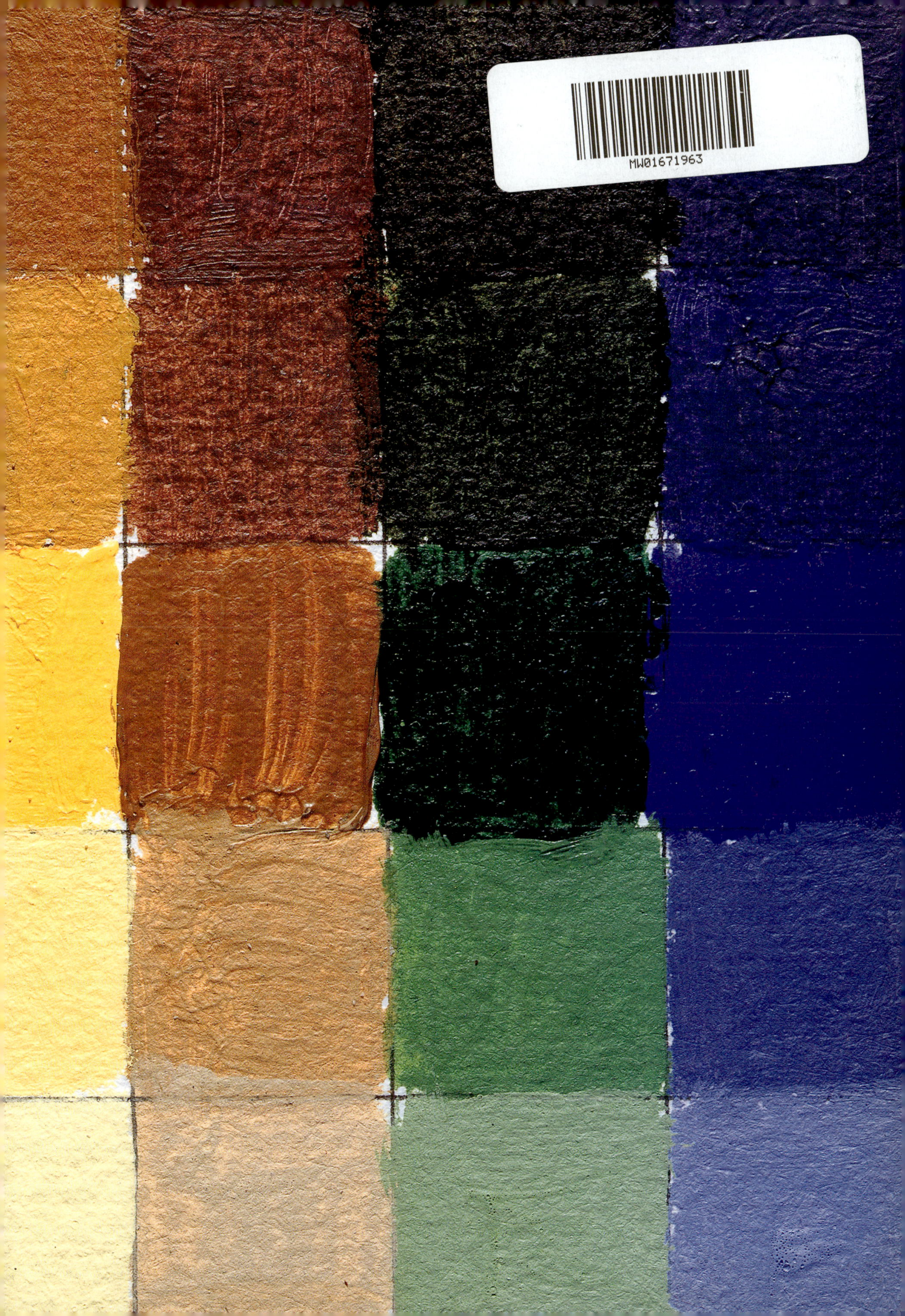

The Painter's Corner

LIGHT AND COLOR

BARRON'S

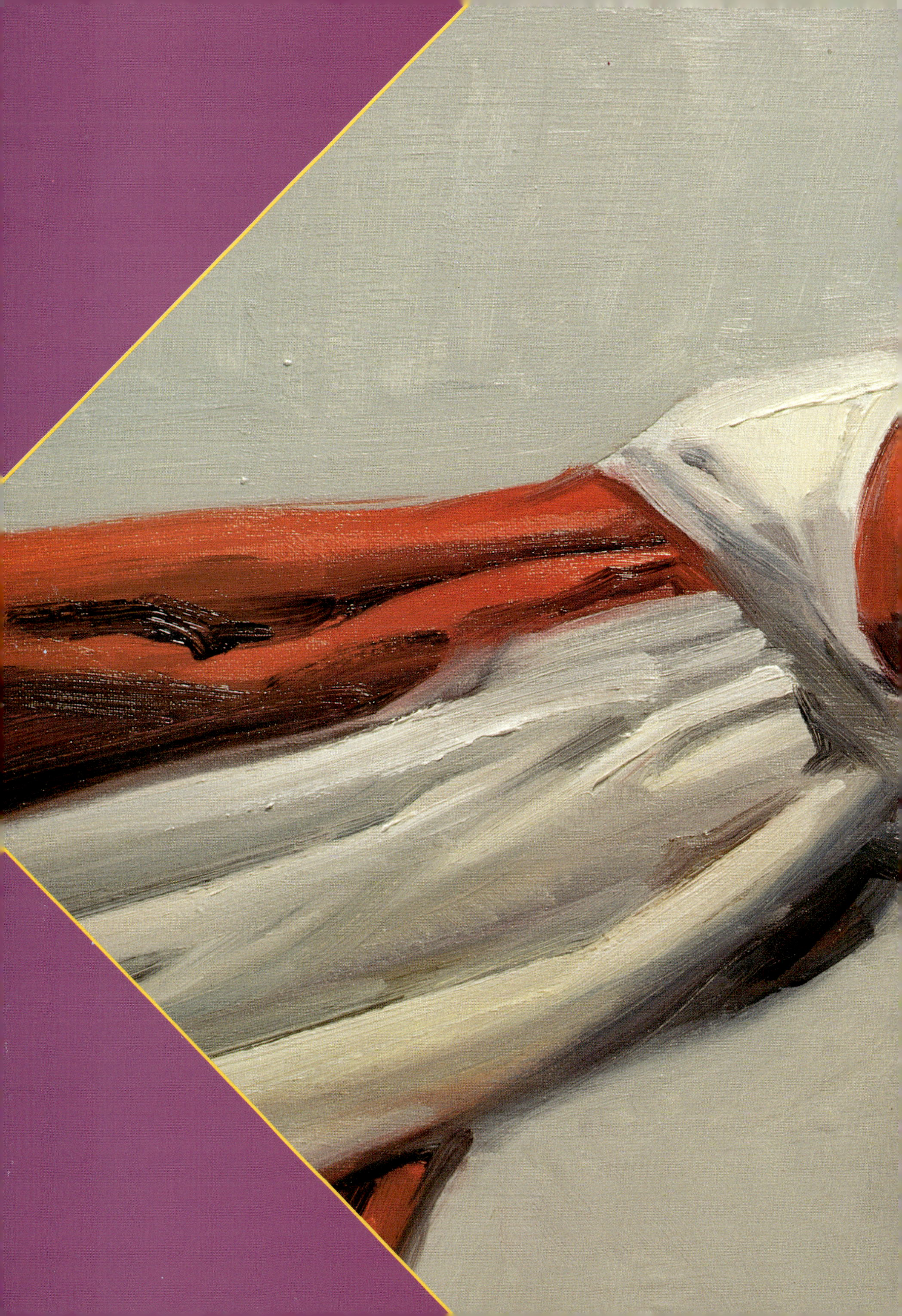

LIGHT AND COLOR

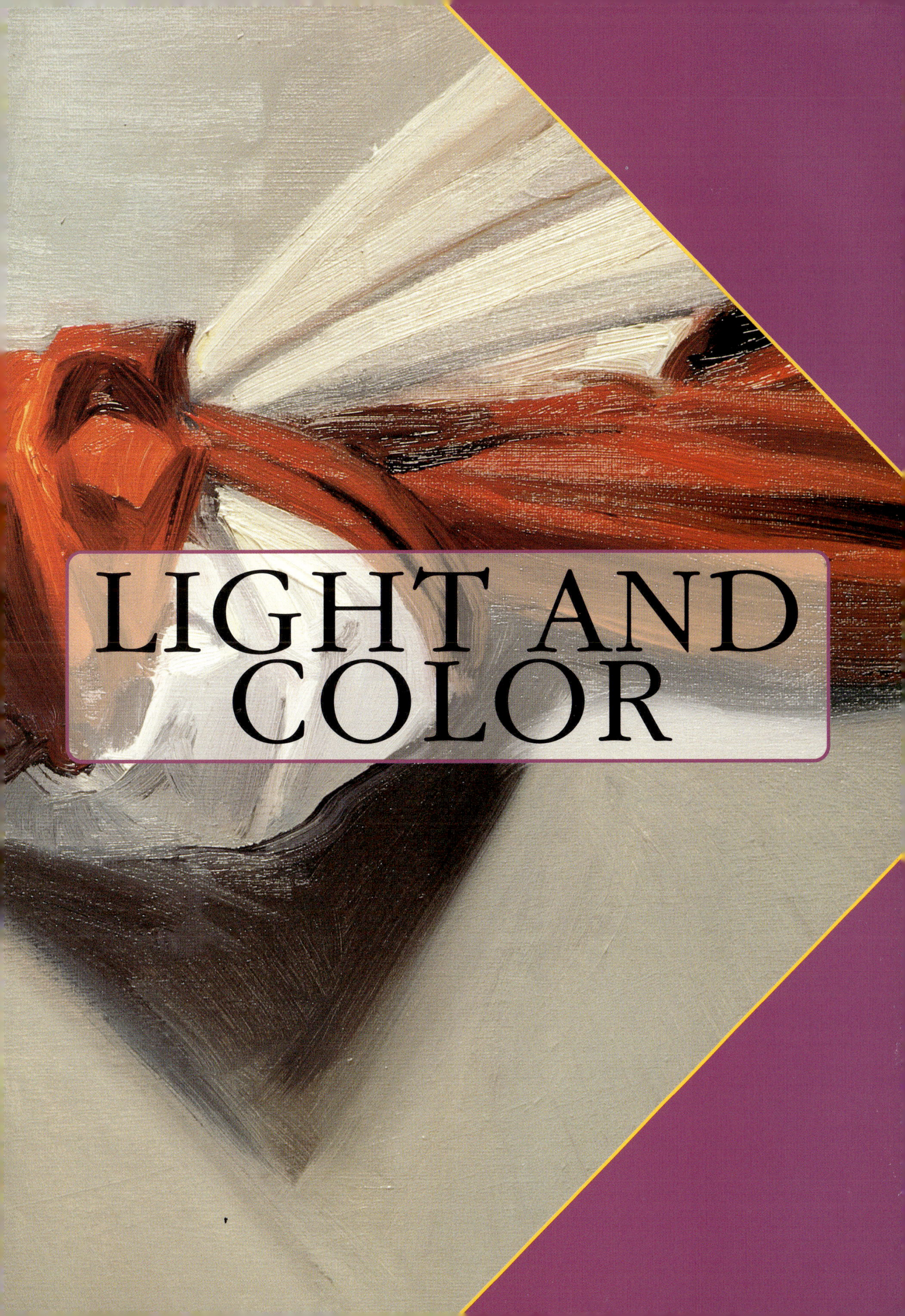

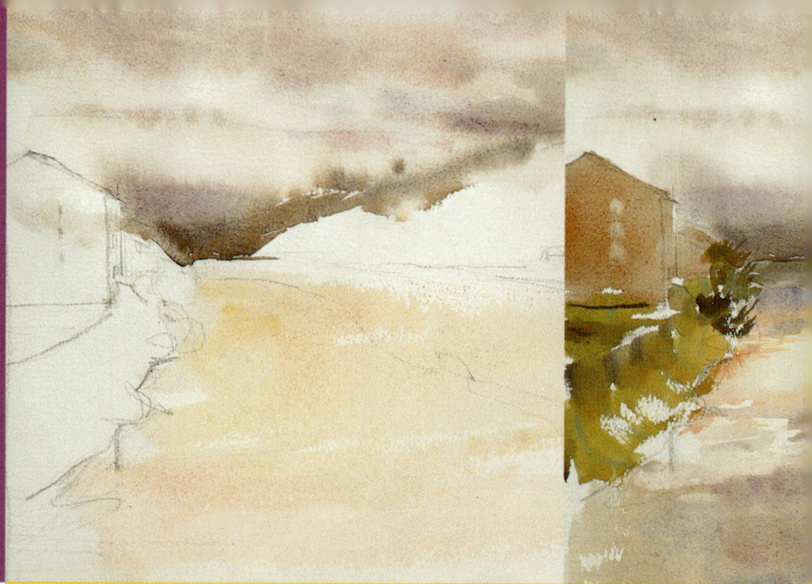

Original title of the book in Spanish: El Rincón del Pintor: *LUZ Y COLOR*

Published by Parramón Ediciones, S.A., Barcelona, Spain

Authors: Parramón's Editorial Team
Text and Coordination: Josep Asunción
Exercises: Josep Asunción, Vicenç Ballestar, Josep Maria Cabané, Mercedes Gaspar, and Ramon Massana
Photographs: Nos & Soto

Translation from Spanish: Eric A. Bye, M.A.

Acknowledgments:
The author and Parramón Ediciones, S.A., wish to express their appreciation to Montse Guasch and Manuel Bofarull for their kind collaboration on this book.

All inquiries should be addressed to:
Barron's Educational Series, Inc.
250 Wireless Blvd.
Hauppauge, NY 11788
www.barronseduc.com

International Standard Book No. 0-7641-5704-3

Library of Congress Catalog Card No.: 2004102805

Printed in Spain
9 8 7 6 5 4 3 2 1

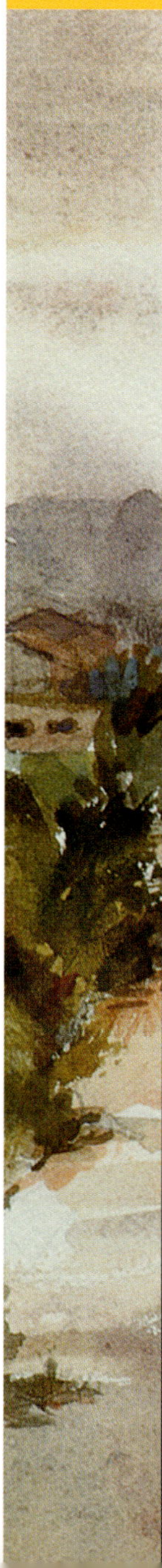

Contents

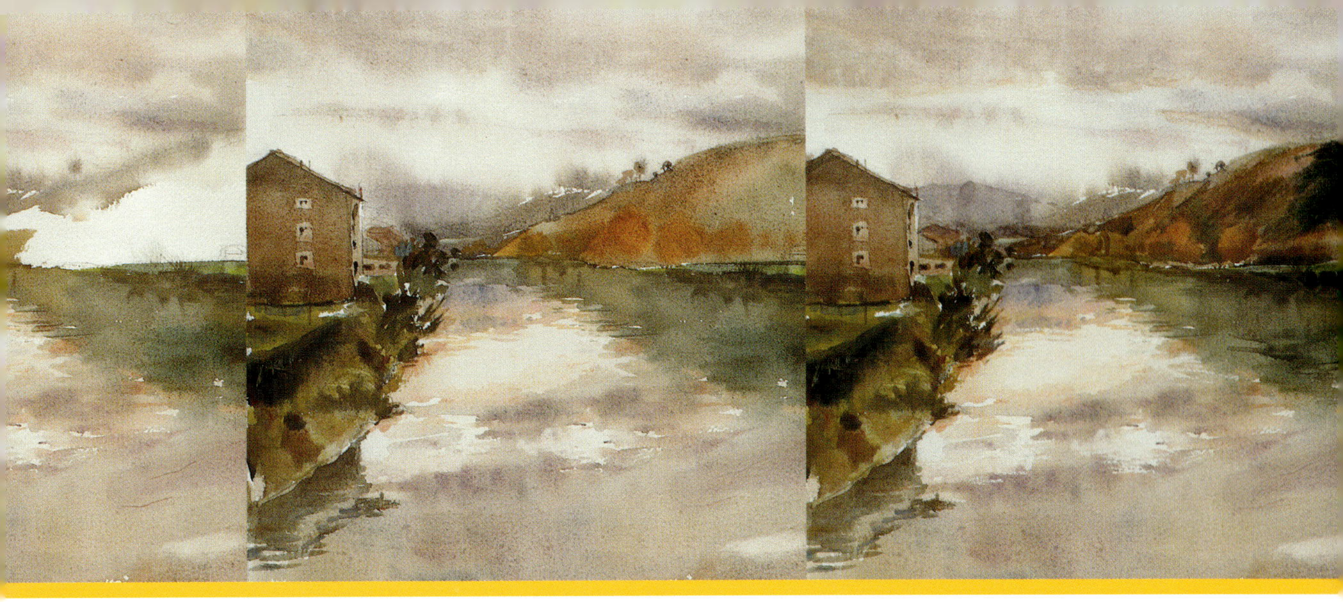

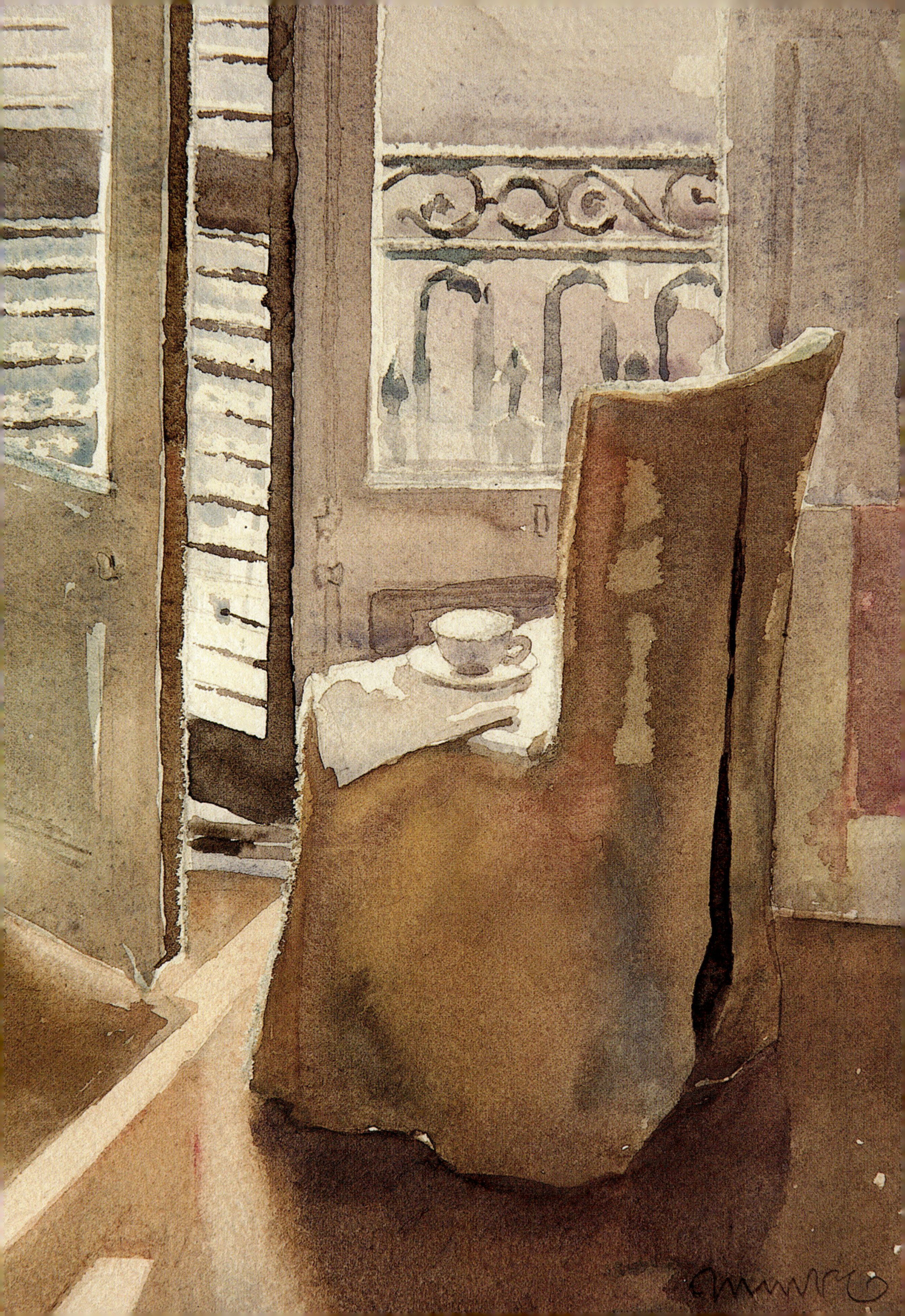

Introduction

Even though they may appear to be two distinct subjects, light and color amount to the same thing. Images have their origin in light, and color is a phenomenon of perception whose *raison d'être* is light. Even if we were to focus strictly on monochromatic chiaroscuro, traditionally in black and white, we would still be dealing with color, since both black and white contain the sum of all colors.

In the first half of this book we will present the theoretical foundations of contrasts involving color and light. The first several pages constitute an introduction that approaches the most expressive dimension of light and color from historical references and the most important concepts. Then we will explain clearly the aspects that pertain to visual perception and color in order to present the theoretical bases for an explanation of the pictorial methods of chromatic chiaroscuro in the chapter entitled "Light Defines Shapes and Space." This first half of the book closes with a chapter devoted to the most commonly used mediums in representing light and color: pencil, charcoal, pastels, inks, watercolors, oils, and acrylics. We will present a vision of the entire field, illustrated with clear examples taken from painters who have approached the subject of light using very different techniques throughout the history of painting. In the second half of the book, the reader will see very clearly how ten practical exercises on very different themes are carried out. These pages analyze the technical and expressive process of each picture. There are ten examples: still lifes, landscapes, interiors, and figures, in which light and color make up the expressive focus of the works.

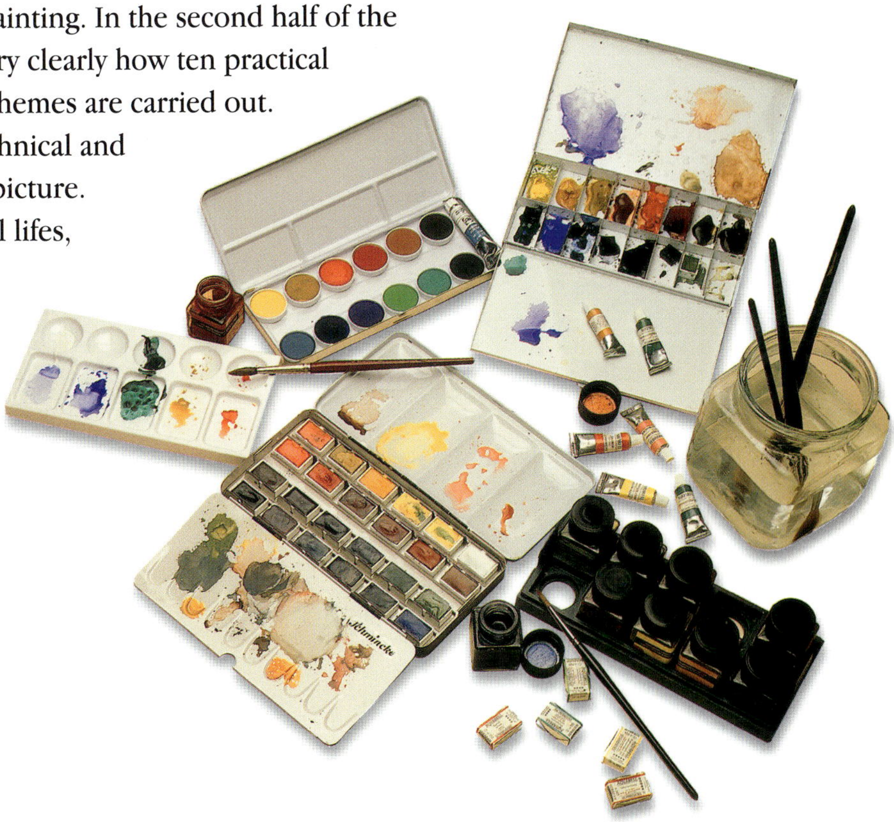

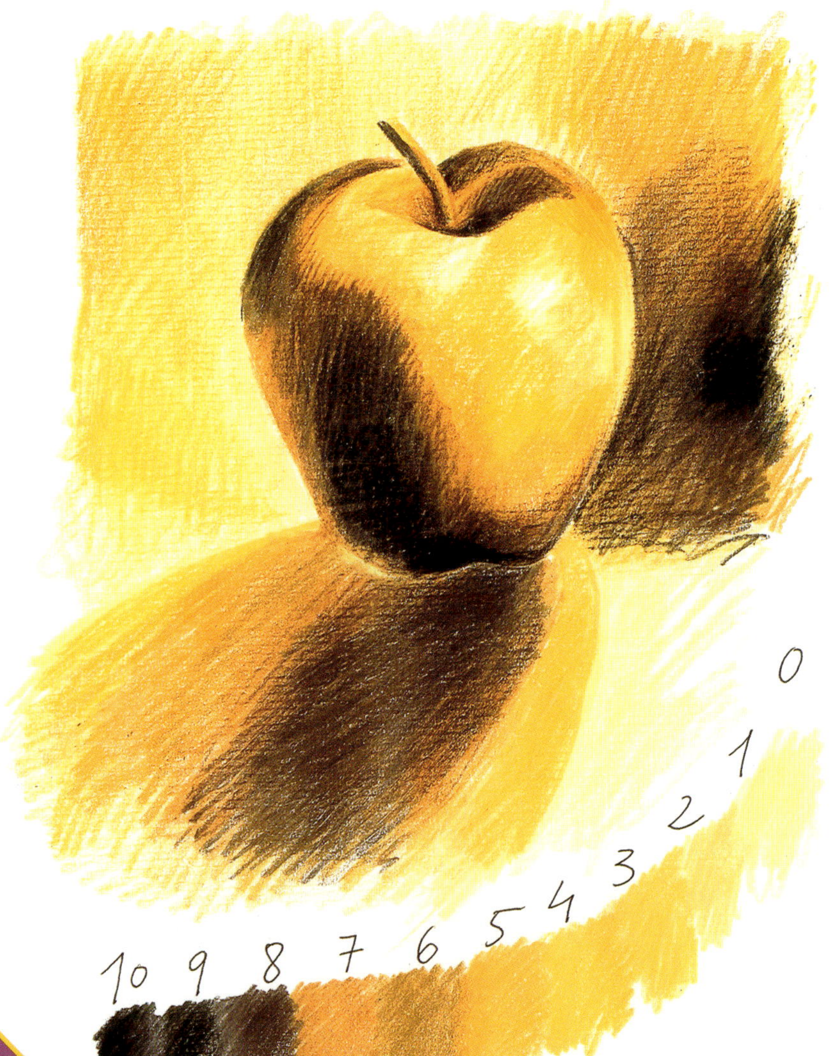
10 9 8 7 6 5 4 3 2 1 0

Light and Color in Artistic Expression

We understand art to be a channel of communication through which there flows a continuum of content that originates in the artist. In this chapter we will deal with the most expressive aspects of light and color, the two elements that create the image.

Up to the twentieth century, the history of painting was made up of a succession of fluctuating moments that would periodically swing from one extreme to another like a pendulum. At one extreme there was art subjected to reason, whose goal was knowledge of nature with a view to dominating it; at the other extreme there was art governed by passion, whose goal was the purest expression of the experience. Thus the classicism of Greece and Rome was succeeded by medieval art, which was more cryptic and mysterious, and whose strength grew out of symbolism. That led to the Renaissance, which was analytical, monumental, and rigorous; that subsequently gave way to the Baroque, which was intimist, emotional, spiritual, or sensuous, depending on the era. Up to the Baroque, artistic periods lasted for centuries, but starting with the nineteenth century they grew shorter, until styles as different as the perfectionism of Neoclassicism and the passion of Romanticism came to exist side by side.

◆

In order to transmit intimism, it was necessary to turn to the baroque chiaroscuro, but a more lavish color scheme in full light was required for evoking great epics.

◆

The way of using light and color was different at every stage. To transmit intimism, it was necessary to turn to the baroque chiaroscuro, but a more lavish color scheme in full light was required for evoking great epics.

With Impressionism, the gates were opened to the artist's personal vision. The painters took their bearings from their own experience, on the "impression" received, rather than in ideals or canons imposed from the outside. Light, which creates impressions, was the main focus of the Impressionists' art.

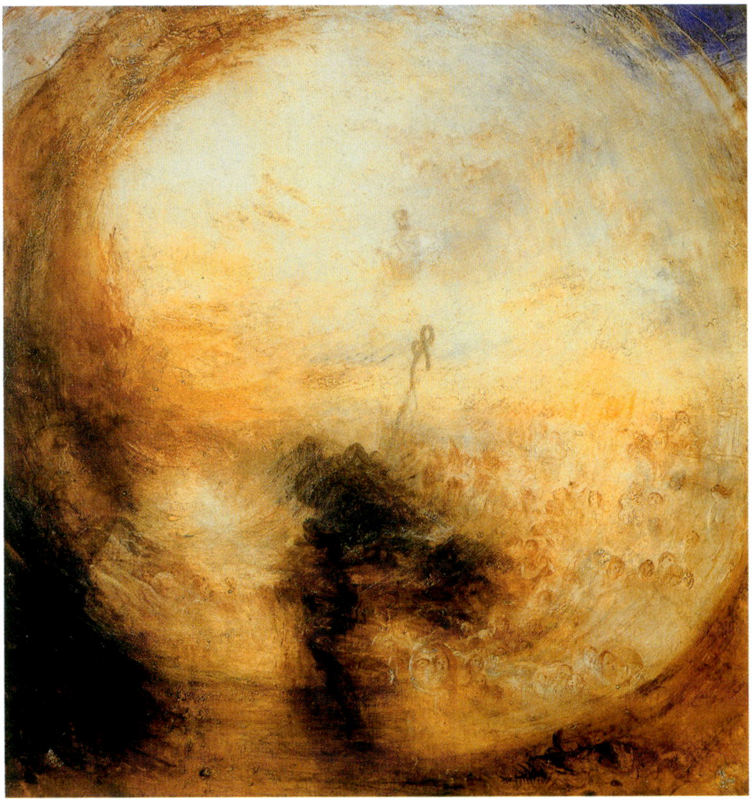

William Turner, Light and Color: The Morning After the Flood. Moses Writes the Book of Genesis, *1843. Tate Gallery, (London, U.K.). Turner was experiencing and transmitting "impressions" before the age of Impressionism. In this painting he treats light and color in a pure state, as a pictorial metaphor of the route to profound perception and knowledge.*

Contrast as a Tool for Expression

When we speak of painting, we speak of image, and every image is formed on the basis of light. In the same way that light, in accordance with physical laws, defines the real image that our retina captures and our mind interprets, the artistic image must follow the same laws so it can be captured and interpreted by the spectator. These laws, which we will come to see throughout this book, can be summed up on a single one: contrast. Without contrast, there is no perception; as a result, there is no expression.

However, the contrast doesn't need to be very pronounced to assure fruitful expression. Sometimes a subtle difference in the chromatic shade or light can awaken strong emotions. Since contrast is based on difference, artists thus attempt to create these differences according to their poetic and expressive intention. In the same way that gastronomy works contrasts creatively at several levels to awaken sensations—contrasts in taste, texture, aroma, and temperature—the contrasts in painting likewise have to be worked at various levels: contrasts of color, light, shape, size, texture, and so forth.

Henri Matisse, Still Life with Red Tablecloth, *1906. Grenoble Museum (Grenoble, France).*
Chromatic contrast, pure color with no neutralization. This was the intent of the Fauvists: rediscovering the purity of the mediums through color relationships. In this case, the green and the red, two complementary colors, are the main features that set up a strong vibrancy.

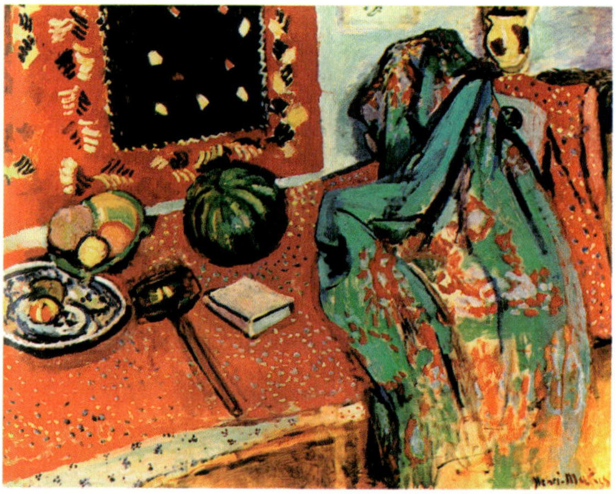

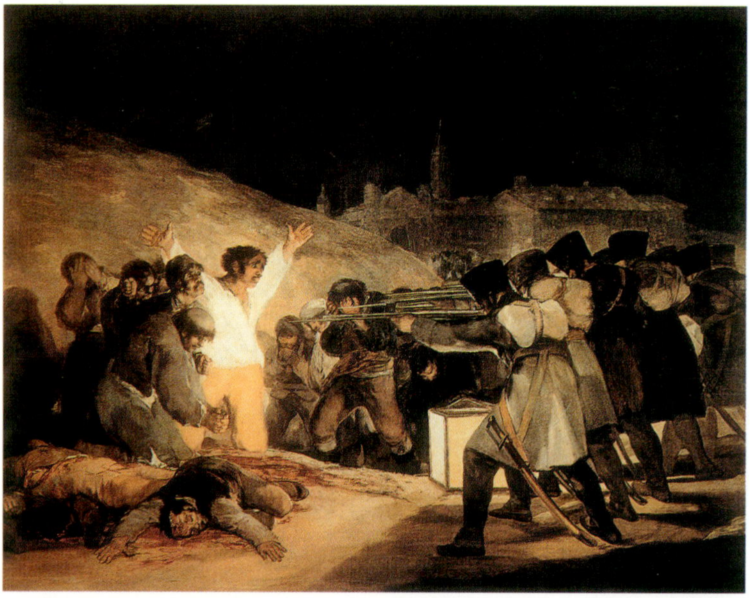

Francisco de Goya y Lucientes, May 3, 1808: Firing Squad on Prince Pio Mountain, *1814. The Prado Museum (Madrid, Spain). For Goya the scene is similar to the crucifixion. Therefore the drama is accompanied by darkness and the contrast with light. White, symbol of purity, reinforces the idea of the victim's innocence. In another, analogous painting by Manet* (The Execution of Maximilian) *the drama is less intense, but only because the scene takes place in full daylight.*

LIGHT CONTRAST AND CHROMATIC CONTRAST
These are the two types of contrast that have most frequently been used in the history of painting: with regard to light value, through chiaroscuro (light and shadow) or through surface (a single point of light shines more than many others); and with respect to chromatic value, through contrasts in shade (such as two complementary colors) or through saturation (a bright color and a more neutral one). However, these are not mutually exclusive avenues, for most of the time they are used together, just as in a single dish there may be a contrast of taste and another of texture, even though one is accentuated more than the other at certain times.

Light as the Subject of Art

The attraction that light exercises on artists goes beyond its practical function as an element that defines shapes and spaces. Light is also an element that has its own very special magic and attraction.

Light symbolizes the immaterial. Only light escapes the law of gravity, and everything that relates to it possesses the same spiritual halo: shadow, color, night, brightness, evanescence, heat... Light is doubtless an element replete with conceptual, symbolic, and experiential content. Many artists have approached it from different angles. In some cases, we encounter a light that creates a very sensual atmosphere, and in others, a blinding light that suggests a supernatural world.

Jan Vermeer de Delft, Girl Reading a Letter by the Window, *1657. Gemäldegalerie (Dresden, Germany). With Vermeer, there is always a natural light, whether warm or cold, that softly bathes the intimate scene. His paintings suggest the meditation and the warmth of the home, tenderness, calm, and well being.*

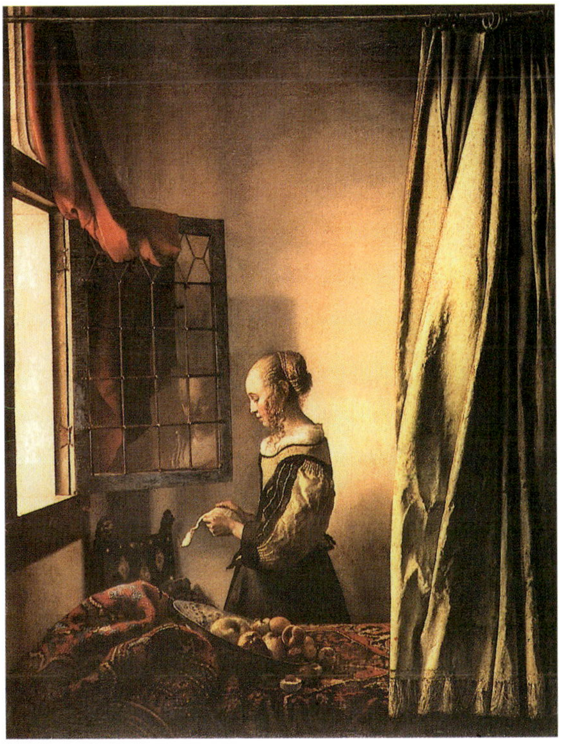

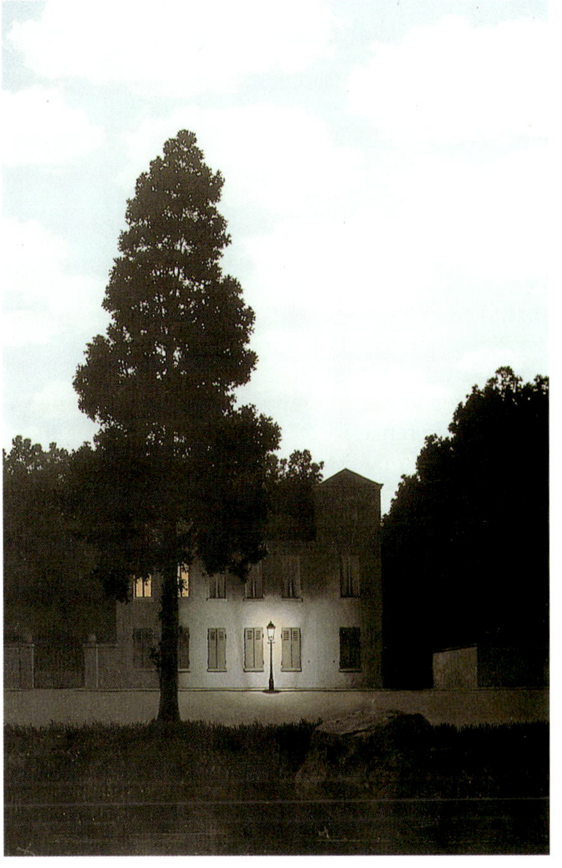

René Magritte, The Empire of Light, *1954. Peggy Guggenheim Collection (Venice, Italy). A surrealist vision: day and night in the same scene. Magritte unites two opposite poles in a single image to produce anxiety and surprise in the spectator and thus stimulate the imagination.*

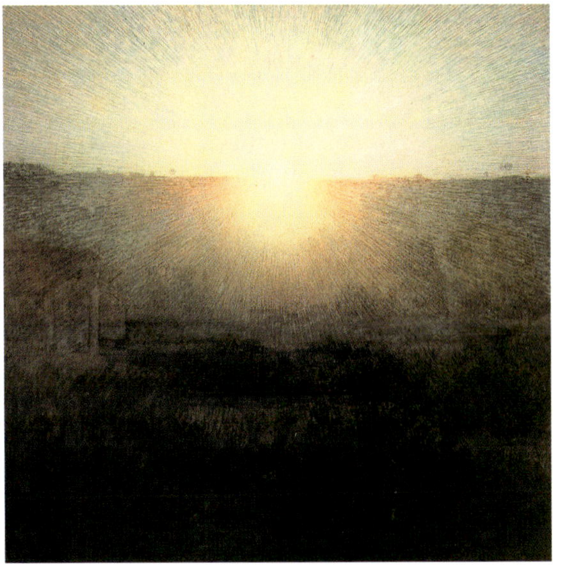

Giuseppe Pelliza da Volpeo, The Rising Sun or the Sun, *1903–1904. Galleria Comunale de Arte Moderna (Rome, Italy). The sole subject of this painting is light: a solar flash that lights up and gives heat and life. At the turn of the twentieth century, dawn was taken to be a symbol of emerging socialism.*

Light and Color in Classical Painting

Classicism is tied to the idea of truthfulness, and it had its origins in ancient Rome. Roman painters started with a very careful drawing and applied a fusion between colorism and shading. Starting in the thirteenth century, after a long period when flat, schematic painting in attractive colors prevailed, painters returned to reality and introduced soft chiaroscuros, even though they still maintained medieval idealism. Flemish art, with its treatment of light and chiaroscuro, anticipated the Renaissance. In large measure, it was an outgrowth of the invention of oil paint, which allows for perfect shading, and a nearly photographic attention to detail.

The Renaissance, with its emphasis on understanding nature, sought thc greatest veracity in representations through visual correction, chiaroscuro achieved through color, aerial and linear perspective, and *sfumato*. The Venetian school, which was more concerned with atmosphere, would give rise to the Baroque. From that time onward, light became a basic element, not only in service to the objects depicted but also in the emotions conveyed.

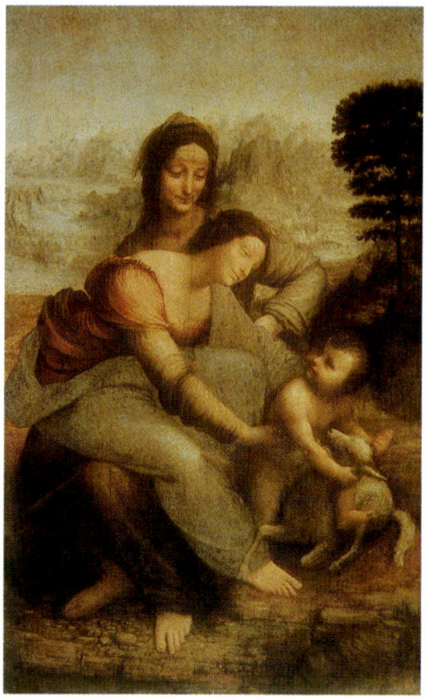

Leonardo da Vinci, Saint Anne, the Virgin and the Child, *1510. The Louvre (Paris, France). A golden, Renaissance light situates the scene in an unreal moment in the day. It floods over everything, modifying every objective color and thus eliminating any trace of realism and naturalness. By means of* sfumato *a "supernatural" atmosphere is created that deifies the characters.*

BAROQUE TENEBRISM

Baroque painting was an experiential painting. Painters sought a theatrical effect and experimented with artificial light that left the background in total darkness. Tenebrism made its appearance. Never before had half-light and darkness been used as pictorial values. It developed that way in the Baroque because it's light that creates the subject, and that imparts reality to the narration. This type of lighting changes the colors of the objects, evening them out in shades of yellow and orange, and makes distant shapes disappear, yielding to a black, deep background.

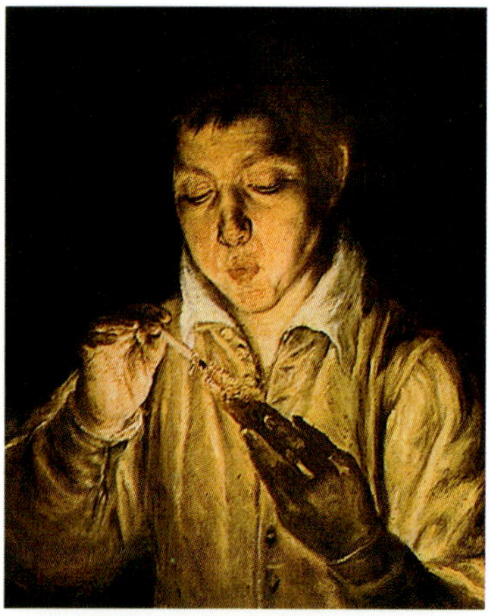

El Greco, Boy Lighting a Candle, *1570–1575. Galleria Nazionale de Capodimonte (Naples, Italy). Darkness and night are common settings for baroque intimist painting.*

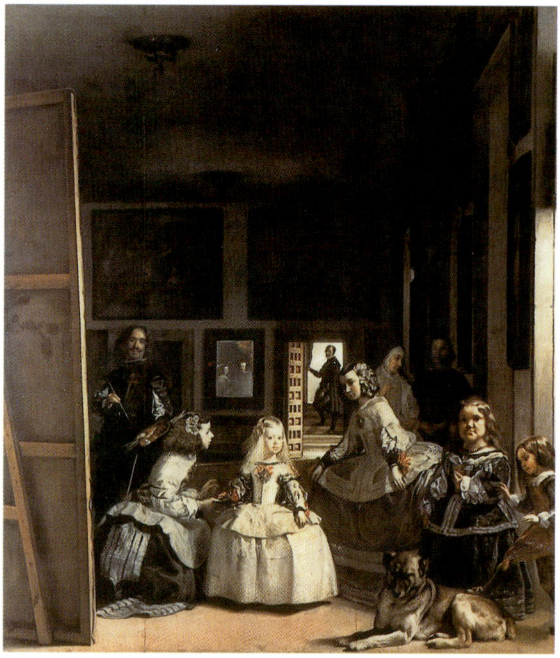

Diego Velazquez, Las Meninas, *1656. The Prado (Madrid, Spain). Two foci of light create the space and the narration: to the right, a window that illuminates the kings who appear in the mirror in the background, and indirectly all the people in the scene; in the background, the door that provides backlighting, and in the middle, the half-light.*

Light and Color in the Nineteenth Century

Academicism would continue the path begun in the Baroque, pursuing the investigation of light and color, but distancing itself from Tenebrism. Daylight would not reach its highest expression until the nineteenth century. "The enemy of painting is gray," declared Delacroix. Light is painted as it is seen, without idealizing it. Then the deviations appeared: the Neoclassics modeled shapes using soft shadings; the Romantics used impastos and glazes more impulsively and nature became a source of spiritual experiences.

With Impressionism, color superseded chiaroscuro and a totally chromatic atmosphere was created. Painters established rich chromatic interplays between warm and cold ranges, modeled complementary shapes, introduced blue into the shadows, and reconsidered the value of the brushstroke.

Historical Avant-garde Movements

In the first half of the twentieth century, there was an emergence of tendencies and styles that had previously been unthinkable: the avant-garde movements. Each one treated light and color as a function of its own tenets. Expressionism and Fauvism, derived from the bold colorism of Van Gogh and Gauguin, both of whom were Postimpressionists, held that light comes from color itself in its maximum, saturated expression, and they worked with strong chromatic contrasts and standardized the use of complementary colors for shadows. With Cubism, Futurism, Surrealism, and Dadaism, color became subjected to the whim of the artists, according to their creative desire and the expressive discourse. They were searching not for an expression of reality, but rather the creation of a new and unique type of work. Every painting was a new reality.

Joan Miró, Nocturne, *1940. Private Collection. This work by Joan Miró belongs to the series of "Constellations" begun during the Second World War. The images are very harmonious. The painter uses graphic signs and altered imaginings to create a poetic effect that displays a celestial kingdom filled with creatures born of pure imagination.*

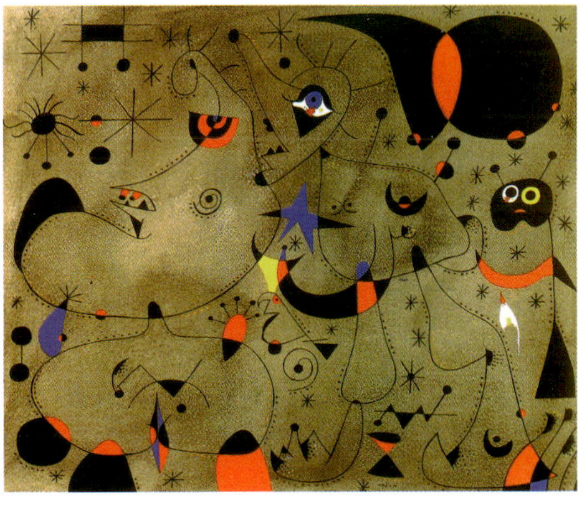

Van Gogh, The Starry Night, *1889. Museum of Modern Art (New York). In the nineteenth century, the night itself has been turned into a pictorial subject. In this work Van Gogh highlights the effects of nocturnal light, which is dynamic, and which, like the sun, also generates psychic and emotional life.*

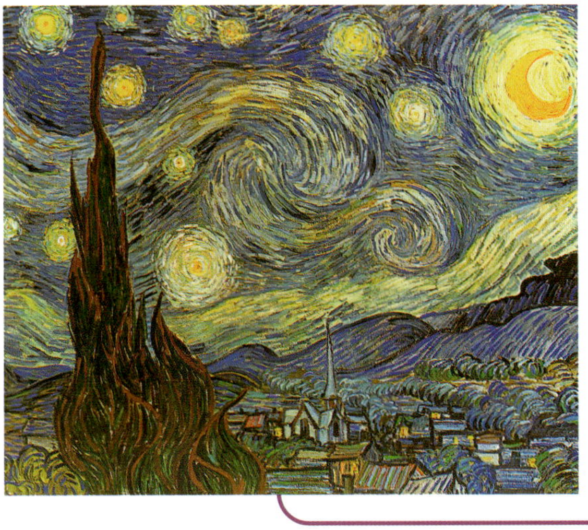

NIGHT

Night has always been a challenge for figurative painting because of the lack of vision it presents. The lack of contrast makes it difficult to produce results. Consequently, there were no nocturnal scenes (except ones that were reduced to a mere bath of moonlight, or a starry sky over an illuminated landscape, with no darkness or mystery) until the Baroque era, with its violent illuminations and nocturnal scenes.

In the nineteenth century, night serves to reveal what is hidden, to introduce feelings and sensitivity into the mystery and the secret. In the twentieth century, the night would come to have its own light and create its own life.

Light and Color in the Still Life Genre

Given the theatrical nature of the still life, this genre makes it possible to manipulate light at will. The artist organizes the scene and introduces light in any way that suits the purpose. The chosen light may be natural or artificial, bright or dim, total, lateral, from above, frontal, from behind, mottled... The painter is always the one who creates the effect. Every decision involves different consequences in both the image and the dramatic effect.

In painting a still life it's important to do a very careful study of how the colors fit together to determine at what point along the spectrum from black to white the most luminous and the darkest values are located. The main problem regarding light and color involves representing the materials, their reflections, transparencies, and textures. This is the major challenge.

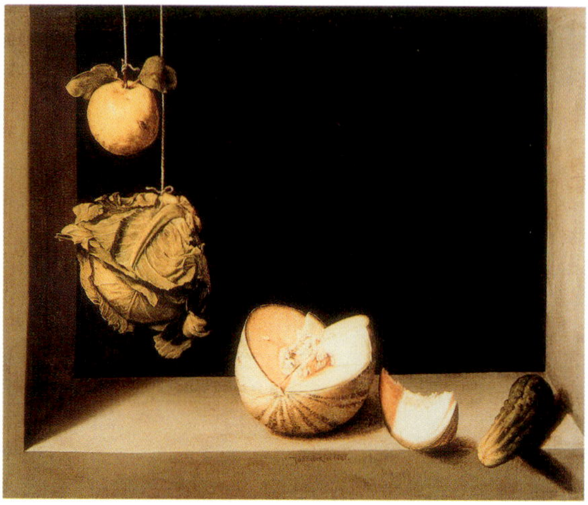

Juan Sanchez Cotan, Cabbage, Melon, Cucumber, and Quince, *ca. 1602. Fine Arts Museum (Granada, Spain). In the still life paintings of this Carthusian monk we see an intensely real presence. Every element in the picture, a sober composition illuminated by a light directed against a deep, dark background, thus becomes an object of contemplation.*

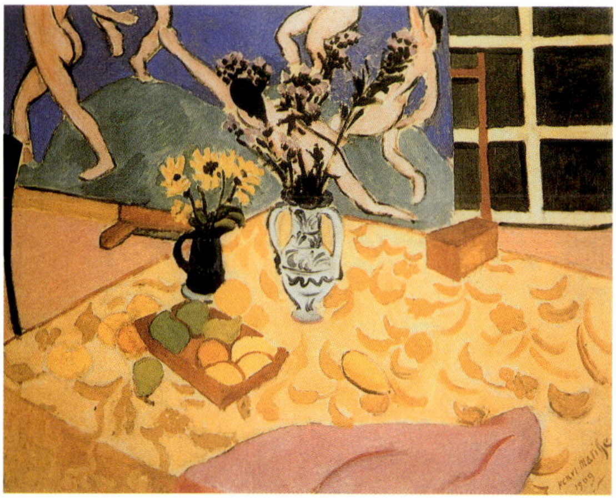

Henri Matisse, Still Life with "The Dance," *ca. 1909. The Hermitage (Saint Petersburg, Russia). The main feature of this still life is the color, which organizes the image based on its relationships and the space it occupies. A completely frontal and global light, which produces neither shadows nor shapes, makes this scene possible.*

CHARDIN, THE GREAT MASTER OF THE EIGHTEENTH CENTURY

This great French still life artist is an essential reference point because of the importance he gives to depicting the effects of light on shapes and surfaces. The use of *sfumatos* and glazes creates a soft, warm light that bathes every object, creating an intimate atmosphere of blended gradations and deep shadows.

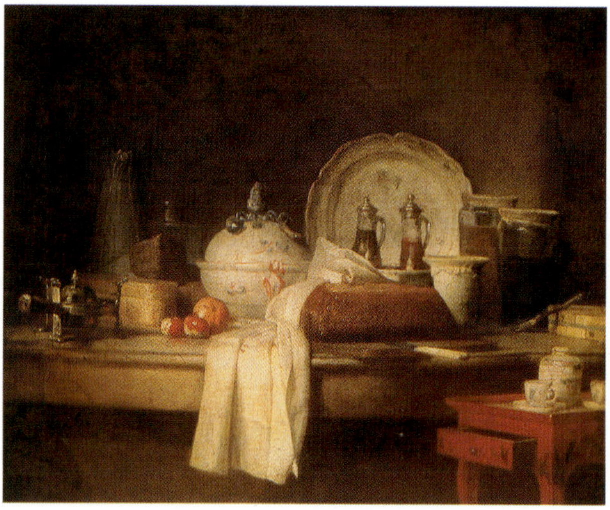

Jean-Baptiste Siméon Chardin, The Kitchen Table, *1756. Fine Arts Museum (Carcassonne, France). The encyclopedist and art critic Denis Diderot said the following about this still life: "Oh, Chardin! This is light and air that you take with the point of your brush and deposit onto the canvas!"*

Indoor Light

Just as still life tableaux focus on objects, paintings of indoor scenes and landscapes focus on spaces. As the very name indicates, indoor scenes represent small, closed areas, habitable spaces that invite the observers to tour them with their gaze and allow themselves to become infused with the atmosphere of the place. Having arrived at this point, the treatment of light is basic. The interplay that is set up among bright or soft lights, half-lights, shadows, hidden corners, and persons or objects bathed by light from the outside or from a lamp makes up the story the picture has to tell.

Indoor scenes have the ability to place the observer in a position of a *voyeur* who is allowed access to private matters, thereby establishing an implied emotional attachment to the scene. As a result, in many indoor scenes the people depicted are not posing, but rather, given the realistic and intimate character of the genre, they are performing some activity in a perfectly natural way. In such cases, light creates the atmosphere.

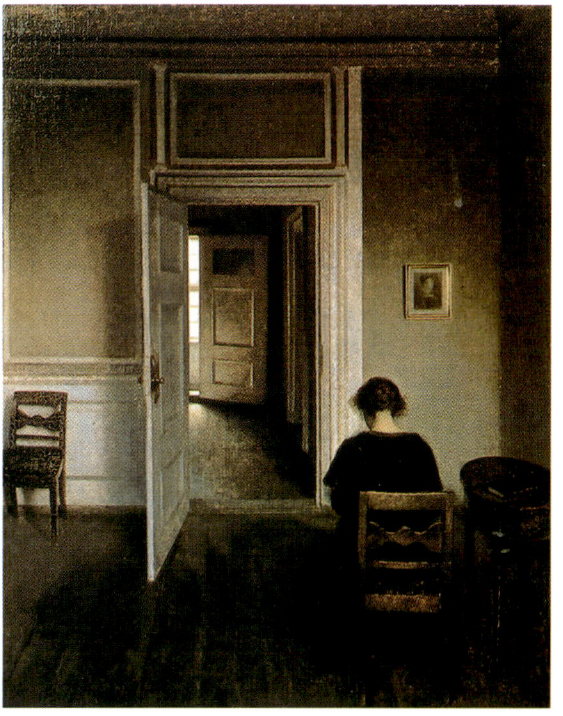

Vilhem Hammershøi, Indoor Scene with Seated Woman, *1908. Musée d'Orsay (Paris, France).*
In the 1880s in Denmark, Vilhem Hammershøi proved one of the great masters in the use of light, and was very well known for indoor scenes with figures seen from the rear. Light is the main subject of his works.

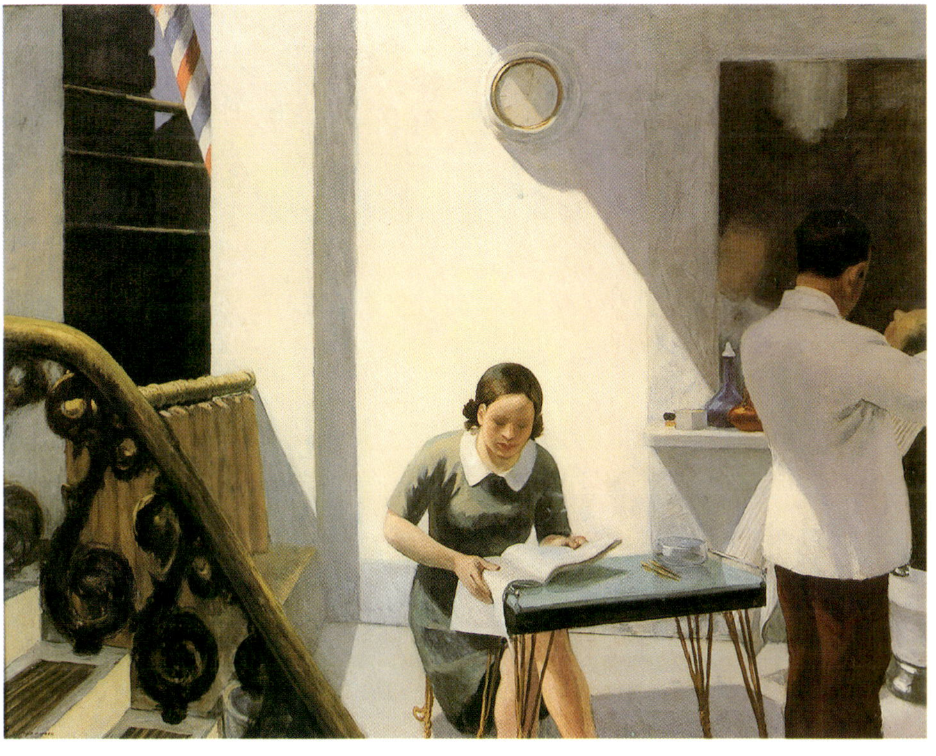

Edward Hopper, The Barber Shop, *1931. Neuberger State Museum (New York). Hopper maintained that his art had no purpose other than to simply "paint the sun's light on the side wall of a house." He painted daily scenes in motels, gas stations, and highways, always communicating solitude and silence.*

Light and Color in Landscape

Light and color are closely linked to landscape. The attractive beauty of a landscape is always related to the atmosphere of light and color: the dawn, the hues of the flowers at noon, shady valleys, summits gilded by the waning afternoon sun, stormy skies, fog in the woods, the tranquil waters of a pond in the morning . . . moments of particular charm in which light always plays a part. The main goal of the painter has always been to capture this light.

There are three major terms, all with obvious meanings, that are used to designate themes inspired by the natural surroundings: *landscapes, seascapes,* and *skyscapes*. Painting a landscape involves painting natural light, whether in a valley, on waves, or in clouds. Undertaking this genre implies being attentive to the time of day, the season, the nuances of color, glare, shadows, atmosphere . . . It's a good idea to paint outdoors to capture this light effectively; and in addition, that is a very stimulating experience.

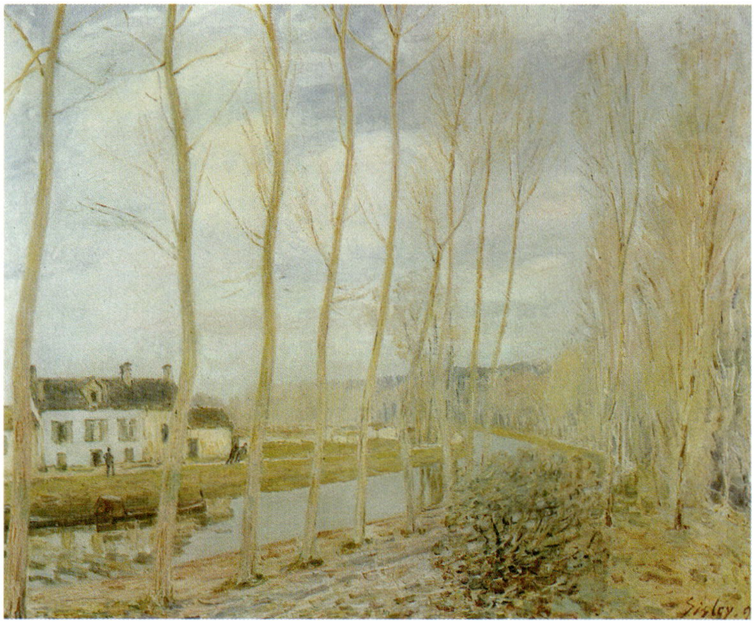

Alfred Sisley, Loing Canal, *1892. Musee d'Orsay (Paris, France). Preoccupied with capturing the luminous atmosphere in the air, Sisley said, ". . . the sky must be more than a background . . . , I place lots of emphasis on this part of the landscape because I hope you will understand the importance it has for me . . . , I always begin a painting with the sky."*

William Turner, Rain, Steam, and Speed, *1844. National Gallery (London, U.K.). These three elements have one characteristic in common: a lack of visibility. When light passes through such dense filters, definition disappears and the features melt together and are reduced to elementary blotches of color. This was of special interest to Turner and brought him close to a type of abstraction that made him an avant-garde painter.*

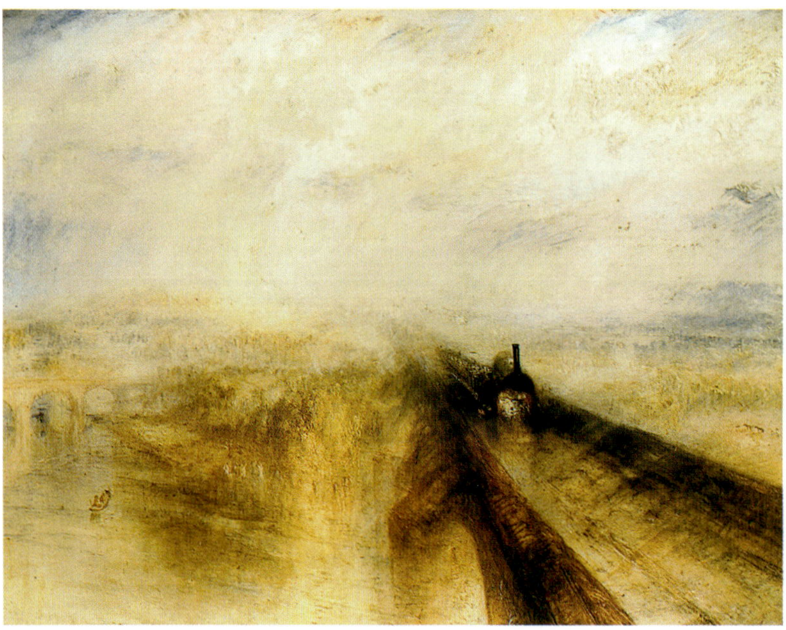

URBAN LANDSCAPES

The interest in depicting the open spaces of large cities or the streets of a neighborhood originated in the twentieth century. Given the geometrical structure of the streets, the buildings, and the furnishings, the urban landscape requires some minimal knowledge of linear perspective. The light also deserves study, since it behaves very differently in a city, with hard, flat shadows and differentiated contrasts, artificial and graying colors, including smoke, fog, and pollution.

Monet and the Discourse of Nature

Monet was clearly an exponent of Impressionism and of his interest in capturing the changing effects of light in nature. The term *Impressionism,* which he coined, is derived from *impression,* which is understood as spontaneous emotion in the presence of nature and as a reflection on the world's mysterious phenomena.

Monet's intuitive sensitivity was born of his fascination with light and color. He experienced nature as a changing and magical world at every instant because of light, which is dependent on the seasons, the time of day, and the message of every element: water, stone, flower, cloud. He worked in solitude and isolation. He worked at a slow pace, despite the appearance of his paintings. He simply sought to create or transmit in his paintings the pure emotion captured in nature, as he explains in a letter to the writer Gustave Geffroy dated June 7, 1912: ". . . I know only that I do what I think to express what I feel in the presence of nature, and often, in order to translate what I feel intensely, I completely forget the most elementary rules of painting, if they ever existed. . . ."

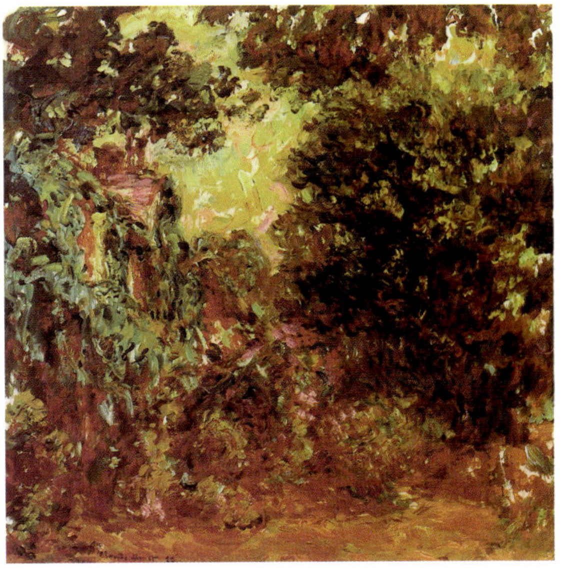

Claude Monet, The Artist's House as Seen from the Rose Garden, *1922–1924. Musée Marmottan (Paris, France). In the last glow of the day lights and colors mix together.*

Claude Monet, Impression, Rising Sun, *1872. Musée Marmottan (Paris, France). With respect to the impression, Monet said, "My strength is knowing how to stop myself in time. No painter can work more than a half hour in the open air if he wants to be faithful to nature. When the object changes, the work must stop." This dawn scene is considered to be the first impressionist painting in history.*

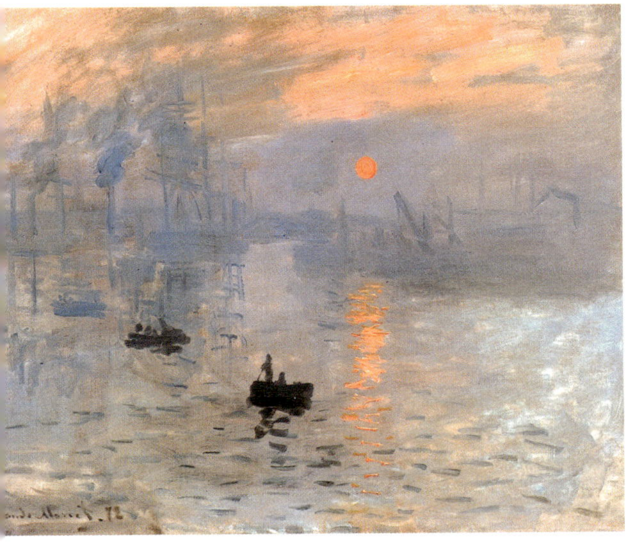

MONET'S GARDEN IN GIVERNY

Giverny is a small village located thirty-six miles (sixty kilometers) from Paris. Claude Monet lived in Giverny from 1883 until his death in 1926. He had water from the river Seine diverted to there, constructed Japanese-style bridges, and raised poultry, peacocks, and pheasants.

He truly devoted forty years of his life to perfecting a house and garden that he painted at all hours of the day and in every season, trying to capture the movement of the plants in the bottom of the ponds and the autumnal hues of the trees.

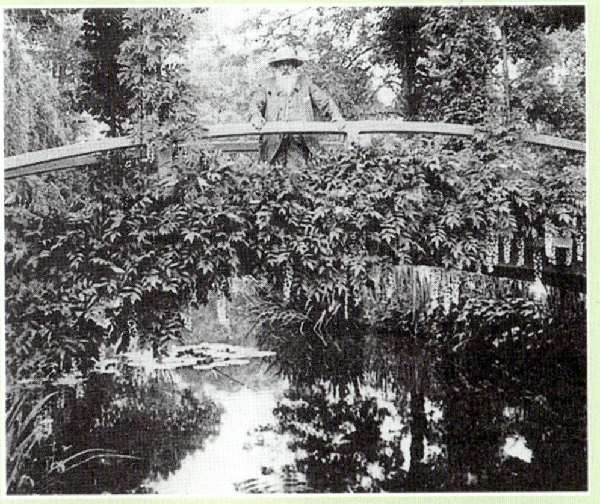

Monet on the Japanese bridge in his garden in Giverny. *Sirot-Angel Collection (Paris, France).*

Light and Color in the Human Figure

The human figure is the most frequent subject in the entire history of art. From prehistoric hunting scenes to hyperrealism, painters have striven to give real and expressive presence to human representations. Light and color have been used in different ways in every artistic period, and we still can't say in all honesty what is best, since there is no single artistic purpose but many, and each one is best adapted to one technique or another.

With respect to light, the principal difficulty is the shape of the human body, with the attendant problems of color in flesh tones and shadow. The second problem is the relationship between the figure and the background. In that regard it is appropriate to observe that magnificent works can be done without emphasis on form, relying solely on the strength of color, and yet without sacrificing a sense of veracity. Nor is it necessary to distinguish clearly between figure and background, as with baroque tenebrism, to make the figure more credible. These are methods that must be observed and experimented with.

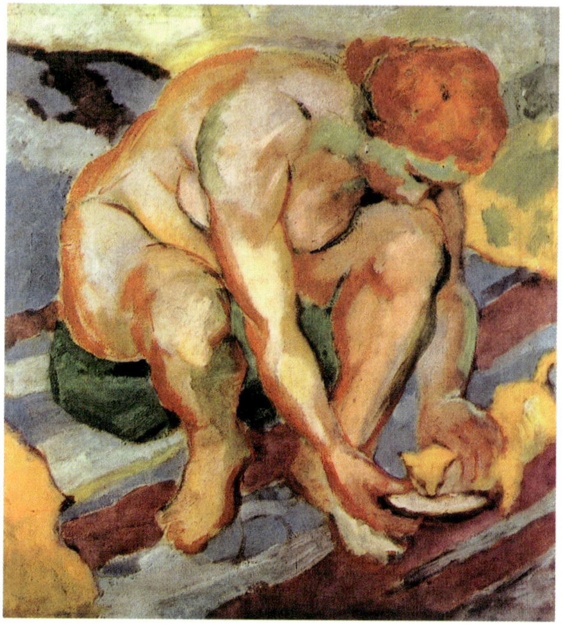

Franz Marc, Nude with Cat, *1910. Städtische Galerie (Munich, Germany).*
A hundred years after Ingres, and under the influence of Impressionism, Franz Marc dared to break down the colors and create a chromatic chiaroscuro. In this work, the flesh tones have warm and cold hues. The warm shades draw nearer and provide light and color, and the cold ones provide distance and suggest darkness.

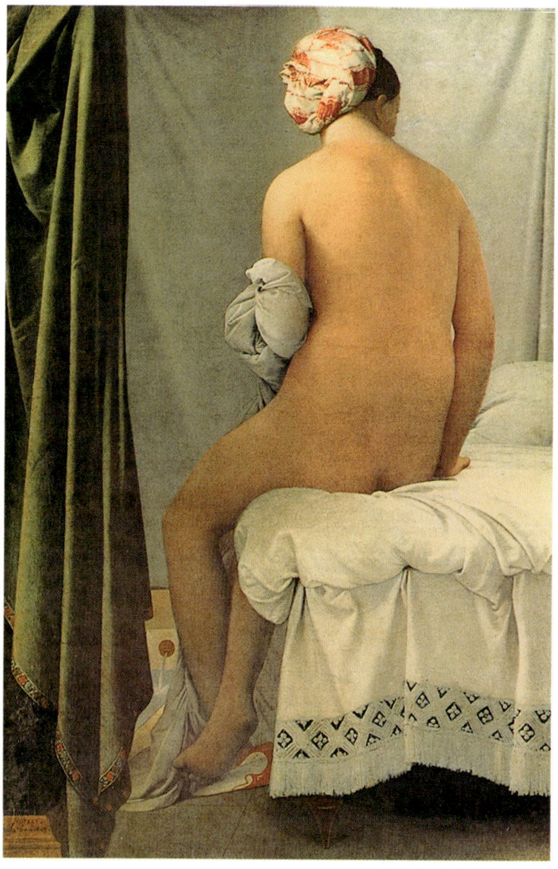

MODELING THE NUDE BODY
In order to model the human body pictorially, one merely needs to be very careful in distributing the values of light and shadow. There is just one avenue for that purpose: careful observation of light, which creates shapes. Every light and every shadow not only adapts to the anatomy, but also defines it, regardless of whether the work involves soft shading or strong contrasts, searching for a more sculptural sense. Nor does it matter if chromatic values are chosen in the Impressionist or Baroque style, as long as the values work together.

Ingres, The Bather of Valpinçon, *1808. The Louvre (Paris, France).*
A Neoclassical scene of great technical perfection, considering that it involves difficult modeling because of the lack of contrasts. The soft shading and the skin color approach photographic realism.

Light and Portraiture

Technically it is no more complicated to depict a face than a body. You proceed in the same manner, starting with a good layout of a drawing that distributes the facial features in accordance with the model, the expression, and the personality.

Regarding skin color, it can be said that there is no single flesh color, but rather many. At the outset, the most frequently used color for the white race is the one produced by a pale orange mixed with and neutralized by blues, plus earth tones for the darkest shades. Many artists work with a base of burnt sienna and use it as a starting point for a broad spectrum of hues. But the skin doesn't have to be bronzed; it can also be grayish, bluish, pinkish, or yellowish without sacrificing realism. One merely needs to compare several portraits to see countless shades of the most disparate types: purple, bluish, brown, blackish, reddish shadows, and more.

Rembrandt, Self-Portrait *(detail), 1659–1660. Kenwood House (London, U.K.). Baroque self-portrait. Short range and very close artificial light.*

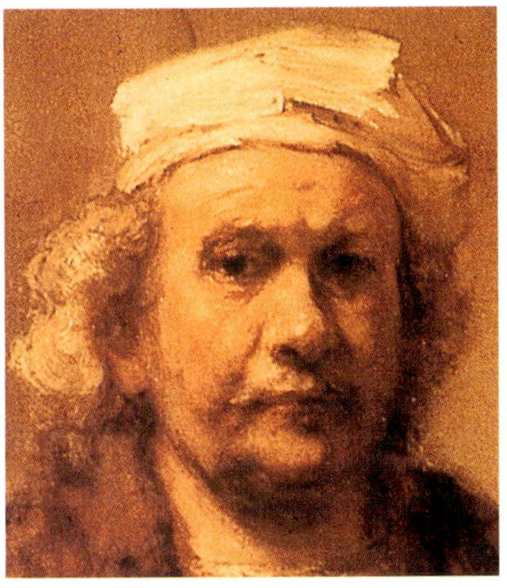

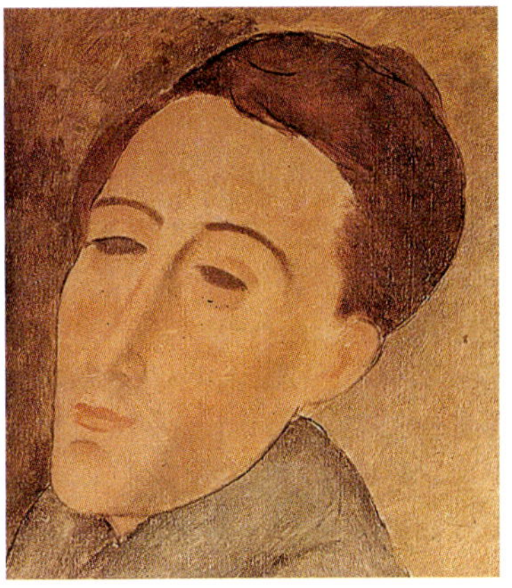

Amedeo Modigliani, Self-Portrait *(detail), 1919. Private Collection. Modigliani gives his face a spiritual quality. Gentle sculpting. The eyes stand out like deep holes in a mask.*

Paul Gauguin, Portrait-caricature of Gauguin, *1889. National Gallery (Washington, D.C.). Postimpressionist self-portrait. Flat colors of great visual violence create an image with a primitivist appearance.*

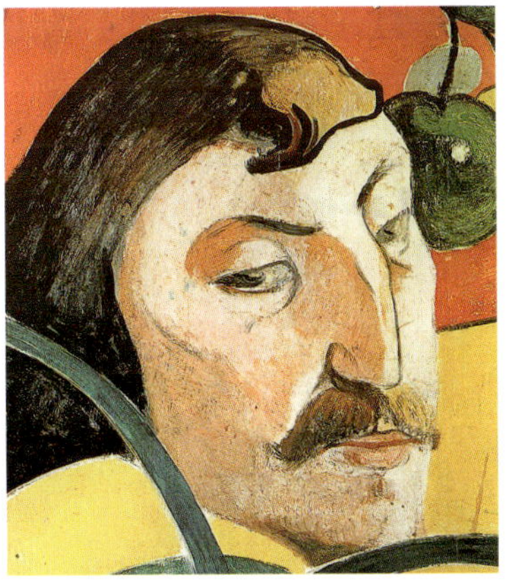

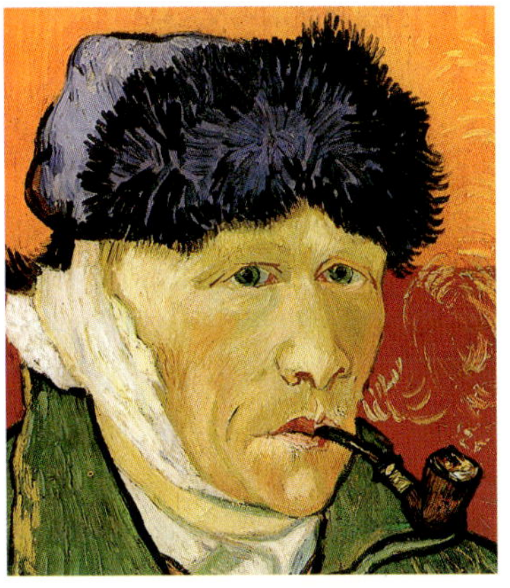

Vincent van Gogh, Self-Portrait with Ear Cut Off, *1889. Private collection. Self-portrait using bright colors that blend in fine but energetic brush-strokes that sculpt the face.*

Pablo Picasso, Self-Portrait, *1907. Národni Gallery (Prague, Czech Republic). Energy and strength are the words that best define Picasso's way of working. Vigorous lines with no sculpting.*

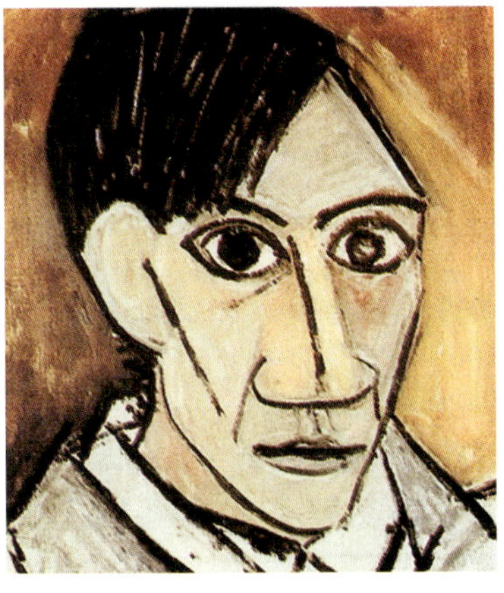

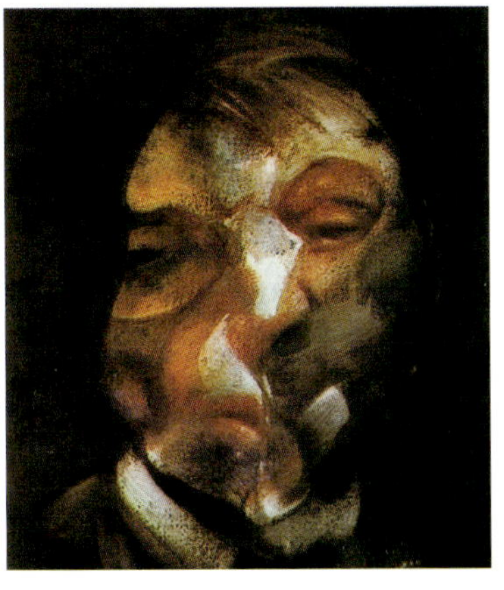

Francis Bacon, Self-Portrait, *1972. Private Collection. Bacon manipulated the interplay of light and color appropriate to classical modeling to create a disquieting and dramatic distortion.*

Light and Color in Abstraction

We usually consider a painting in which we can recognize no features of visual reality to be abstract, even though it may suggest such features to us. Abstraction always involves an absence of discourse of the descriptive narrative type, which is not considered essential if we remember that painting is nothing more than color, shapes, and textures on a flat space, vibrating in a poetic way.

Color and light continue to construct the pictorial image, no matter how abstract it is, unless the visual contrast involves nothing more than texture, matter, shape, or space, as is sometimes the case with some minimalist painters or topical painting. But this construction functions differently from that of figurative art, since light and color don't behave according to the laws of nature, but rather follow the laws of the painting itself.

Mark Rothko, Orange, Red, and Red, *1962. Dallas Museum of Art (Dallas).*
Rothko played with chromatic contrasts involving shade, value, and saturation. His paintings took a long time to create and were very cerebral. Nowadays they are seen as authentic icons of emptiness and nothingness, for contemplation and meditation.

MARK ROTHKO

Many abstract painters rely on the strength of color to communicate non-narrative messages. One of the most important painters in that regard was Mark Rothko, who used simple blotches of superimposed colors to create vibrations with great communicative force. The light is in the color itself, which acts like a living mass, sometimes producing tension and, more frequently, sucking the observer in. The boundaries between these masses and the background color are the areas of greatest visual tension and expressive force of his paintings.

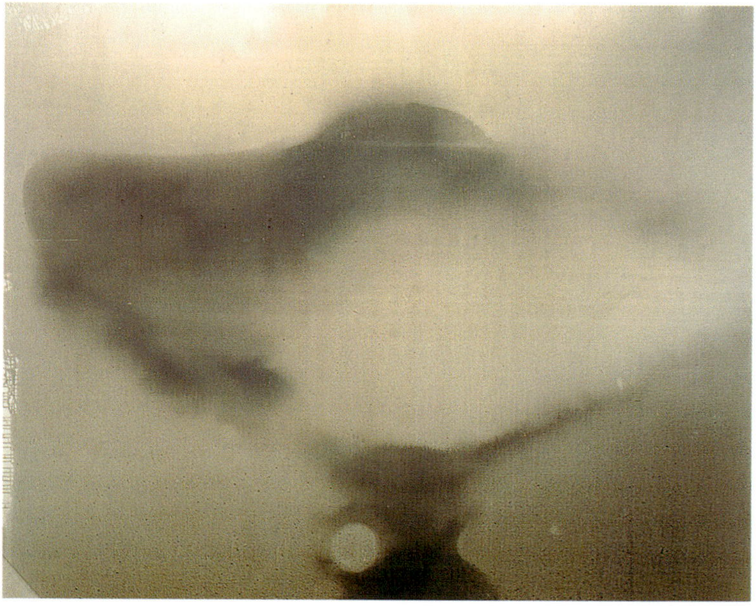

Vicenç Viaplana, Sentimental Theory, *2000. Private Collection. Here is a delicate and subtle interplay of monochrome chiaroscuros. Viaplana's paintings possess the magic of things suggested, like visions perceived through veils or translucent windowpanes that impede resolution of the image.*

Light and Visual Perception

Without light, the eyes can perceive no form or color, and painters, who are more preoccupied with the creations of light than by the light itself, have studied its laws to learn how to depict it.

For several centuries painters didn't bother studying the laws of visual perception. It was Leonardo da Vinci, during the Renaissance, who was the first to analyze how we perceive reality, in order to figure out how to represent it accurately. One of his greatest discoveries was aerial perspective, which advanced the representation of depth in landscapes. With Newton and the advances achieved by European scientists in the study of light and color in the nineteenth century, the future bases of painting became grounded science.

In this same century in England, the painters Turner and Constable, witnesses to the new discoveries and theories, influenced the art of the following ages by applying those discoveries to their works. Impressionism closed the nineteenth century with a real high point in the observation of light and color, focusing its artistic production on that point.

Light not only defines visual reality physically, but also presents it on a sensory and emotional level, breaking through the limits of representation to arrive at expression. The same can be applied to color as a phenomenon of light.

Light not only defines visual reality physically, but also presents it on a sensory and emotional level.

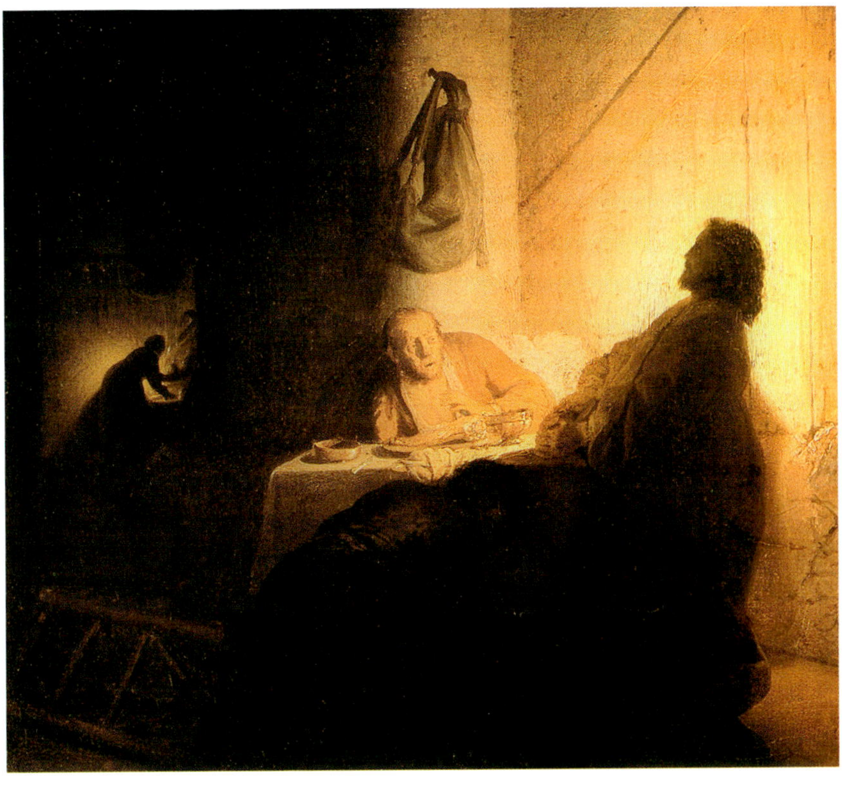

Rembrandt, Dinner in Emaus, *1628–1629. Jaquemart-André Museum (Paris, France). Rembrandt's greatest strength is using light on a pictorial level in a magisterial way, and it is his secret for captivating the observer. With a few elements and the right play of light, the painter manages to tell stories charged with emotion and mysterious symbols.*

How We Perceive Visual Reality

Perception is not a passive phenomenon, but rather an active process. In the act of perceiving, we act on the stimuli in the following way: we explore them, select them, and analyze them; we capture the essentials, proceed to an abstraction, and finally synthesize them by relating them to our previous experience. As Arnheim states, "there is no basic difference between looking at our surroundings and thinking with our eyes shut," because the eyes are merely the sensory organs, but it is the mind that creates the perception based on the stimuli received and the mental models acquired through past experience.

Studies on perception by Gestalt psychologists have revealed that we perceive stimuli in a related way; therefore the relationships among the perceived elements are more important than the elements themselves. This affects both chiaroscuro and color, as we shall see in the following pages. In the second place, they showed the importance of the preexisting mental model, which strongly conditions perception, to the point that we see what we already know in what we observe, and not what we are really observing.

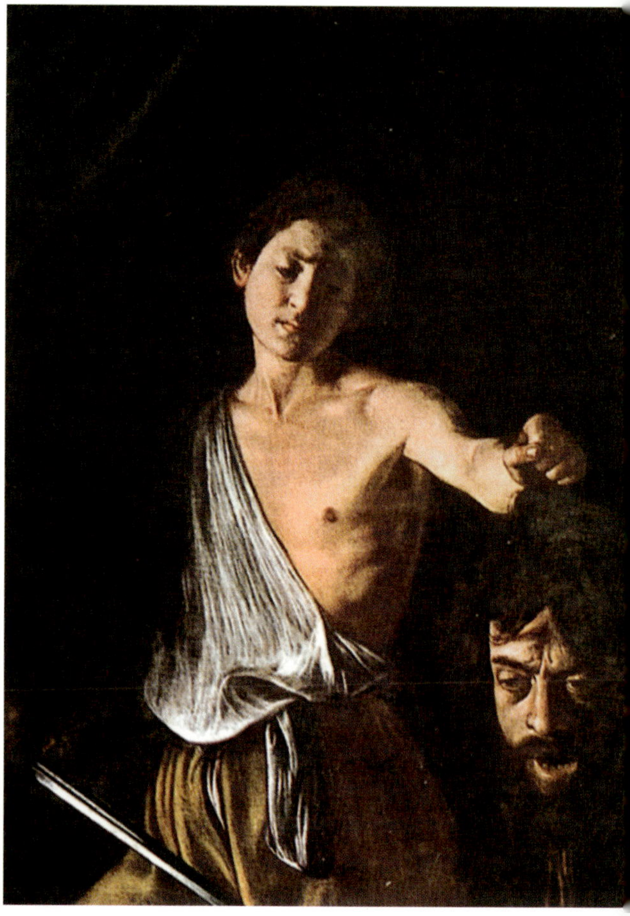

Caravaggio, David with the Head of Goliath, *ca. 1605. Galleria Borghese (Rome, Italy). Even though the tenebrism hides David's arm that holds the sword, we still perceive it due to the law of pregnancy, which makes it possible to mentally fill empty spaces and correct errors, always seeking perceptive perfection.*

Andres Macara, The Badminton Game, Tenerife. *Private collection.*

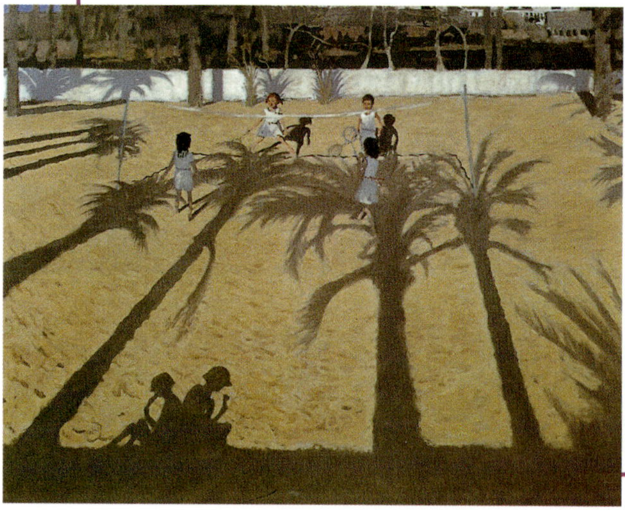

ANALYSIS OF A PAINTING ACCORDING TO GESTALT LAWS

Based on sensory experiments, psychologists of the Gestalt theory discovered that perception follows common laws. We will apply them to this work. According to the law of *proximity,* we group the parts that are closest: the group of girls who are playing and the ones who are eating ice cream. By the law of *equality,* we connect elements of the same class: shadows or children. By the law of *closure,* we perceive the figures even if they are unfinished, in this case, the palm trees. And finally, by the laws of *destination* and *common movement* we perceive direction: the shadows form a unit (the palm grove) because they recede toward the same point.

General Factors in Chiaroscuro

When light enters a space, it bathes everything in its field of action, creating the visual image. Depending on the light source, its quality, and distance, it will have a greater or lesser impact on the image. In any case, the light always produces a relationship of contrast, since it involves the presence of shadows. Light and shadow are two sides of the same coin.

But there will also be other phenomena as a consequence of the interplay between light and shadow: on the one hand, the visual creation of the third dimension through sculpting the shapes and defining the limits or the fields of the space—depths, planes, hollows, etc.; and on the other hand, all kinds of reflections, since light bounces from materials that normally act as reflectors. When the materials have special characteristics of textures or transparency, still other effects appear, such as reflections of the image or visual distortion. In addition, if the air is dense, it acts as a filter that creates hazes and atmosphere, which are common elements in landscapes.

ANALYSIS OF *BOYS ON THE BEACH* BY JOAQUIN SOROLLA

Sorolla was one of the best impressionist painters at capturing light and color. His creations are decisive and free, so that with just a few judicious strokes he could define effects of light on bodies and figures in special situations, such as these children at the beach, bathed in light and water. Let's use this work to consider these effects in detail.

Joaquín Sorolla, Children at the Beach, *1919. Casón del Buen Retiro (Madrid, Spain).*

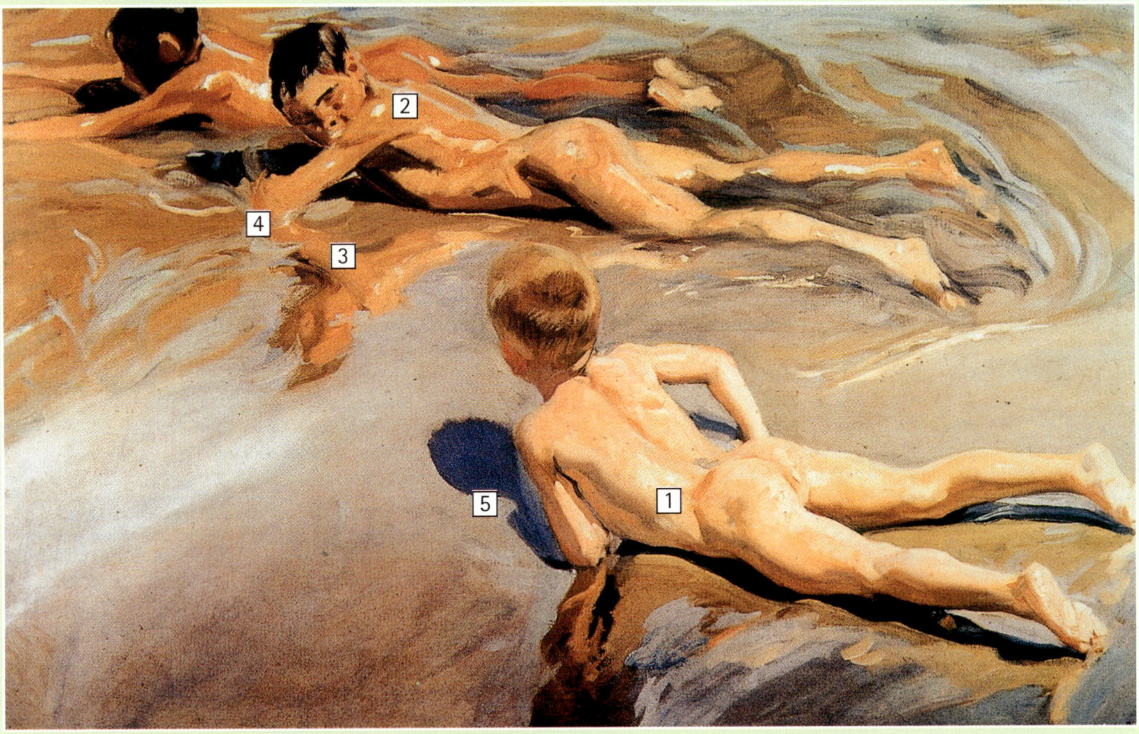

1. Sculpting
The passage from light to shadow depends on the nature of the light. In this case, the shading is viscous and of strong contrast in order to indicate the wet skin and the intense sunlight. Note the presence of blue in the shadows.

2, 3, 4. Reflections
Because of their smoothness or their liquidity, some materials, such as water, reflect everything around them like a mirror. Here, the water and the children's skin reflect several features: reflections from the light source (2), blurred images due to the water's movement (3), and colors as simple blotches without shape (4).

5. Projected Shadows
These are projected by the body, even with distortion and a slightly different value than true shadows.

Natural and Artificial Light

We cannot speak of a single natural light, since light changes radically according to the time of day, the seasons, and even altitude and geographical latitude. Gauguin and Van Gogh moved to the south of France in search of purer light, and Paul Klee returned to Tunisia because he was fascinated with its golden light.

Natural light, when it's white, has little effect on colors, but it produces a bluish shade in the shadows. We have to keep in mind the influence of atmospheric phenomena, such as snow and rainstorms, as well as the many possible combinations of sunlight and rain, morning mists, and stormy skies. In each case, we have to create different shadows, almost always soft, unless they are the result of direct sunlight.

Artificial light is commonly used in interior scenes and still lifes. Whether it comes from a bulb, a halogen lamp, a fluorescent light, or some type of combustion (candles, gaslights, or oil lamps), it will always modify the color of objects. The shadows will be hard or soft depending on the quality and intensity of the light. Its effect is always more dramatic.

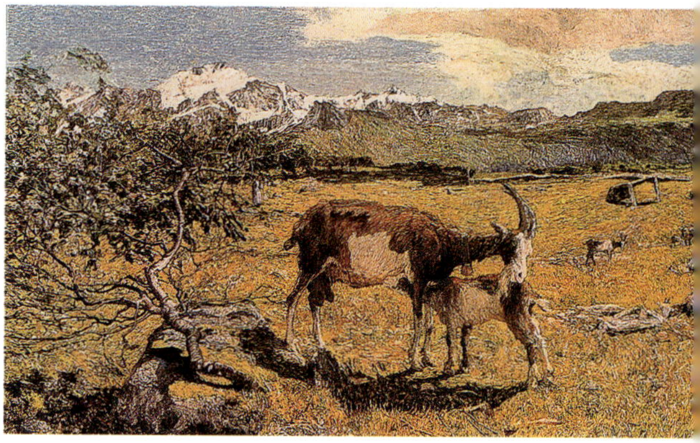

Giovanni Segantini, Alps in May, *1891. Private collection. The clear, clean light of mid-morning. The sun inundates the scene of peace and tranquility. Note the wonderful work in the textures of the grasses in the meadow and hair of the goats, which seem to absorb the overall light.*

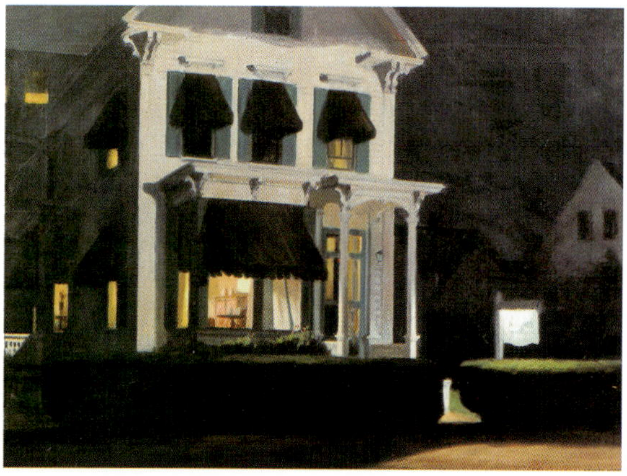

Edward Hopper, Tourist Rooms, *1945. Yale University Art Gallery (New Haven, Connecticut). A night scene with two focuses of artificial light. On one side, there is a large streetlight; even though it doesn't appear in the picture, we deduce its presence from the shadows on the porch. On the other side, there is an illuminated sign that's visible; it's less striking, but brighter.*

LIGHT FACTORS

- The type of light: natural or artificial
- Brightness: half-light, dim, strong, or full
- The nature of the light: hard, normal, or diffuse
- The direction: from the side, from the top, backlighting, from the front, emphatic or atmospheric
- The objective: precise (a single or several points in the scene), partial (one or more illuminated areas), or total (the entire scene).
- The color: white, golden, cold, lunar, from artificial colored light . . .

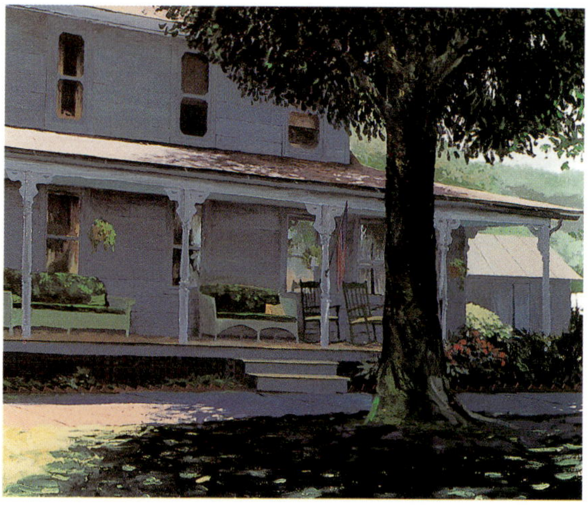

Bryn Craig, Marland House. *Private collection. A daytime scene that corresponds to noontime sunlight. The presence of porches, projections, and the crown of a tree create areas of shadows and strong contrast. Despite the contrast, perception is clearer than in the preceding painting by Hopper, with its artificial light.*

Natural Positions of the Light Source

A natural position of the light source is one that would exist in nature. Depending on the time of day and the location of the object, the light would be from the side, from the front, or from above.

When the sun rises and sets, the light is low and can produce frontal or back lighting, depending on whether the spectator is situated facing the sun or away from it. The nature of this kind of light is hard; it produces long, hard shadows with marked contrasts. In the middle of the morning or afternoon, the direction of the sunlight is from the side; its brightness is medium, and its quality is normal. An examination of midday sun from overhead reveals a very hard illumination, with scarcely any shadows. In general, the quality depends in large measure on the condition of the atmosphere; if it is very clean and the sun is shining in a clear sky, the shapes and shadows will be hard, but everything softens and blends on a cloudy day, due to the filters that the light encounters when it passes through the atmosphere.

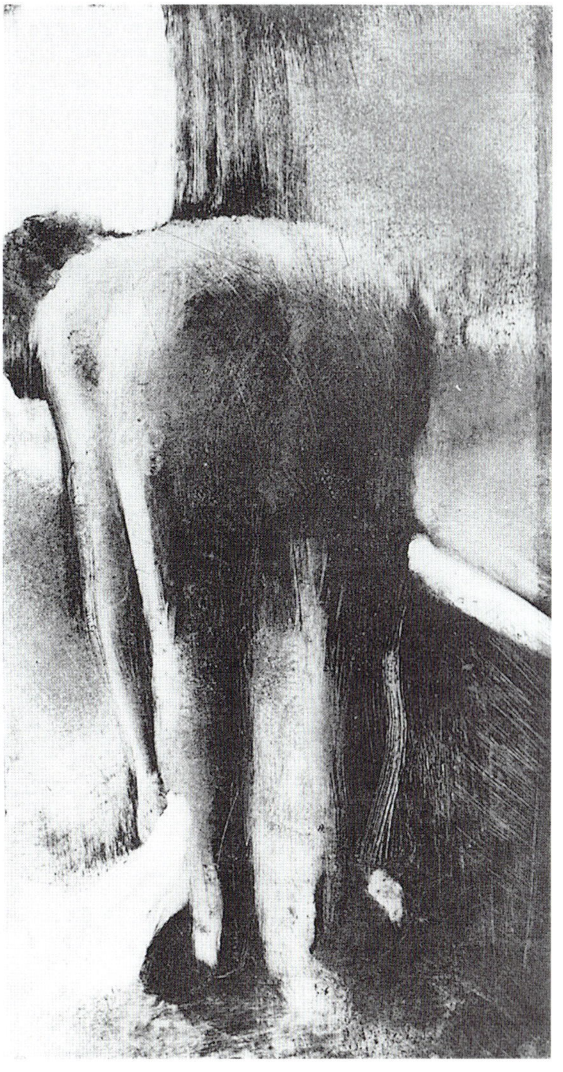

Edgar Degas, Nude Woman Drying Her Feet, *ca. 1879–1883. The Louvre (Paris, France). In this engraving, Degas has chosen backlighting to emphasize the frontal plane of the bather's forced position. This device creates a tension of suggestive eroticism, since this type of illumination interfered with a clear vision, due to the dark shadows it creates.*

Rembrandt, Annunciation, *1660. Narodni Gallery (Prague, Czech Republic).*
This example of lateral illumination in the baroque style is characterized by its obedience to a direction connected to the theme. It involves an annunciation in which the archangel Gabriel doesn't appear physically, but rather in the form of a light source, the light that floods Mary.

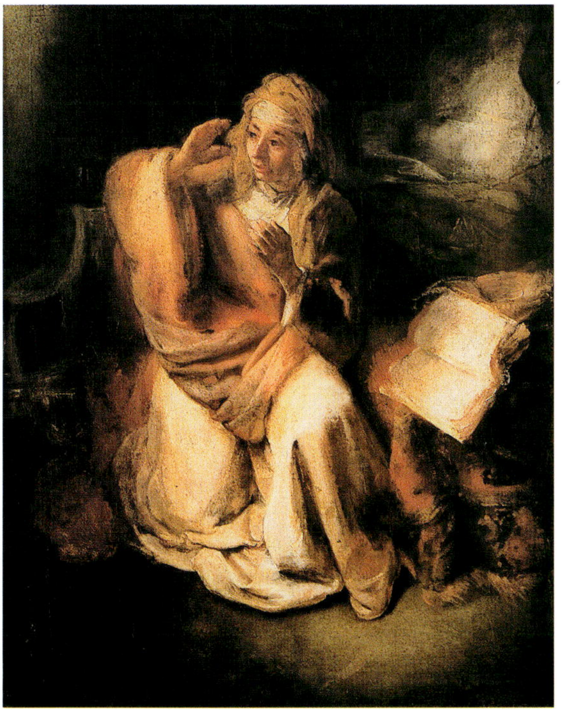

NATURAL SETTINGS WITH ARTIFICIAL LIGHT
Artificial light can be used to re-create natural illumination. To paint an interior scene with or without a human figure, or a still life, the light can be modified in terms of quality and objective by applying filters (curtains, screens . . .) or by locating reflectors to soften the shadows or set up areas of brightness.

Forced Illumination

Even though there is some spectacular lighting that occurs naturally due to the position of the sun in combination with low clouds, the theatrical nature of the moment doesn't take away from its naturalness. Forced illumination is artificial illumination that is manipulated for specific purposes, and which goes against natural laws, such as shadow plays, pinpoint objectives, exaggerated tenebrist effects, and a combination of hard and soft shadows in the same plane.

As a rule this type of illumination has a specific expressive intent, such as creating a certain pictorial climate, highlighting a detail, distorting features for dramatic purposes, or surprising the observer by locating the light inside the object rather than outside it. Most nighttime illuminations are forced, and they create new realities that are very different from the light of day.

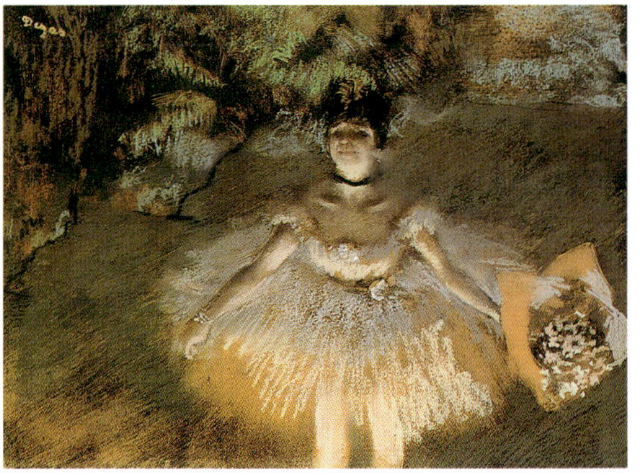

Edgar Degas, Ballerina with Bouquet Bowing to the Audience, *ca. 1876. Private collection. Emphatic, exaggerated light of a theatrical nature, since this is the only position of the light source that is not available in nature. Edgar Degas often resorted to this in his dance scenes, transporting the observer to other fictitious and magical realities.*

Vincent van Gogh, Café Terrace at the Place du Forum, *1888. Rijksmuseum Kröller-Müller (Otterlo, Netherlands). Van Gogh immersed himself in nocturnal light to capture the night atmosphere. Objects change color and take on the yellow hues of the pinpoint lights of the streetlights and the sliver light of the moon.*

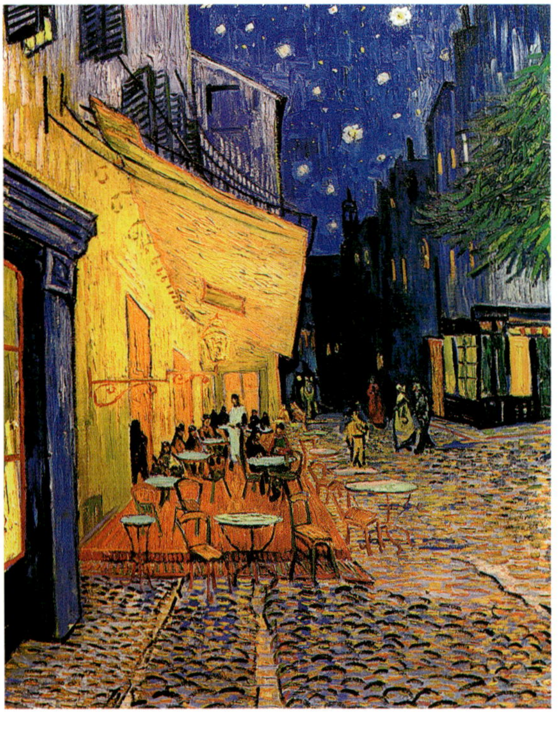

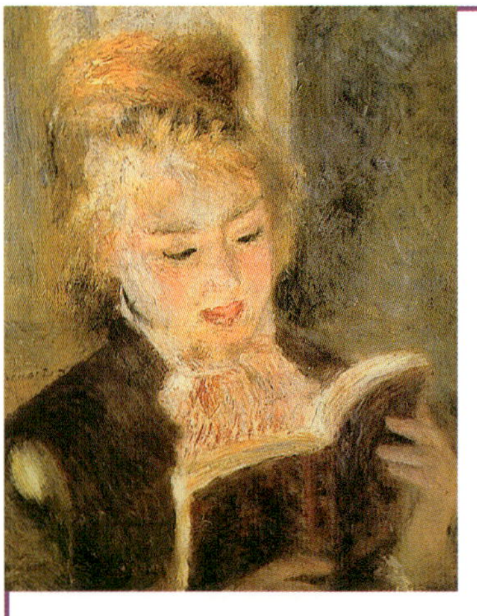

Pierre-Auguste Renoir, The Reader, *1875–1876. Musée d'Orsay (Paris, France).*

RADIANCE

Radiance is a phenomenon that is located between the light source and the object illuminated. An object that radiates light can be seen as a source of light when in fact it merely reflects the light, as in the case of the moon and the sun. In order for the gleam to be perceptible in a certain area, there has to be illumination located higher than what we expect. The use of reflectors causes this effect, as with the book in *The Reader* by Renoir, which illuminates the shade of the face and increases the sensation of full light.

Light Value

Capturing light involves learning to evaluate, or in other words, to compare. The way to evaluate light involves contemplating the scene as a succession of spots of light. It may be helpful to close your eyes to a squint to blur your vision and compare the contrasts in various areas. In practice, it's helpful to do preliminary sketches in which you work only with indefinite spots of light and shadow, without getting into details; that way, the chiaroscuro advances progressively and can be adjusted and corrected.

In general, there is a tendency not to contrast very much for fear of excess, or to fall into the opposite situation by deciding that the greatest point of light will be the white and the darkest part the black, filling in the scale to the fullest, but that too is a mistake. Often the lightest value is a medium gray because there is not much light in the scene or because the model is made of some dark material; in fact, pure white rarely appears. The same is true of absolute black: it is rarely found in the scene. The most advisable method involves devising a scale before starting to apply the definitive colors to the image.

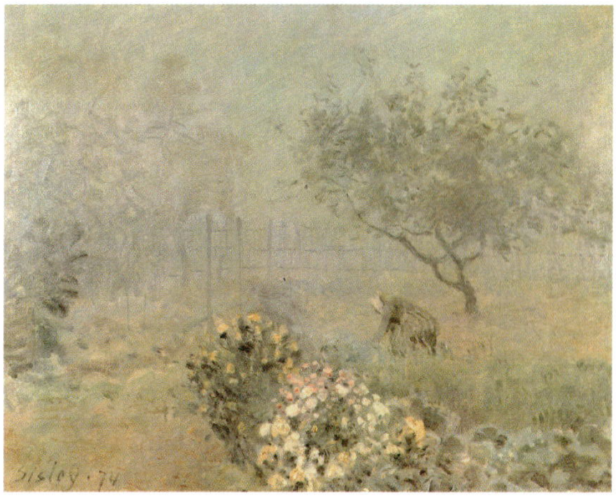

Alfred Sisley, Fog, *Voisins, 1874. Musée d'Orsay (Paris, France). "Which painters do I like?... all the ones who have loved nature and have felt it with force," replied Sisley in an interview in 1892. This painting reveals perfectly his fascination with the mysterious light of foggy mornings. The color scale he used is situated in an intermediate band, without great contrasts, and that's a prerequisite for depicting fog.*

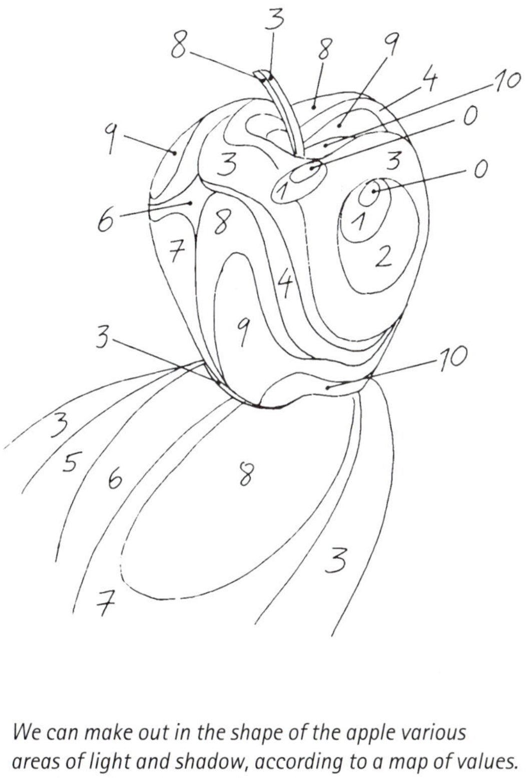

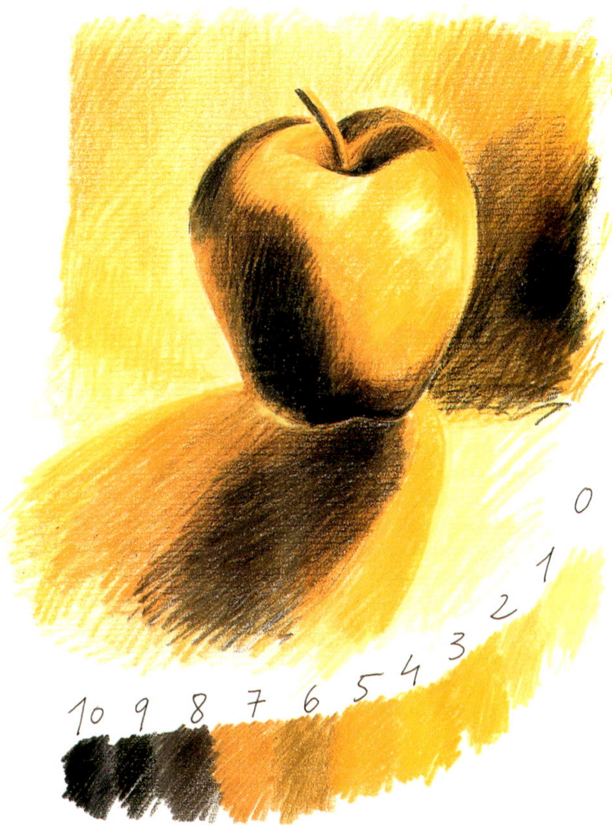

We can make out in the shape of the apple various areas of light and shadow, according to a map of values. A color scale will be helpful in determining the extremes between which the chiaroscuro will develop.

Relative Luminosity

A white handkerchief in half-light is still perceived as being white even though it sends to our retina the same light as a black handkerchief in sunlight, because luminosity doesn't depend solely on the capacity of the object for absorption or reflection of light, but rather on the distribution of the light values in the entire scene, which is something more complex. The white handkerchief appears to be white in half-light not because it gives off much light, but rather because in that half-light it gives off more light than the other objects, even though it is not white.

The physiological adaptation of vision to each light situation allows a valuation of the chiaroscuro so that that particular scene is the one represented and no alien scale of color values is applied. With respect to color, as we will see shortly, precisely the same thing happens. Even though we know that a handkerchief is yellow in conditions of full light, under moonlight it's no longer yellow, but rather gray, and that specific gray is the one that's required and correct for those conditions.

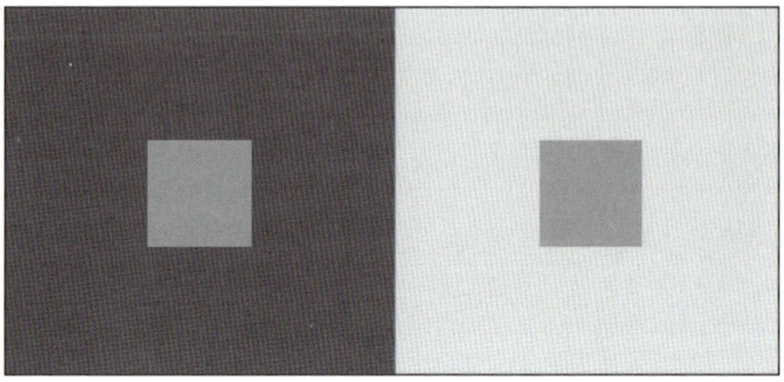

Even though the two central squares have the same tonal value, they are perceived differently because of the background.

The entire stripe is the same shade of gray, but the shading in the background changes how it is perceived.

Edward Hopper, Eleven O'clock in the Morning, *1966. Private Collection. This painting is a clear example of relative luminosity. What could turn out to be a dark color in front of the window would be light in any place in the general half-light. Nothing is light or dark in and of itself, but rather in relationship to its surroundings.*

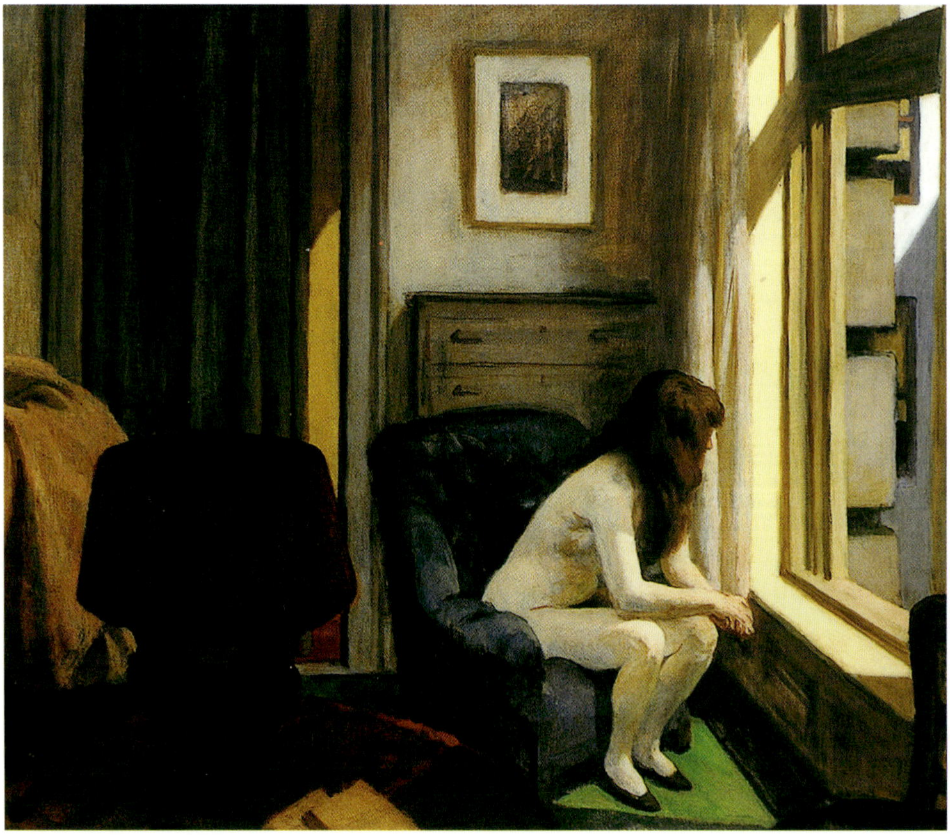

Color Is Light

Every one of the colors that make up white light corresponds to a certain wavelength. The human retina is not sensitive to all electromagnetic waves, but only to certain lengths, the ones in the chromatic spectrum.

We don't know precisely why a tomato is perceived as red and not blue, but we do know that it absorbs all the colors of the spectrum except the one that it reflects, and that one is red. Depending on the type of light it receives, an object takes on one color or another in our vision. In reality, the tomato is not red; rather it is perceived as red under white light, but in the shadow it is brown, and if it's illuminated by a candle it's orange . . . So what in fact are light and color? In referencing a color we always use daytime white light because it contains the entire spectrum of colors, and the color of the object is named according to that light.

That same tomato will exhibit different colors as a function of its surroundings: an objective or local color, which is the color of the object under conditions of pure white light: red (Delacroix called it "the true color"); other tonal colors, which are variations of light and darkness of that color as a function of chiaroscuro: pinks, browns . . .; and finally, colors reflected on the surface: yellow reflections if, for example, there is a lemon next to it. There is another factor that plays a part in the color of a landscape: the atmosphere, which cools the colors to the point that the brownish woods are seen as blue in the distance.

When we perceive the colors of a painting, in reality we are seeing the light that falls on it reflected in multiple waves according to the pigments in the painting.

But we don't paint with light, but rather with pigments. Every pigment has characteristics that make it react to light by reflecting the waves that correspond to its color. That way, when we perceive the colors of a painting, in reality we are seeing the light that falls on it reflected in multiple waves according to the pigments in the painting, and that reflected light forms the ultimate chromatic image in our system of perception.

Under certain conditions, when white light passes through a glass prism, it breaks down and forms the color spectrum. This is the same phenomenon that occurs when sunlight passes through raindrops: a rainbow.

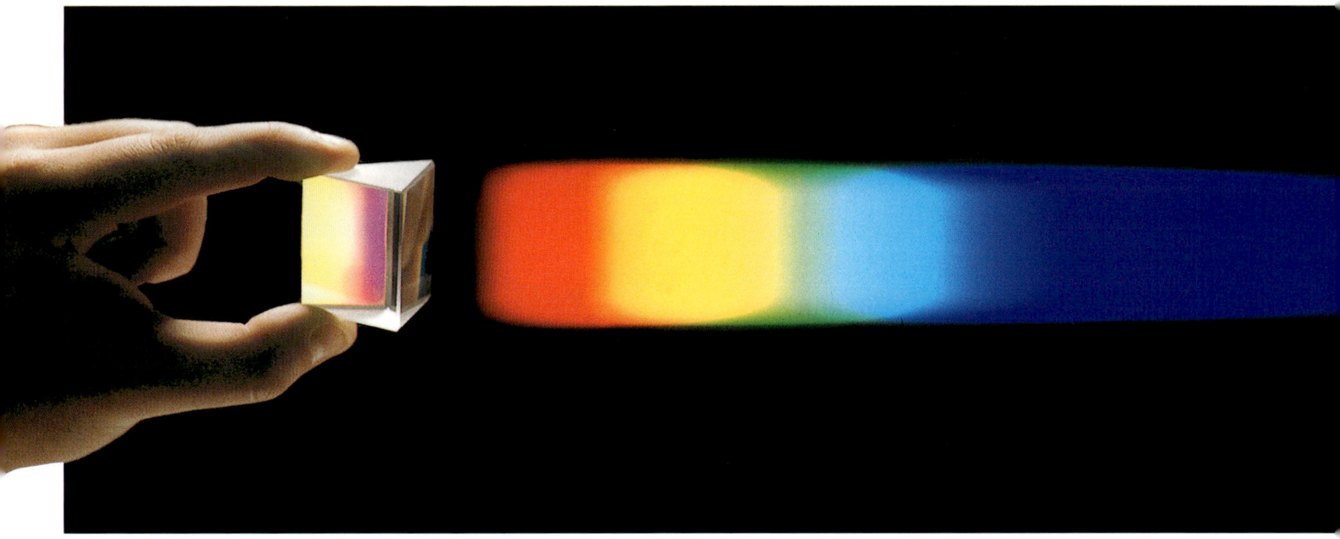

Description of Color

A color is defined according to three factors: shade, saturation, and value.

• The shade, also called the hue, indicates the color's position within the chromatic circle: green, blue, purple, yellow, etc. Changing the shade or "tinting" involves displacing the color toward a neighboring or adjacent one (adding blue, orange, or red, for example).

• Saturation, which is sometimes called brightness, refers to the purity of the color. A saturated color is one that is accompanied by none of its complementary color or black; it is an active color with its maximum chromatic energy. The opposite of saturation is neutralization, which consists of subtracting chromatic energy from a color. A neutralized color is a passive color that has faded or grayed, by mixing with its complement.

• The value is the level of luminosity. In order to give more light to a color without changing its tone, we must add white or dilute it. To darken it we can use several techniques, although the best one from the viewpoint of color theory involves mixing it with its complementary color or with black. Every color has its own light level, which can be very high, as with yellow, or very dark, as with purple.

SCIENCE AND COLOR

Newton established the foundation of color theory by observing that the color spectrum is produced when white light is broken down. Maxwell developed an electromagnetic theory of light. Rood worked on optical mixing. Goethe developed a theory on the physiological, psychological, and symbolic aspects of color. Chevreul observed how shadows become tinged with the color that complements the color of the object. In addition, there were Ostwald, Young, and others—a long list of scientists who have contributed to our understanding of color. Painting has advanced thanks to their research.

Vincent van Gogh, Portrait of Dr. Gachet, *1890. The Louvre (Paris, France). In his works van Gogh incorporated all types of chromatic scales. This painting can serve as an example of how certain colors are defined.*

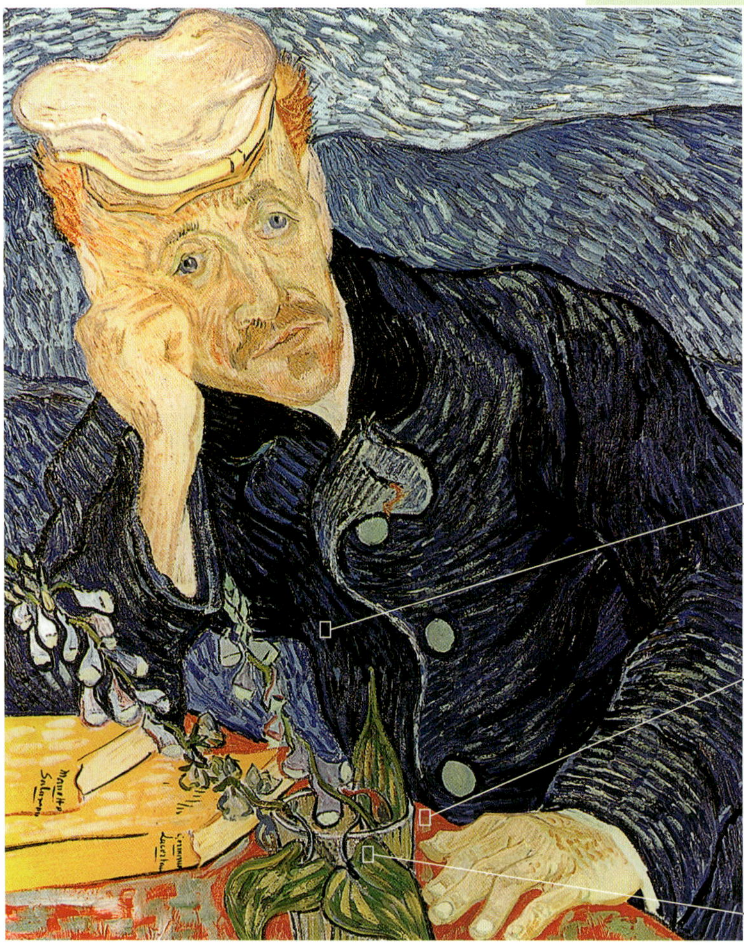

• Grayish blue. Much of the blue has been neutralized by mixing in a little orange, its complementary color.

• Bright red, with no added colors. It retains its light and purity.

• Dark green: This green has been darkened with its complement, red, although just slightly, in order to preserve its shade and avoid creating a very neutral gray.

The Color Wheel

All the colors in the spectrum can be situated on a color wheel. There are three basic or primary pigment colors that cannot be produced through any mixture: lemon yellow, magenta red, and cyan blue; we could also substitute carmen for magenta and Prussian blue for cyan. If these three primary colors are mixed, they produce the three secondary colors: orange-red, blue-violet, and green. Mixing a primary and a secondary color produces a tertiary color: greenish blue, orange yellow, and so forth, until the circle is divided into as many variations of hue as necessary. Starting with any shade, new colors can also be produced by adding white to lighten the color, or by mixing in its complementary color or black to produce new, muted color scales.

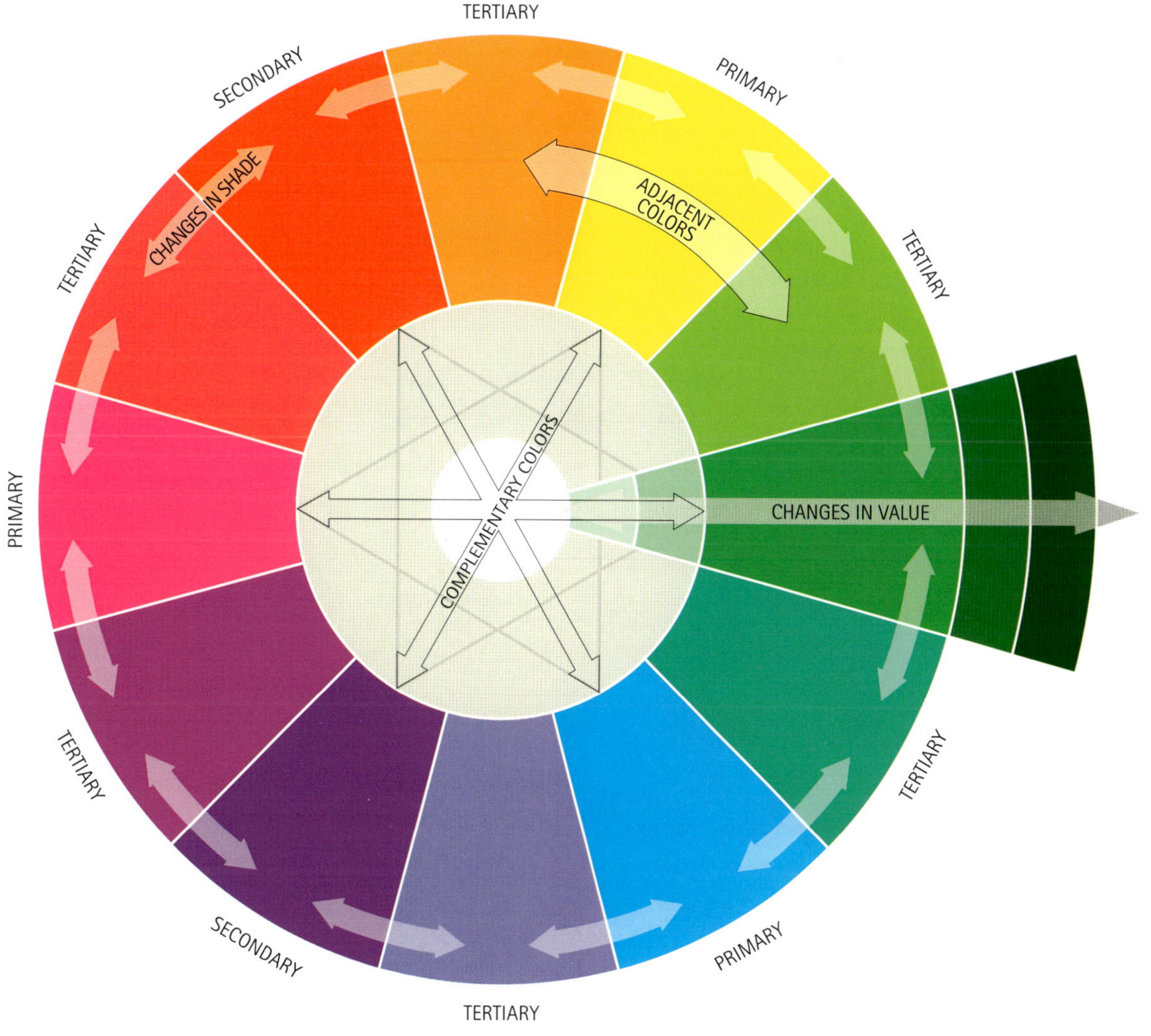

COMPLEMENTARY AND ADJACENT COLORS
When two colors are located at opposite sides of the color wheel, they are complementary: green and magenta, blue and orange, yellow and purple, etc. When they are next to one another they are adjacent: red and orange, yellow and green, and so forth. On the basis of these two relationships it is possible to work up a color by changing its shade if it is mixed with an adjacent color, or by neutralizing it—with attendant darkening—if it is mixed with a complement.

Lightening and Darkening Color

In lightening a color we have two equally valid options: adding white to it or diluting it. In the first instance, the result is a pastel shade of the same color, since the white pigment also has its own density and body. In the second case, the color is lightened with a greater sensation of light and without varying its shade as long as it is applied onto a white substrate.

To darken a color, we need only mix in its complement, and that is the general rule; however, if you don't want to produce any graying of that color a better option is to use the darker adjacent color. For example, red for orange, blue for green, purple for blue, and orange or green for yellow, as appropriate. There are also variations of light in each color depending on the pigment. Thus, in practice this factor means that a cobalt blue is lighter than a Prussian blue and darker than a cyan. Black is almost never used for darkening, since it produces shades with little gradation that sometimes appear dirty.

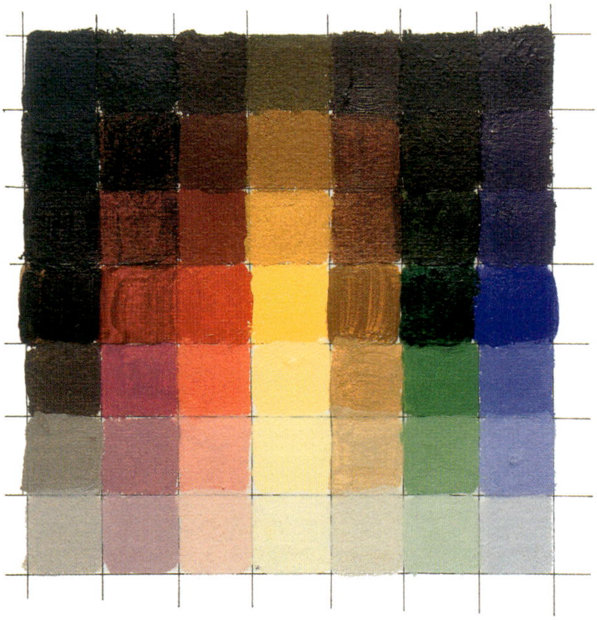

Putting together a color chart like this with values from light to dark is a very useful exercise for learning to lighten and darken colors by any technique. Note that it becomes necessary to use black in producing the darkest values of a color.

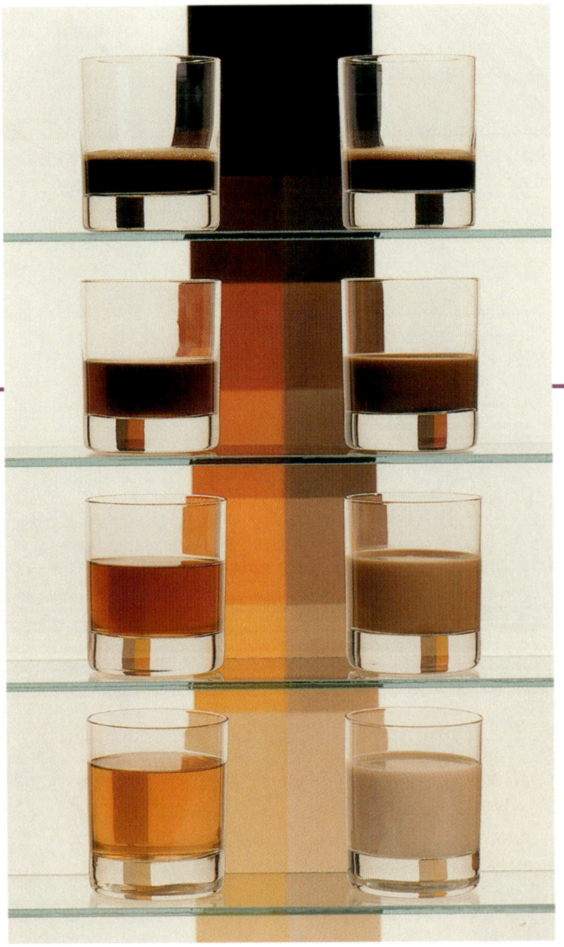

If we put coffee into two glasses and lighten it with water and milk simultaneously, we can observe that the water lightens the color of the coffee without changing its shade, whereas the milk adds a pastel quality. This is what happens with any color; the quality of the light is neither better nor worse, only different, but it must be kept in mind depending on the desired effect.

THE DANGERS OF ABUSING BLACK AND WHITE

Too much white adds a pastel appearance to the point that the color appears milky. Sometimes this can be avoided by mixing a color with its more luminous adjacent color. For example, it can be worthwhile to use yellow to add light to green and avoid turning it into a pastel shade, or to use oranges and earthy colors, which in combination with white produce salmon and creamy colors. Using too much black dirties the color and becomes monotonous, since it allows too little room for maneuvering. If we darken red with black, for example, we produce a darker red, but by always passing through the same garnet colors. Mixing it with greens, on the other hand, produces more variety in dark shades.

Color Interaction

At the turn of the twentieth century, Joseph Albers conducted a thorough experimental study of the influence that colors exert on one another. Two different colors can turn out the same if they are surrounded by appropriate colors, and vice versa.

Chromatic influence is also connected to the extent of each color. For example, the effect that a touch of red produces on the rest of the colors in a composition is not the same as that of a huge patch of red; any gray in that blotch will appear greenish or bluish. Another factor is the intensity of the light, whose interaction we have already examined (p. 28). Finally, it's worth noting that the interaction is produced with greater or lesser explosiveness depending on the borders between the colors (whether shaded or sharply defined).

A century before Albers, Delacroix had declared, "Give me mud and I will paint the skin of a Venus . . ., as long as I can paint the colors around it that I want." There is one clear lesson that we can deduce from all this: one must paint the entire canvas at the same time, never one section at a time, since all the colors interact with and thus change one another.

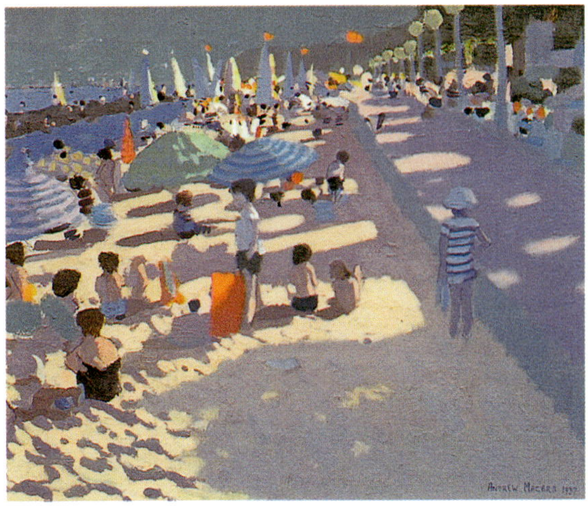

Andrew Macara, The Beach, *1987. Private collection. The neutralized colors in the shadows vivify the saturated colors bathed in sunlight. The fact that the lights have yellow tones and the shadows purple ones produces a greater light and thermal shock between the heat of the sunlight and the coolness of the shadow due to the interaction between the two complements.*

OPTICAL MIXING
Also called *retinal mixing,* this is based on the Bezold effect. Bezold was a meteorologist in Berlin who discovered that certain bright colors distributed homogenously transformed the effect produced by the carpets that he made as a hobby. Color distributed in that way, in small, scattered points, mixes on the retina rather than on the palette, contributing its hue to the whole. Pointillism exploited this resource to the utmost, creating suggestive atmospheres and shapes in paintings based exclusively on retinal mixing.

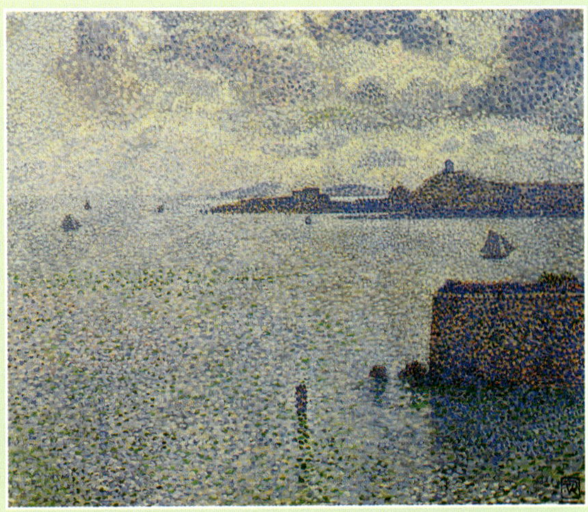

Thea van Rysselbergue, Sailboats and Estuary, *ca. 1892–1893. Musée d'Orsay (Paris, France). Tiny, distinct brushstrokes of blue, carmine, yellow, orange, green, and white form the image on the observer's retina.*

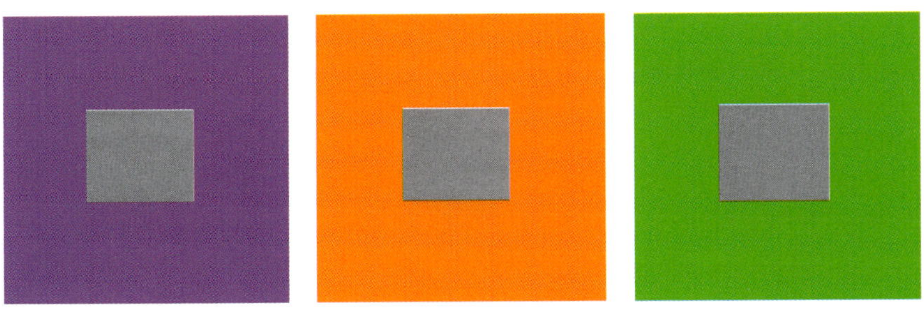

The same gray is seen as more yellowish when the background is purple, more bluish if the background is orange, and more reddish if the background is greenish. Each color forces the neutral tone toward its complementary color.

Chromatic Harmony

Harmony is the internal coherence of the painting. When we say that there is harmony of light and color, this doesn't mean that it's a serene composition devoid of tension, rather that any imbalance, shock, or tension has a purpose, even if it is the search for a violent contrast of value and tone between complements.

Harmonizing involves creating a relationship between the parts to establish cohesiveness, to create unity within the variety. On a chromatic level, this is done intuitively by discovering as the work advances that certain colors don't go well together and must be modified, or that others create the necessary counterpoint to tie everything together. Next we will see some examples of classical harmonization that can assure a certain degree of success to painters without much experience.

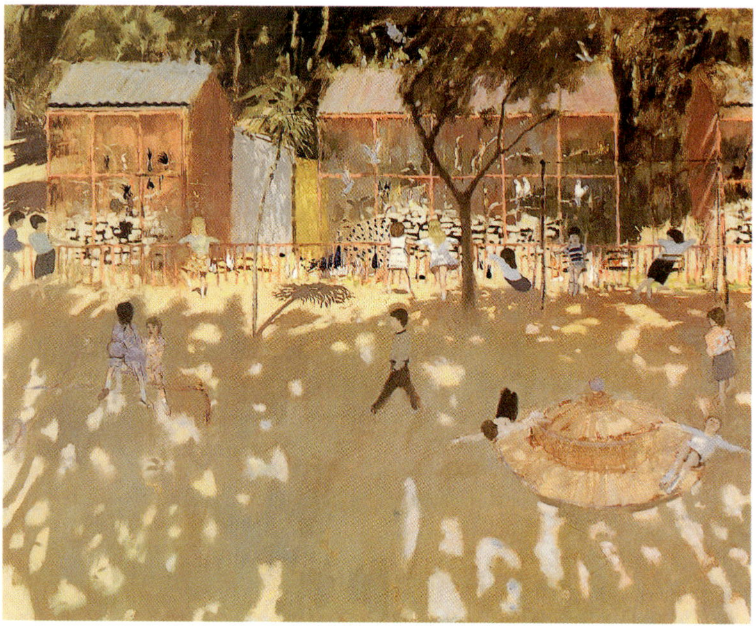

Andrew Macara, Rethymnon, Crete. *Private Collection. Here is a good example of a simple melodic scale. The dominant shade is yellow. In addition to very bright and luminous, pale, dark, orange, and greenish yellows, we also find their adjacent colors: greens and oranges. The counterpoints of their complementary color, purple, heightens the effect.*

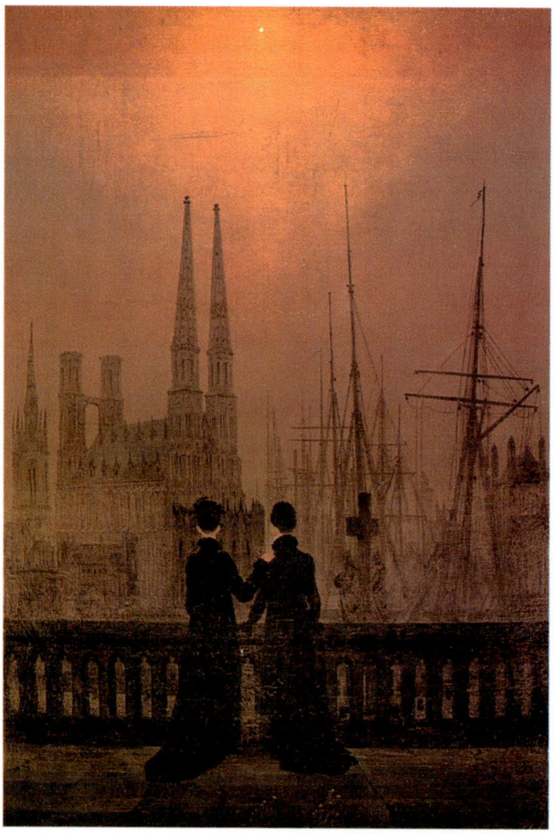

Monochrome and Dominant Tone Melodic Scales

Taking a single color as a base, the entire image is created by using changes of value and tone. If only the value is modified by using black and white or the complementary color, the result is a monochrome; if the tone is also changed, we speak of a simple or a dominant tone melodic scale. In this case, the base color is mixed with other colors to produce shades while maintaining the general character of the dominant tone. For example, a simple melodic scale with a dominant tone in red will admit different reds (cadmium, vermilion, or bright red . . .), oranges, purples, crimsons, pinks, warm grays, earthy colors, salmon, etc. There is also the possibility of adding counterpoints in another color as long as they don't create an excessive contrast. Recall the blue and rose eras of Picasso.

Caspar David Friedrich, The Port at Night (The Two Sisters). *The Hermitage (Saint Petersburg, Russia). The purple shade of this romantic painting contributes an atmosphere of mystery and fantasy by situating the scene in the night. Using few changes in value and tone, the artist creates very suggestive monochrome harmonies.*

Harmonic Triads and Tetrads

Harmonization through harmonic trios is accomplished by combining three colors that are equidistant from one another on the chromatic circle. They form an equilateral triangle, as with the three primary colors, the three secondary ones, three tertiary ones, and so forth. This type of harmonization is very common, since the three colors always compensate for one another on an active and luminous level, although it's important to keep in mind that there is no complementary relationship among them, so the tension is always low. The same operation can also be done on the color circle using squares or rectangles; in that case the result is harmonic tetrads, with similar effects, but with richer nuances of color.

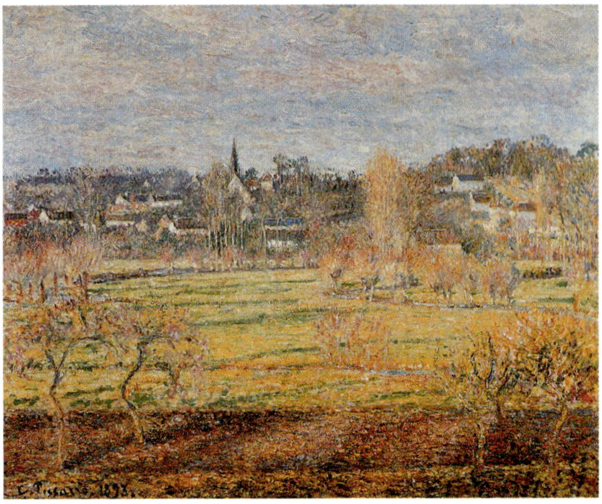

Camille Pizarro, February Dawn, *Rijksmuseum Kroller Müller (Otterlo, Netherlands). Triads of secondary colors are used in many impressionist landscapes: green fields, orange earth, and mauve shadows or skies.*

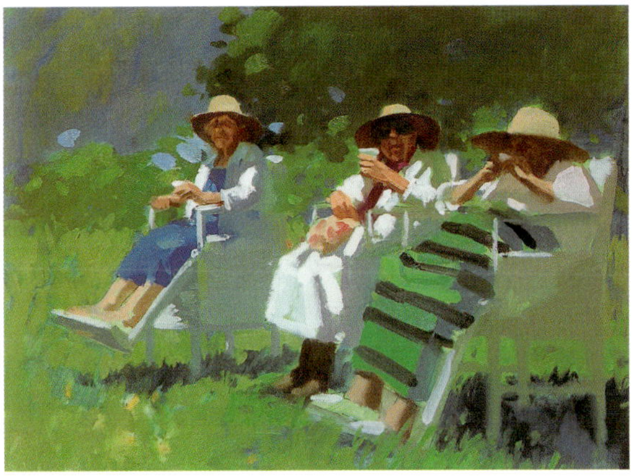

Charles Sovek, The Three Graces, *private collection. Here is a harmonization in a cool color scale, with green as the base. In this case, the white also acts as a cool color, imparting freshness to this scene filled with sunlight.*

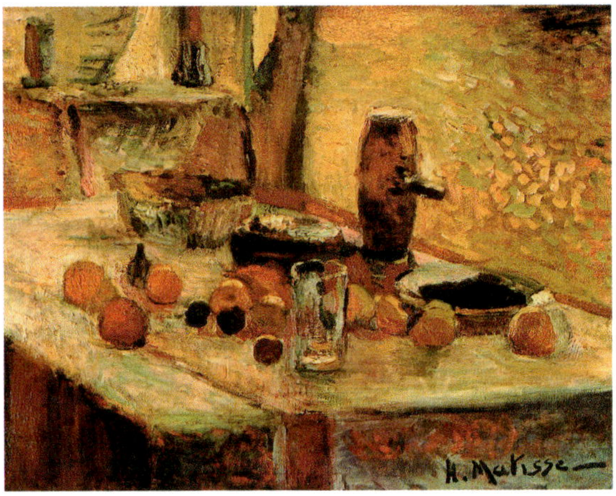

Henri Matisse, Orange Still Life, *1899. Musée National d'Art Moderne (Paris, France). "Stating that color has regained its expressiveness is the same as telling its history" (Matisse). A completely warm color scale: reds, oranges, warm greens, yellows, purples. Black is used undiluted in order to highlight the colors even more.*

Thermal Color Scales: Warm and Cold

In his theory of colors, Goethe established a polarities chart in which colors were associated with hot or cold, with their consequent effects on perception. The phenomenon of temperature in color is subjective, since it is produced only in the mind on a level of perception, but it's very effective. In perceiving a certain color, we associate it with a temperature experience in which this color played a part (the yellow and orange of fire, the red of coals, the blue of water and the sky, the green of plants, and so forth).

Warm colors are considered to be the ones that go from purple to yellowish green, passing through reds and oranges. Black, even though it is neutral, quickly adds heat. These colors produce nearness and dynamism, in contrast to the cold colors, which suggest spatial depth and passiveness. The cold colors are the blues and greens, along with the bluish purples. White adds more cold than heat, even though it too is neutral.

Harmonizations Between Complementary Colors

The relationship between complementary colors is that of greatest chromatic contrast. Two complementary colors have nothing in common; they are totally opposite one another, and they establish a relationship of compensation and tension. If we look at a color for a long time and then close our eyes, we see its complement. We have already seen that a neutral gray surrounded by an active color is perceived to be tinged with its complement. This type of chromatic shock can be used to produce very dynamic harmonizations. We can draw a comparison with the difference between a sweet and a salty food. One color would be the sweet, and its complement the salt. If we eat something salty right after something sweet, the contrast is extreme. But this vibrancy can exist only as long as the colors are not mixed together, since they would cancel one another just as mixing the two foods would annul them both.

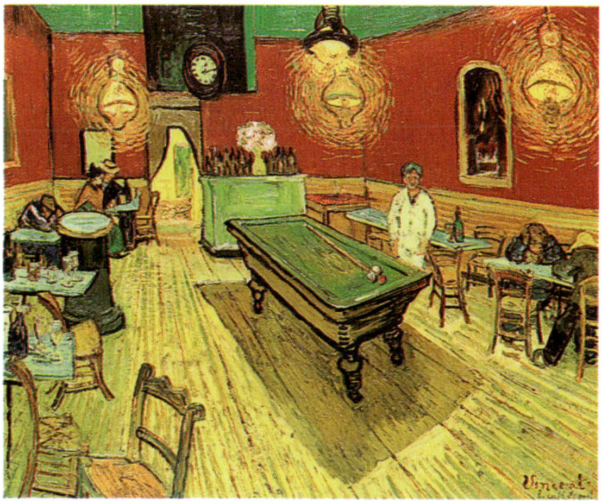

Van Gogh, The Café at Night, *1888. Yale University Art Gallery (New Haven, Connecticut). An application of the contrast between complementary colors in a radical and concentrated form, using red and green.*

HARMONIZATION BETWEEN COMPLEMENTARY AND ADJACENT COLORS

This follows the same mechanism as the harmonization between complementary colors, but in this case one color is combined with another that is adjacent to its complement, such as orange and green or orange and purple, but not orange and blue, because they are direct complements. Nor is it necessary that the adjacent color be very far from the direct one; with that same orange, a blue-green or a blue-purple would work.

Neutral Ranges

Despite the famous declaration by Delacroix, when I assert that "the enemy of painting is gray," one thing is certain: the neutral combinations always turn out well harmonized and may be exquisite for their elegance and suggestiveness. Working with neutralizations balances the whole, for no colors are excessively vibrant, and all are present in some way on the entire surface, and the chromatic vibrancy is subtler because it places emphasis on light values. The neutral scales mean that any saturated color stands out and gives off its own intense light. For example, if there is a touch of cobalt blue in a general harmonization of gray tones, it will appear to be very luminous because of the chromatic energy of that pure blue. This is a resource that's commonly used to create very beautiful effects of light.

Anders Zorn, Summer Dance, *1897. National Museum (Stockholm, Sweden). Zorn painted this tableau at the request of his friend and fellow painter prince Eugene, with the intention of depicting a dance that was celebrated in Sweden during the summer solstice under the aurora borealis. The broken shades are appropriate to a late afternoon.*

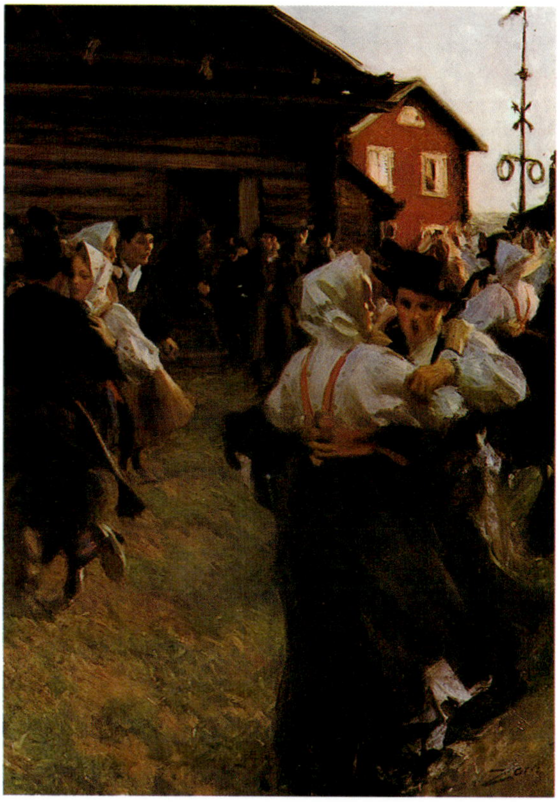

Light Defines Shapes and Space

When we look at the full moon, its relief appears as flat spots, but when the moon is in the crescent phase, the relief is seen as real craters, with mountains and depressions. All this information varies according to the type of illumination.

There is a double value to luminosity and color: on the one hand, the local luminosity and color, which are the ones that belong to the object and depend on the material—a lemon is luminous yellow and a coconut is dark brown—and on the other hand, illumination, which imposes shapes and color changes that are transitory—they depend on that specific luminous moment that will have a decisive effect on the definition of that object. It's not the same to perceive the lemon or the coconut in the half-light as under the direct beam of a nearby light source for, depending on the illumination, other colors, shapes, and textures will be detected besides the luminous yellow and the dark brown.

Light defines space and shapes by contrast, that is, the chromatic and monochromatic chiaroscuro.

Light defines space and shapes by contrast, that is, the chromatic and monochromatic chiaroscuro. Chiaroscuro is an interplay of light and shadow. We see two types of shadow: shadow on the object and shadow that the object projects. The former is right on the object and part of it; we don't think about it when we see the object. The projected shadow has the same physical nature, but it is perceived as being very different from the former, since it involves the imposition of an object that has a strange power to create darkness on another object. The shadow on the object is not subject to distortion, but rather always adapts to the shape of the object; however, a projected shadow always distorts the object, since it is conditioned by the nature of the space or shape onto which it is projected, as well as by the illumination, and there is more distortion with artificial illumination than with natural light. Shadows on an object create shape; projected shadows always create space.

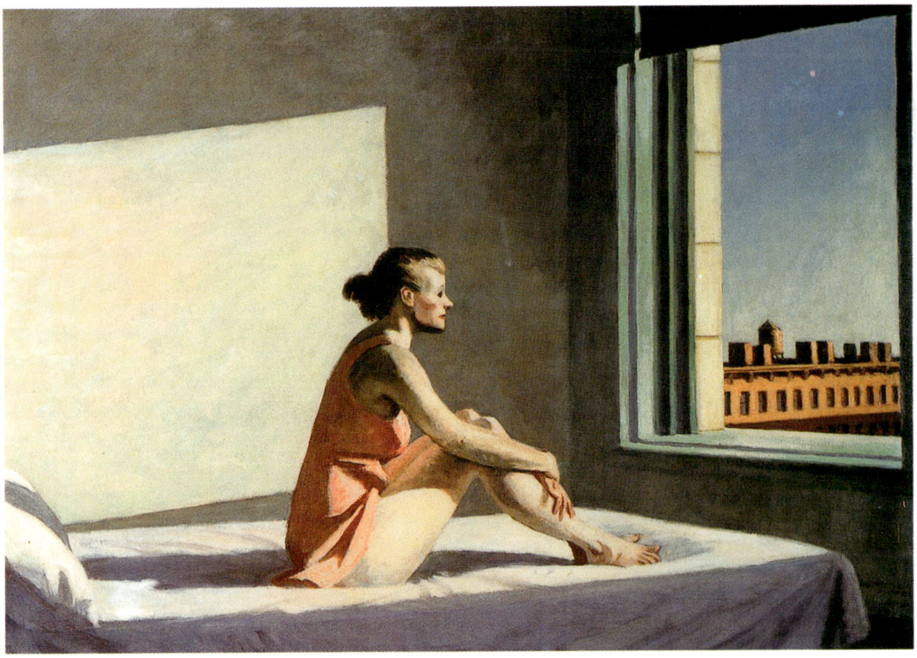

Edward Hopper, Morning Sun, *1952. Columbus Museum of Art (Columbus, Ohio). Fascinated by the effects of light on figures and space, Hopper focused in his paintings on interiors and exteriors in which a wall, a highway, or a piece of furniture takes on tremendous poetic weight.*

Creating Shapes Through Chiaroscuro

Modeling defines the shape through correct application of light values and shadows to the object. For that purpose, every brushstroke or line has to be adapted to the morphology of the object with respect to size, direction, and value.

In order to capture value and its extension, the methods of observation previously described (page 27) must be applied. With respect to the direction of the brushstroke or line, the following advice may serve as a useful exercise, especially for artists without much experience. This involves using the brush as an instrument of touch, imagining that you are touching the object. The direction that the hand would take is the one to follow with the brush.

The passage from light to darkness in modeling, whether using colors or crosshatching, can go from a soft shading to a hard contrast. In any case, there will be modeling as long as there is a scale of values. If the light source is too close to the object it destroys the modeling, since it annuls the gradations and reduces the shape to just two planar values. Diffuse light, on the other hand, offers more shades and details in the modeling.

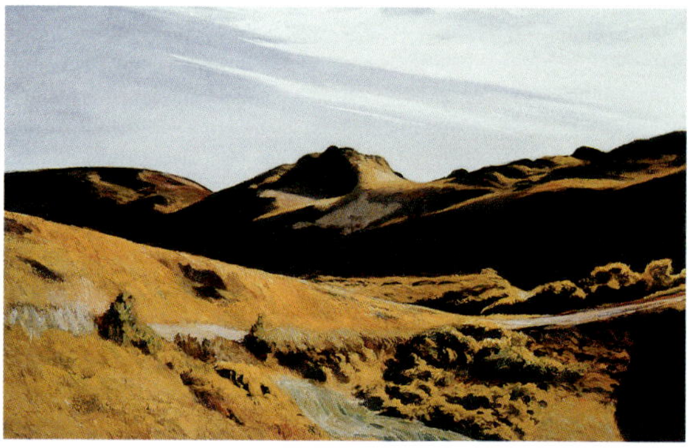

Edward Hopper, The Camel's Hump, *1931. Proctor Institute Museum of Art (Utica, New York). Certain landscapes are perceived to be similar to other shapes, but in larger scale. The modeling here defines the orography of the landscape.*

Two different ways to create gradation: crosshatching and shading.

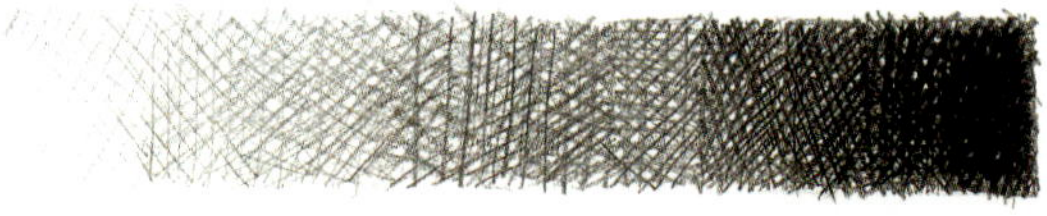

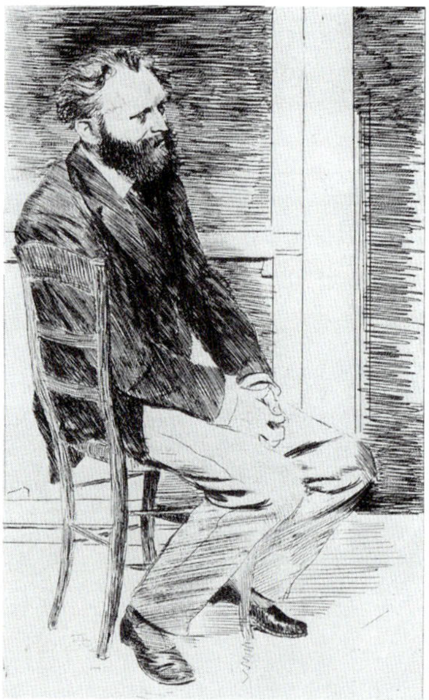

Edgar Degas, Edouard Manet Seated, Turning Toward the Right, *ca. 1866–1868. Musée des Beaux-Arts du Canada (Ottawa, Canada). In working with lines, one must use crosshatching to create different grays.*

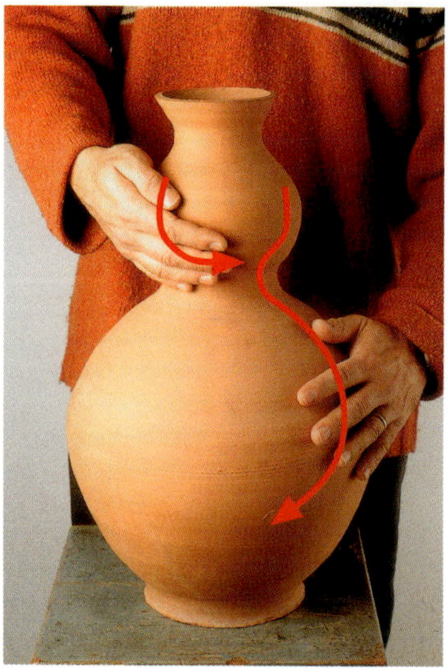

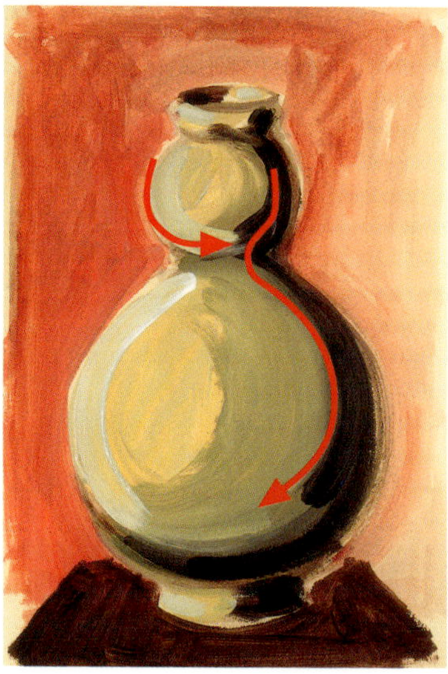

The direction of the brushstrokes in modeling mustn't go against the natural shapes of the object. One efficient method for capturing these shapes effectively is to imagine that you are running your hand naturally over the object. The direction that your hand would follow is the one to use with the brush.

Modeling Clothing

All painters have worked with clothing, either as preliminary studies for other works or as a project for analyzing shapes and textures. In theory, depicting clothing is no different from any other type of modeling, although at a higher level of specificity one more problem is added: representing textures, since a silk is not the same as sack cloth or velvet. Every material responds differently to light.

Coarse, rough fabrics absorb more light, and it's easy to model them: passages from light to dark with intermediate values. The texture can be defined by the type of stroke. The smoothest fabrics reflect more light, even producing satiny luster in the instance of some natural silks, or a nearly brilliant shine on synthetic fabrics. The color of the clothing is also important. Using the same illumination, a white fabric moves in the high light zone with dark touches, and a black fabric in the low zone with touches of light, as we can see in the painting by Isaac Brodski.

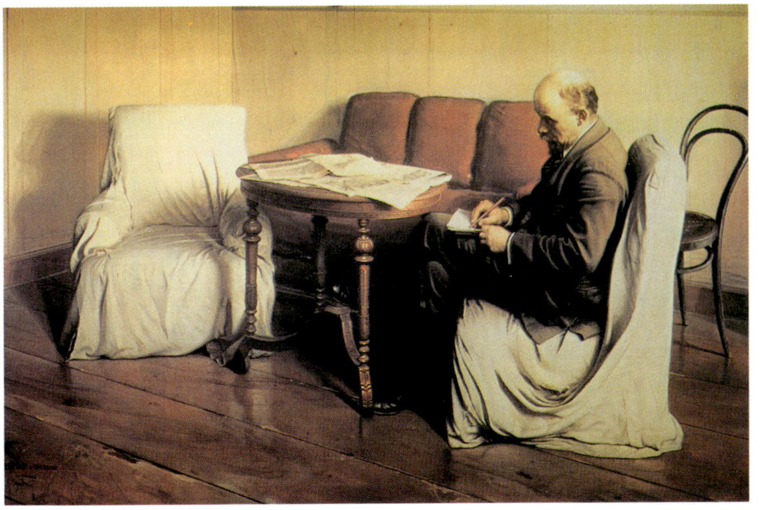

Isaac Brodski, Lenin in Smolnyi, *ca. 1920. Tetriakov Gallery (Moscow, Russia). Wonderful apparel in this painting of photographic realism that is a page from the artistic chronicle of the Russian Revolution.*

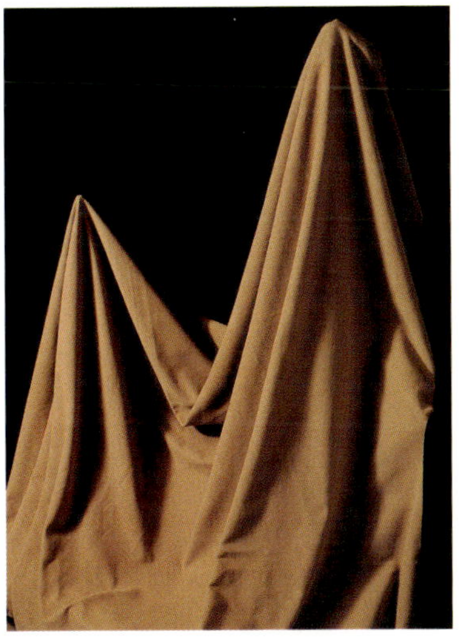

Every fabric has its own personality. Before painting it, you have to study its characteristics of texture, draping, luster, and color, since these characteristics, in combination with the light they receive, produce a particular effect.

1

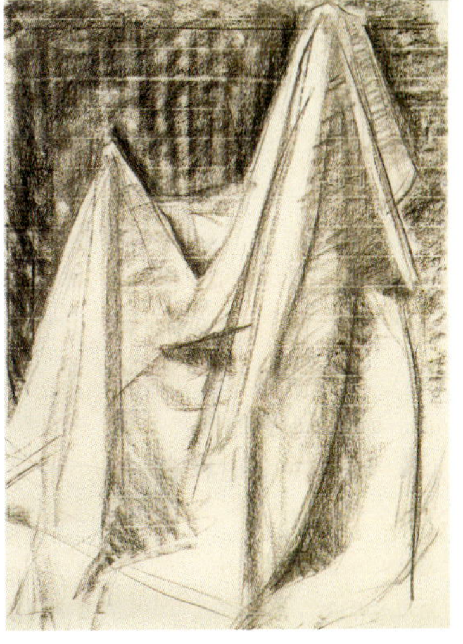

2

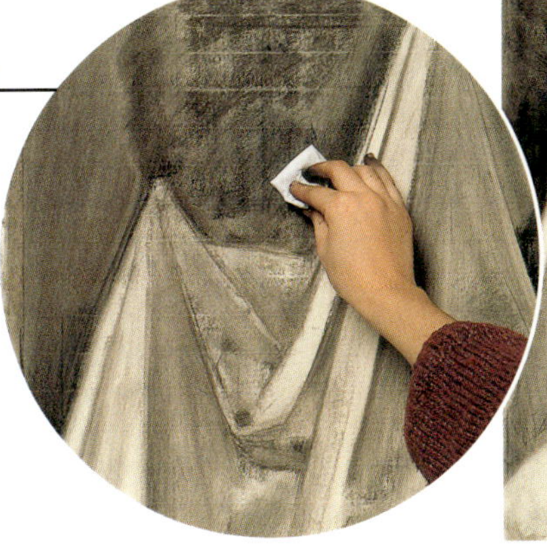

3

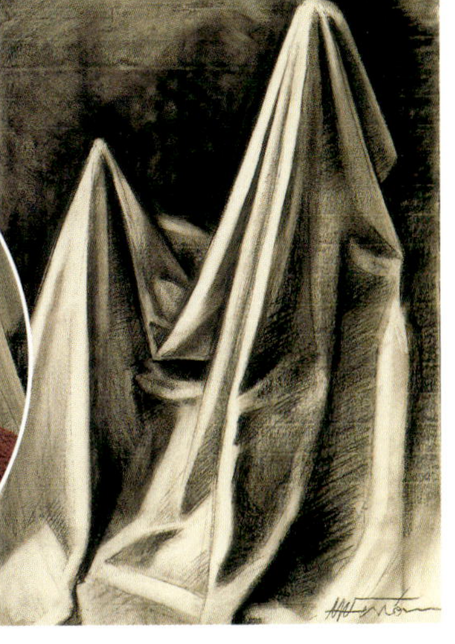

1 The first strokes set up the basic shape.

2 The areas of color are shaded more or less as a function of the fabric. As the shading fills in the empty pores of the paper, it provides more or less body to it. Light areas can be created by erasing.

3 Here is a finished charcoal drawing by Myriam Ferrón.

Projected Shadows

Projected shadows are an extension of the object in the space produced by the light, and although they are part of the object, they also constitute it from the projection space and everything that it reaches. A projected shadow reproduces only the silhouette of the body, with no shades or values, and it is almost always distorted.

The color of these shadows is the color of the space on which they are projected (the ground, a wall, or another object), not the object that casts the shadows. That color darkens, as we have noted in the chapter on color. In addition to shape and color, we also have to pay attention to the nature of the shadow, defined by the contrast and the determination of its limits. A very hard shadow will set up a strong contrast and have very specific limits, but a very soft one won't create much contrast and will have limits that are not clearly defined. Finally, the point of view of the scene has an influence on how the shadows are seen, since they adhere to the perspective in precisely the same ways as the objects that produce them.

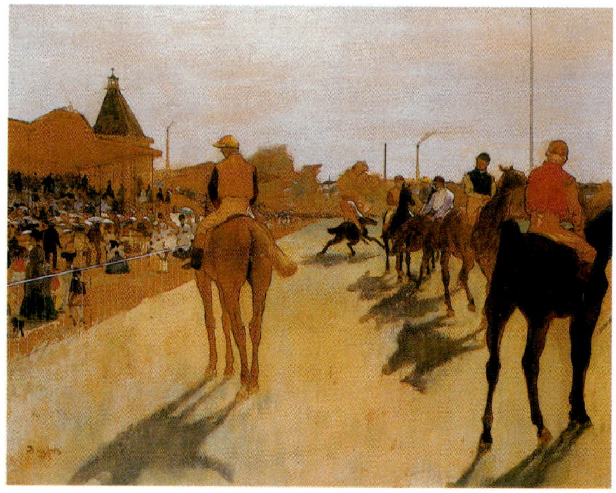

Edgar Degas, Race horses in front of the Grandstand, *1866–1868. Musée des Beaux-Arts du Canada (Ottawa, Canada). An excellent painting in which the projected shadows are as important as the figures themselves. Without them there would be no clear perception of the ground plane, the horses would lose their appearance of height, and the low afternoon light would not be captured.*

SHADOWS WITH ARTIFICIAL LIGHT
Artificial light sources emit their light rays in a radial shape, spreading out from a point (the light source). The shadows also propagate in divergent fashion, starting with the projection of the light source on the ground. Shadows from artificial light are highly distorted due to the lack of parallelism. The edges tend to be less clearly defined, since there is not always a single light source, and that causes several combinations of shadows.

Direction of shadows with artificial light. The light spreads out from the source, and so do the shadows cast on the ground.

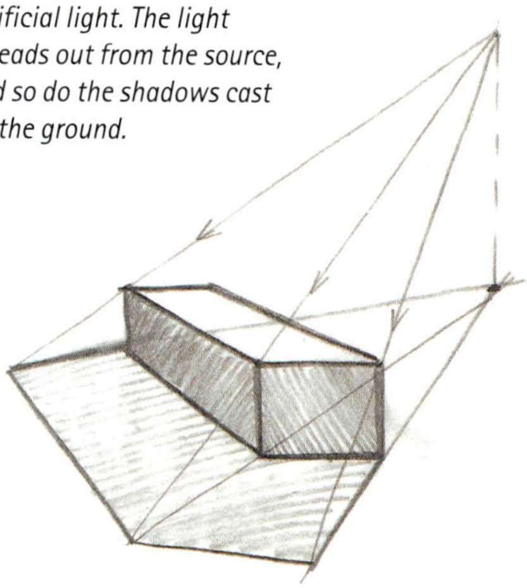

SHADOWS WITH NATURAL LIGHT
Due to the tremendous distance from the light source, the sun, the light beams are parallel. The shadows are likewise projected in parallel, except when the sun is in front or behind, in which case the shadows fall on the line of recession. Depending on the hour of the day, the shadows may lengthen, and that must be kept in mind when painting landscapes.

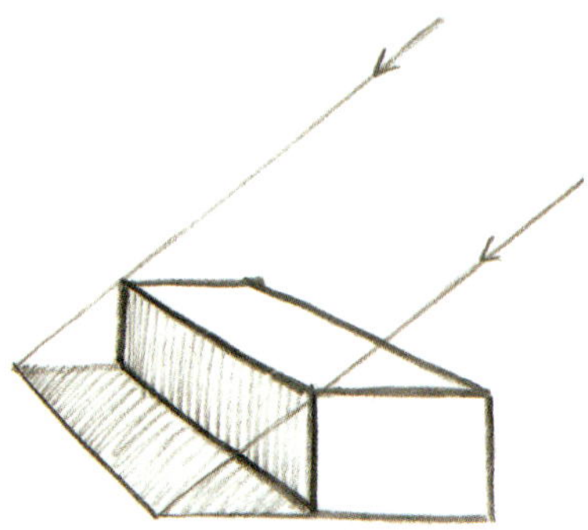

The direction of shadows with natural light. The light beams are parallel.

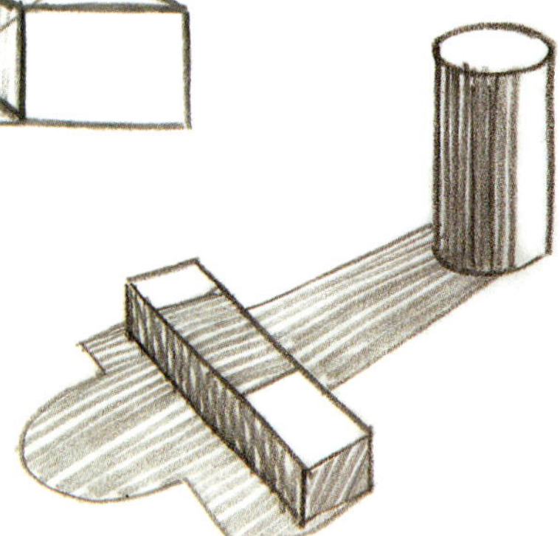

The shadow always adapts to the orography of the ground and the obstacles located in its projection.

Highlights and Reflections

Everyone knows that black surfaces absorb light and white ones reflect it, and that perception exists because of reflections of visual reality onto the retina. But these reflections don't go toward the retina exclusively, for the light is also spread throughout the scene, since every object, depending on its color and composition, acts like a reflective screen.

There are four phenomena produced by the reflection of light in an image:

• Radiance: reflections of light that bodies produce as they illuminate one another by acting as reflective screens, especially white surfaces.

• Highlights: reflections from the light source: the sun, light bulbs, fluorescent lights, windows, etc.

• Color reflections: objects that are very close reflect their color onto one another, especially the most luminous and active ones.

• Image reflections: especially on polished surfaces, including the mirror effect. Objects and the surrounding space are reflected: walls, surrounding shadows, etc.

Jan Vermeer of Delft, Young Woman with a Pitcher, *1660. Metropolitan Museum (New York).*

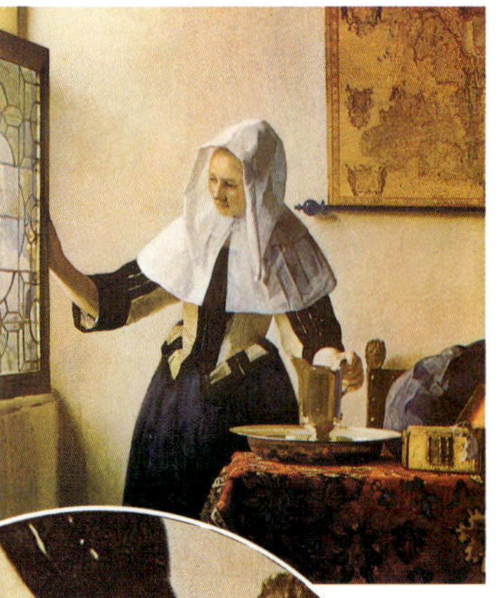

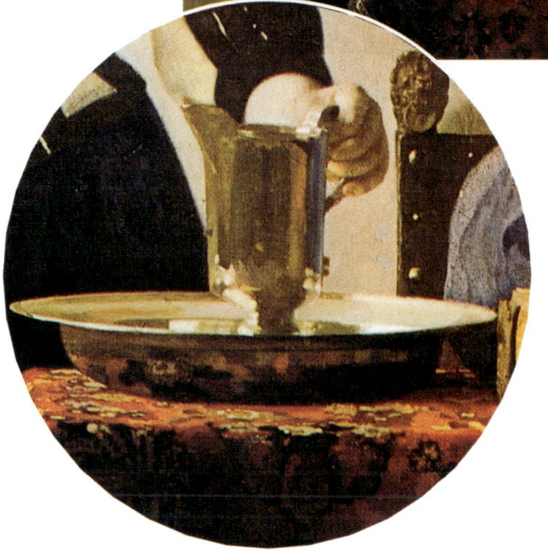

Take a close look at the details on the pitcher and the basin, which reflect the surrounding space (walls, lights, and shadows), the objects (the tablecloth), the colors of the surroundings, and the light sources and reflections. The basin acts like a reflector for the pitcher, and vice versa, because of their polished surfaces.

REFLECTIONS IN WATER

Water, like most liquids, acts like a polished surface, causing multiple reflections according to its movement. The greater the movement, the less distinct the reflected image, until the ambient light is reduced to multiple reflections, as in the current of rivers or the sea. Stagnant water, which is much more still, can act like a true mirror as long as the air is not moving.

Valentin Serov, Pond with Weeds, *ca.1900 Tetriakov Gallery (Moscow, Russia).*

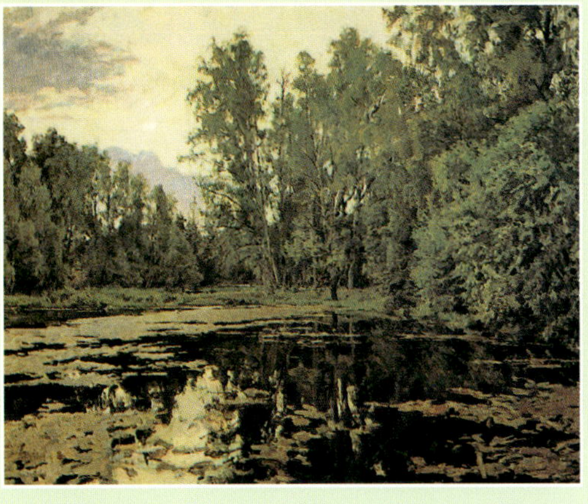

The reflection on the polished surfaces of objects conforms to the shape, producing a contrasting effect with clear delineations. Reflections on matte surfaces simply model the shape with gradations.

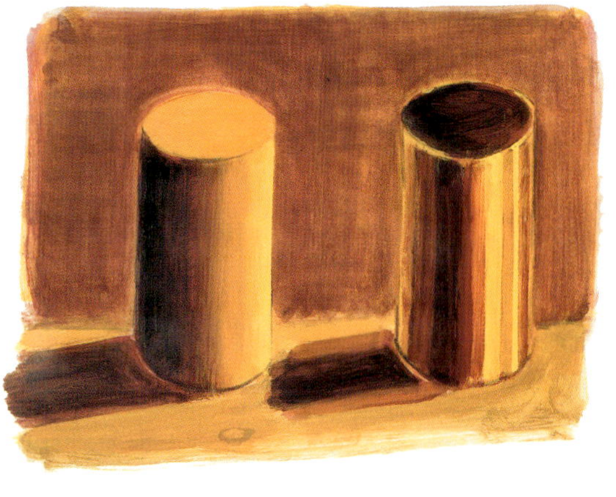

Transparency

When an object is not entirely opaque, special luminous effects are produced in the object itself and in the shadow it projects. This involves transparency and filtered light. Depending on the degree of opacity, there will be total transparency or a greater or lesser degree of translucence. This affects the color and the shape of everything located inside and behind the object.

If the transparent body is not a plane, the light penetrates the walls of the shape and produces surprising effects of chiaroscuro. We observe lines, shading, and unexpected reflections: we merely need to look at glass bottles. These effects lose definition if the object is translucent and can be converted into diffuse streaks of light and shadow. If the object is colored, it will act with light like a chromatic filter, coloring everything near it like a colored light bulb. Another effect to keep in mind is that light passes through the body and invades the projected shadow, even producing soft glints inside it.

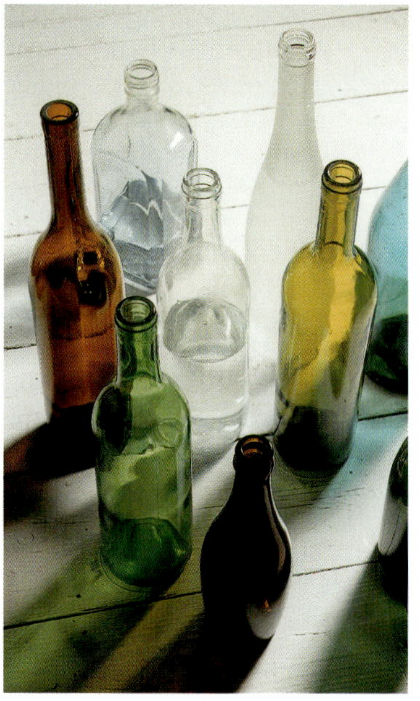

Note in this photo from life the visual phenomena that are normally produced in transparencies: distortions, color reflections, color changes, light inside projected shadows, reflections of shapes, and gleams of light.

A transparent glass beaker allows us to see what is behind it even though it produces distortion. The smooth surface and the liquid it contains also reflect the surroundings. The gleams of light become more intense as the background darkens.

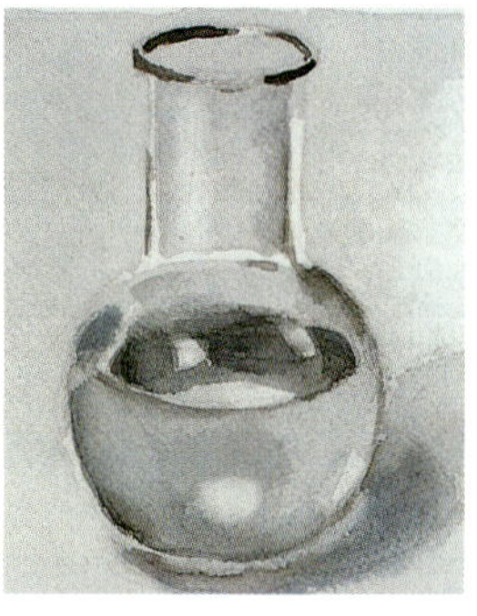

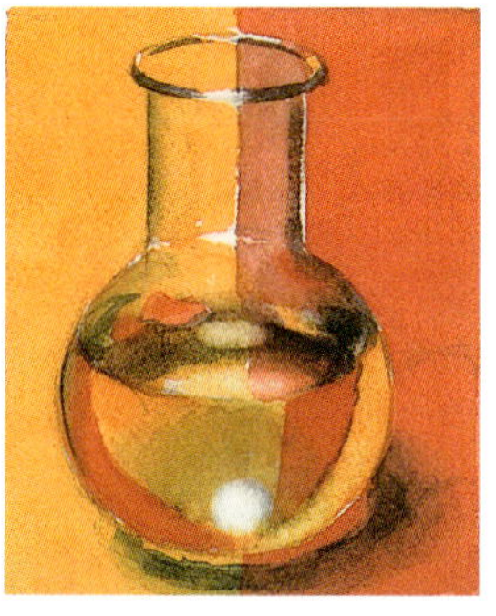

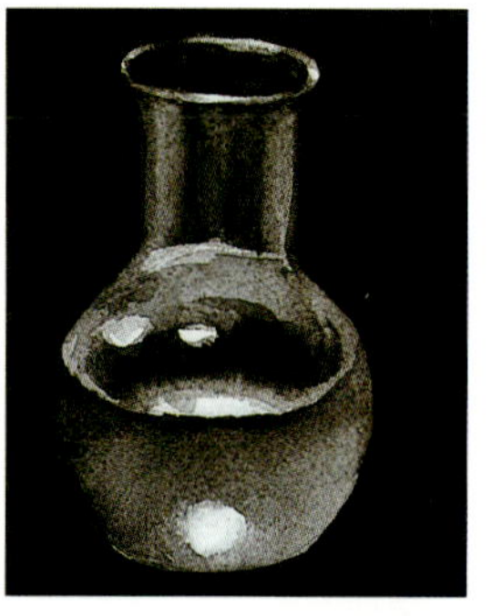

FILTERED LIGHT

Types of filters include fabrics, curtains, blinds, awnings, arbors, and the very foliage of trees. It's a good deal easier to represent this light if the cause of this effect is included in the scene, for that helps the observer understand the changes of color or quality, as well as the curious shapes of the lights and shadows—sometimes rays or points of light—produced by blinds.

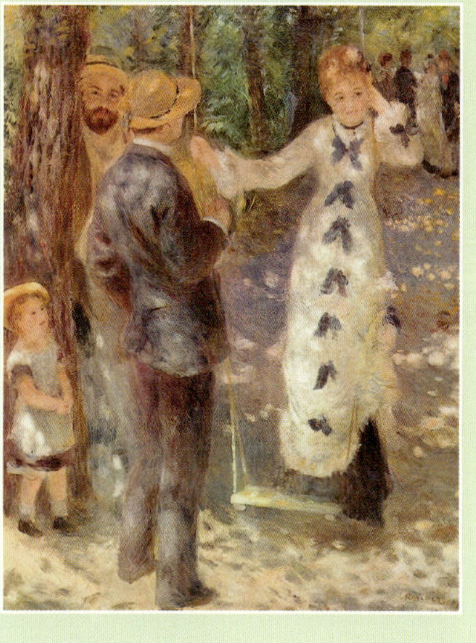

Pierre Auguste Renoir, The Swing, *1876. The Louvre (Paris, France). The light filtered through the foliage of the trees produces a light play in the general shading that gives the scene a special magic and charm. It's important that every point of filtered light conform to the shape or space on which it lands.*

Light Defines Space

Space appears to be structured visually by a fairly clear distribution of contrasts in light. Spatial limits are perceived through factors involving distance and corporality (such as walls, ground surfaces, horizons, and corners), or abstract sensations involving space (depth, recession, emptiness, an abyss, hazes, etc.). One clear effect of spatiality is gradation, which implies the transition from light to darkness and vice versa. In terms of perception, light creates nearness, and darkness distance; thus, gradations create depth. Increases in luminosity help create increases in distance. The distance increases if a change in illumination is added to a change in size between an object in the foreground and another one farther away.

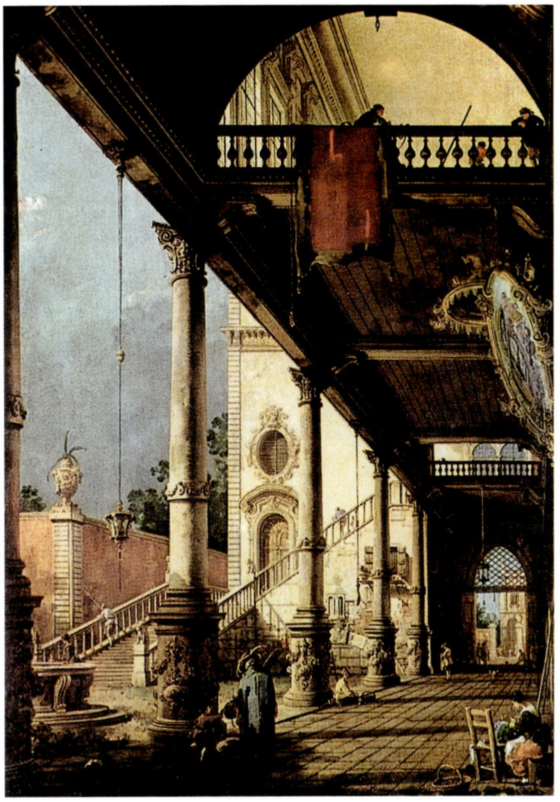

Canaletto, Caprice with Portico and Hallway, *1765. Galleria dela Accademia (Venice, Italy). This work by Canaletto shows depth created with perspective and a spatial division between the interior of the porch and the outside, created through the distribution of light and shadow.*

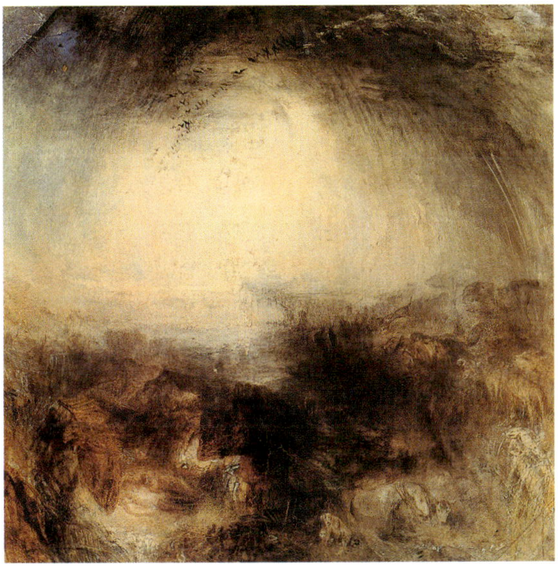

William Turner, Shadow and Darkness, the Afternoon of the Deluge, *1843. The Tate Gallery (London, U.K.). Despite the fact that the lights and shadows rest on no object, the interplay between areas of light defines spaces and depths, masses, densities, and openings.*

Some luminous phenomena that define space: A simple gradation is all that's required to suggest depth of space (A). The perception of a single shape may vary according to how the shadows are arranged (B). Changes in luminosity between the foreground and background help reinforce increments of distance (C). The arrangement of reflections indicates a cavity or a bump (D).

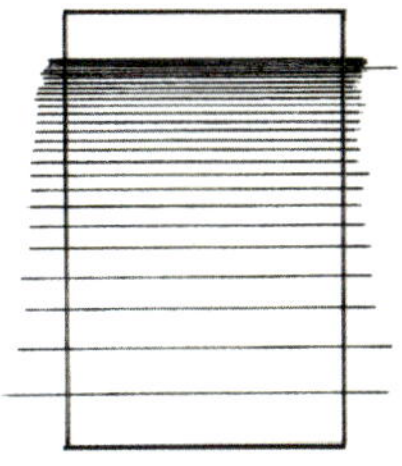

A

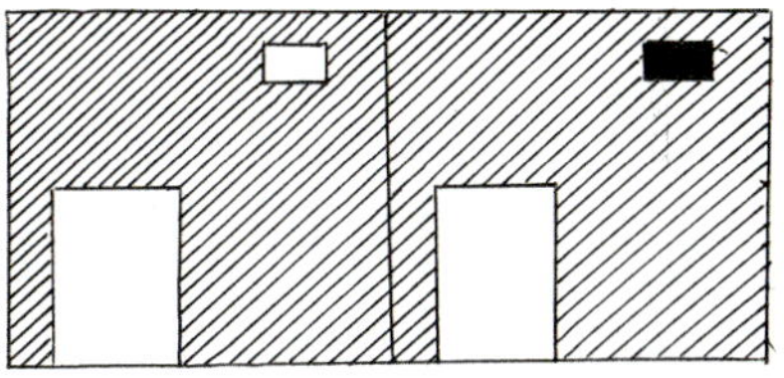

C

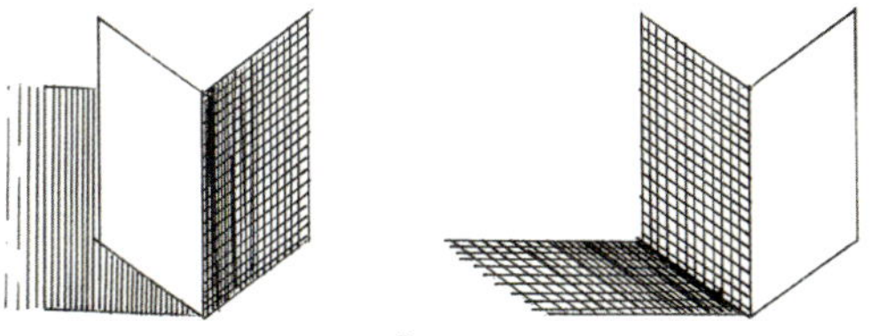

B

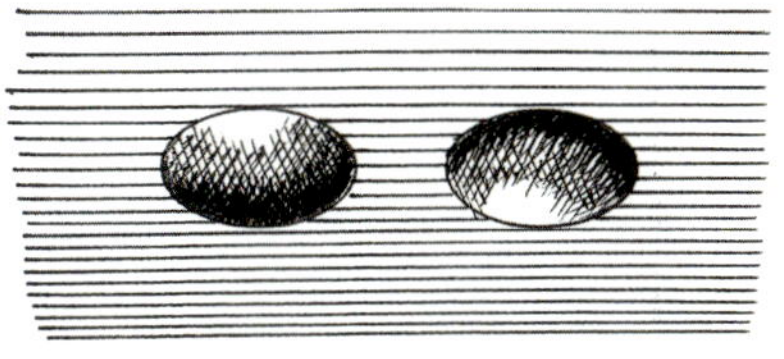

D

Light and Linear Perspective

Linear perspective is a graphic resource for suggesting depth. This method is based on the very effect of human vision: a horizon line located on a level with the observer's eyes on which truly parallel lines converge in vanishing points. According to this system, a road that has the same width for its entire length is perceived in recession in such a way that the width decreases as it approaches the horizon. Any geometric shape is perceived in the same way, and it can create one or two vanishing points, depending on whether it is presented frontally or at an angle.

In reality, outlines or borders don't exist, not even in our perceptions; they are merely a convention used in drawing. There are differences in value between planes created by light effects, and the outlines are the limits between one plane and another.

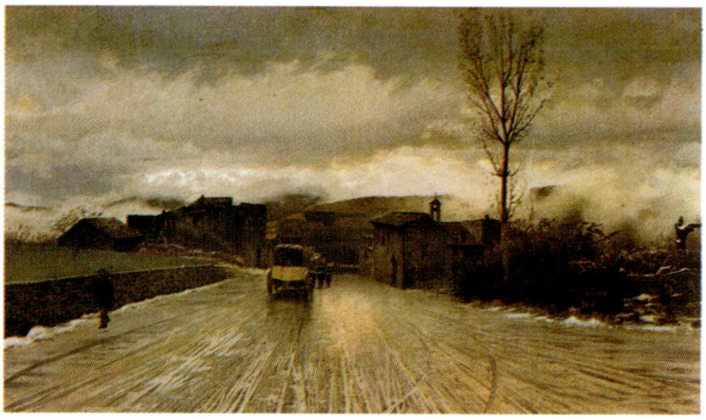

Giuseppe de Nittis, Crossing the Appenines, *1867. Galleria Nazionale de Capodimonte (Naples, Italy). Note the application of linear perspective to landscape. Roads, highways, and rivers are defined on the basis of vanishing points where their borders merge, on a horizon that may or may not be visible. The tire tracks in the frozen road also follow this law.*

DIFFERENT SPACES IN THE SAME PERSPECTIVE
Within a single linear perspective, the sense of depth can be controlled by working the gradations and contrasts among receding planes. Also, light interspersed among objects, and the location and quality of the illumination, can create very different atmospheres and perceptions. Illustrations 2, 3, and 4 demonstrate this factor clearly, for even our perception of the room's spatial dimensions (1) changes.

1

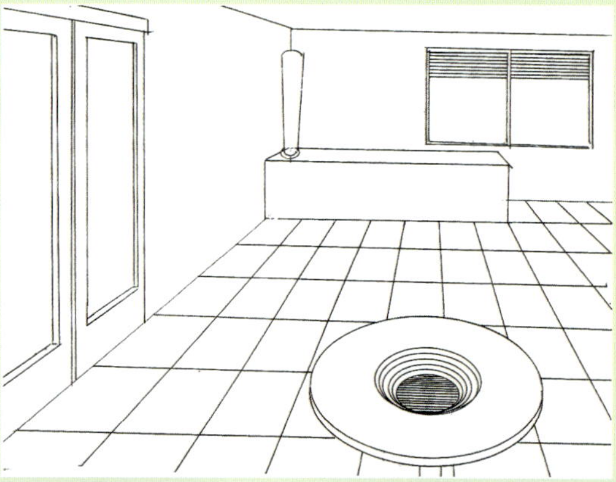

2

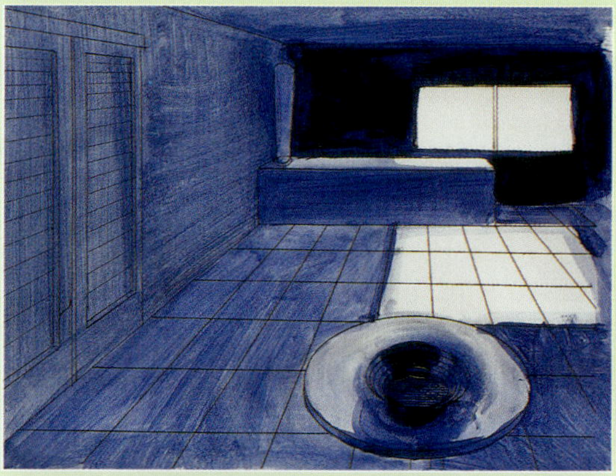

3

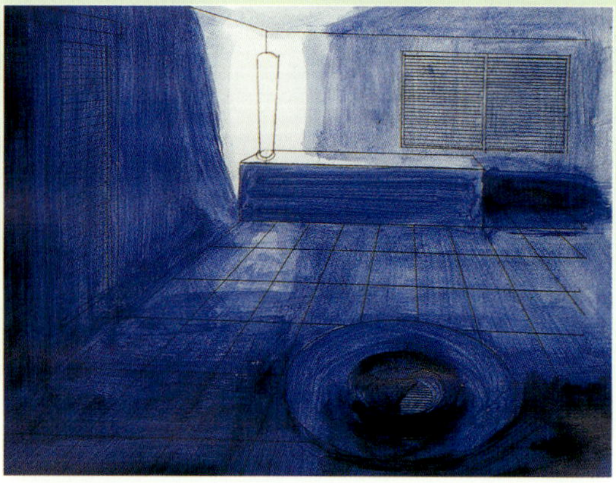

4

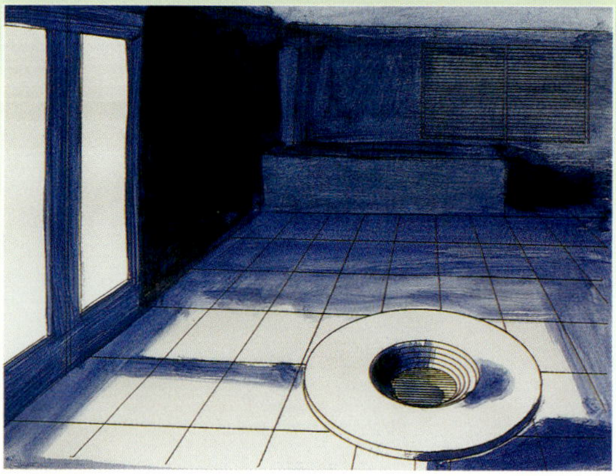

Aerial Perspective

When the space is not hemmed in by linear borders, it's impossible to apply linear perspective. A field of wheat, a mountainous landscape, a valley, a marina, and a lake are represented according to other laws that are based mainly on the perception of shapes and space according to the effect of light in the atmosphere. This set of laws defines aerial perspective, which was described by Leonardo da Vinci in his treatise on painting.

Due to the effect that atmospheric mass produces on space, three great phenomena are produced. First, it creates a lack of definition; this is obvious when the atmosphere is heavy or very vaporous, but there is a lack of definition with things that are far away even on a clear, sunny day. Secondly, there is a reduction in contrast; the farther away an object is, the less contrast it exhibits, appearing more gray and neutral. And finally, colors become cooler as distance increases, and if they are very far away, they appear bluish.

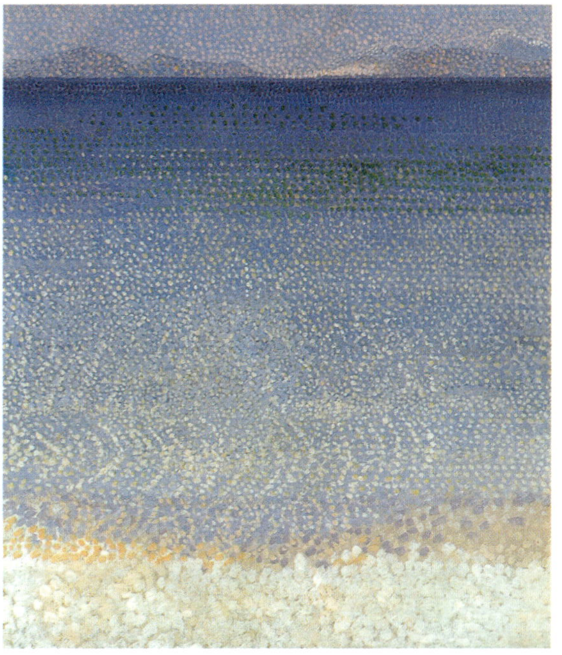

Hendi-Edmont Cross, The Islands of Gold, *1892. Musée d'Orsay (Paris, France). In this painting, the composition is based on the simple overlaying of strips of color (the sand, sea, and sky) in a gradation that cools the colors as a function of their distance until arriving at the vaporous silhouette of the islands at the top of the painting at the level of the horizon.*

FOUR LAWS OF PERSPECTIVE IN LANDSCAPES

- Distance reduces definition.
- Contrast is greater close up.
- Distant hues become cooler due to the atmospheric mass, and become bluish.
- The farther away an object is positioned, the smaller it appears.

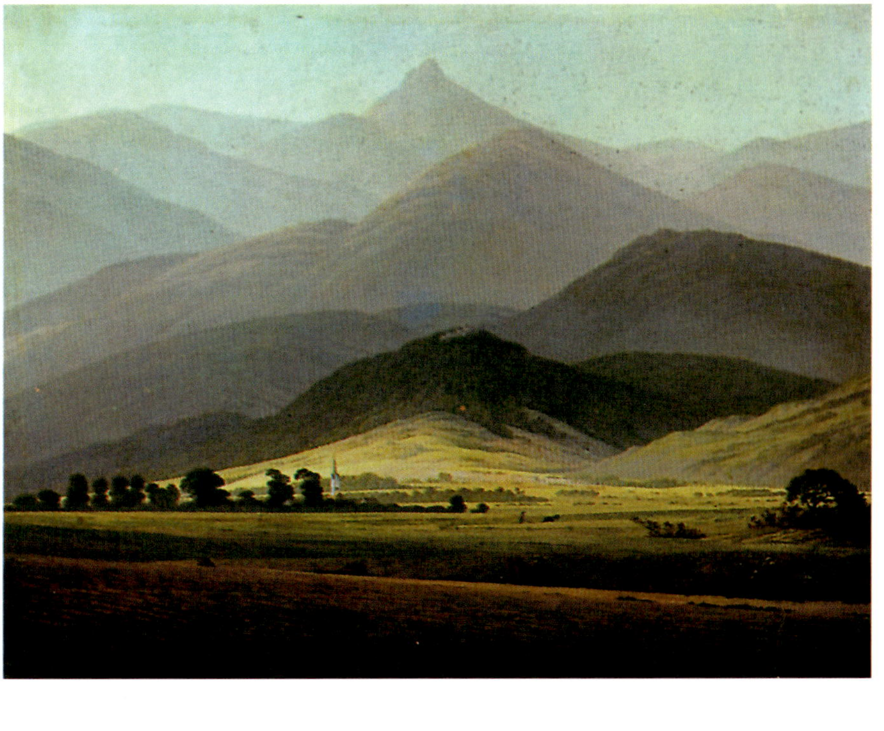

Kaspar David Friedrich, Mountainous Landscape. *Pushkin Museum, (Moscow, Russia). The sensation of spatial grandeur is a perfect example of the application of aerial perspective. The mountain chain recedes in the distance as it gains altitude and depth, and its colors become diffuse and cooler in the space.*

Chiaroscuro and Composition

The arrangement of lights and shadows in a scene is organized on the basis of compositional intent. Composing involves arranging the parts as a function of an overall sense, creating visual directions that go from the points of greater importance toward the more marginal areas of the image.

Setting aside the picture's narrative, we can consider chiaroscuro to be a composition of masses on one plane. The darkest masses have more weight than the light ones, and that weight factor needs to be balanced as on a scale unless a destabilizing effect is desired. Before starting a painting, it's a good idea to do a few preliminary sketches to arrange the main features in an attractive way and study the light masses. There must always be a center of attention, a visual focus that draws in the observer's gaze and acts as a door through which to enter the work. Finally, it's worthwhile to point out that every color has a different weight; to verify that, you can photocopy a color card and observe the equivalent gray shades of every color.

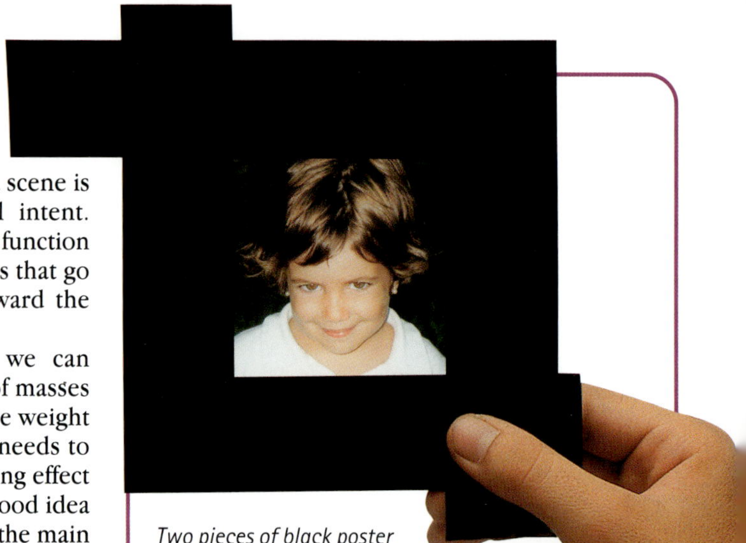

Two pieces of black poster board can be used to make a frame that's adaptable to any format.

PHOTOGRAPHIC FRAMES

Aside from traditional compositions, such as central, symmetrical, pyramidal, and diagonal ones, there are more personalized framings that can be used for any scene. Sometimes all the poetry of a picture is in the contrast between a dense mass and a large, airy space, or in a very heavy object located at the top of the composition that creates an unexpected tension.

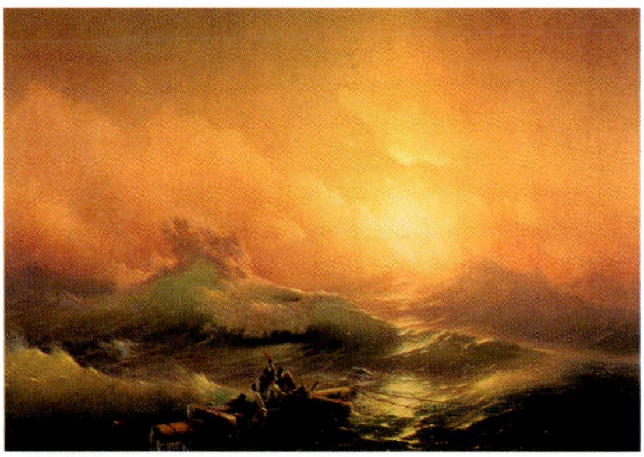

Ivan Avazovski, Ninth Wave, *1850. Russian Museum (Saint Petersburg, Russia).*
In this magnificent sample of pictorial Romanticism we observe the spectacle that combines tragedy and beauty. The light of dawn produces a chromatic explosion that becomes the center of attention in the picture. The whole scene unfolds from this point of light.

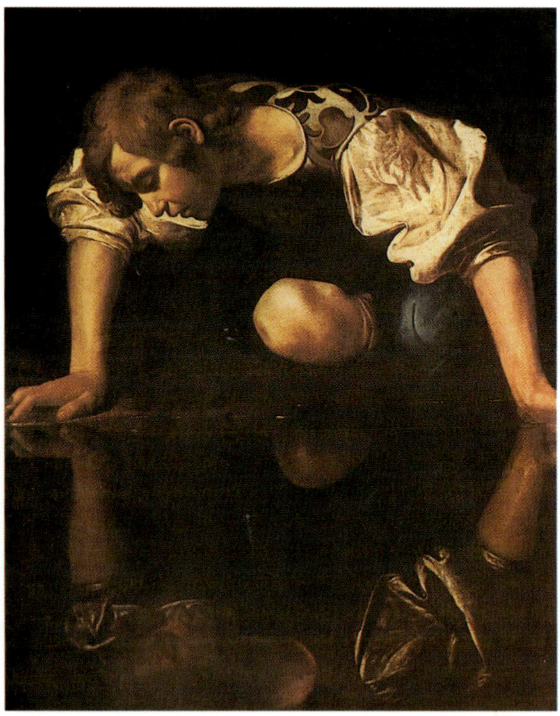

Caravaggio, Narcissus, *1600. Galleria Nazionale d'Arte Antica, Palazzo Corsini (Rome, Italy). Caravaggio structured this Narcissus in a simple but effective symmetrical composition based on a horizontal axis to create a mirror effect. The illumination is stronger in the upper part to indicate that it is real, whereas the lower part is a reflection.*

Resources for Representing Light

The different materials and procedures express very different artistic values, since every technique has its own language. The light effects in a scene are perceived as charged with expression or poetry depending on the medium used.

Every medium has its own personality, and none is superior to another, only different, like the instruments in an orchestra. It's as important to know how to choose the right instrument for each composition as it is to know how to play it to deliver the musical piece with all its beauty to the audience. In the following pages we will treat from a theoretical viewpoint the possibilities of the most commonly used media; we will then examine some specific examples in the subsequent chapter.

In speaking of mediums, it's inevitable to refer to music. If we want a fine, elastic sound, we will use a flute or a violin, but not a drum; similarly, if we want a fine line of variable intensity, we will use a pencil and not a brush loaded with paint. When we intend to represent and highlight the effects of light using these mediums, it's crucial to know the possibilities that each one offers so we can make the best choice. Oils are a good choice for creating a tenebrist chiaroscuro because of the shading and the depth of the colors; charcoal and graphite are good choices if we want a tableau in black and white, but watercolors are not because they are too luminous and transparent. On the other hand, watercolors are a good medium for conveying the reflections of light on the sea and a clean, luminous, atmosphere, but not pastels, and charcoal even less. Some mediums are more limited technically than others, just as with musical instruments, but that doesn't make them less interesting. Oils and acrylics are the most versatile, and of the two, oils offer the greatest chromatic richness for depicting light and color, although some pastel works convey a very special atmosphere. It's worthwhile to experiment with them all.

◆

When we intend to represent and highlight the effects of light using these mediums, it is crucial to know the possibilities that each one offers so we can make the best choice.

◆

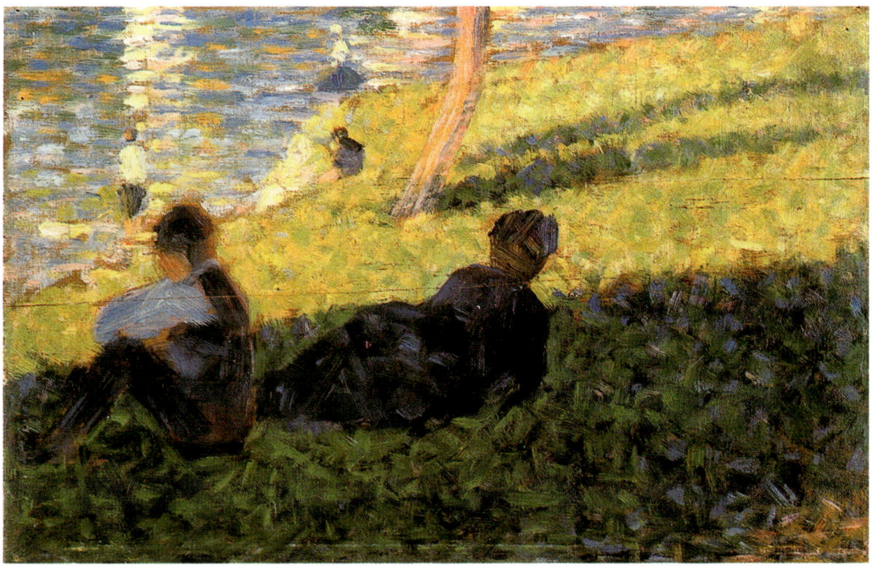

Georges Seurat, Study for "Afternoon on the Island of Grande Jatte," *1884. Musée d'Orsay (Paris, France).*
A quick sketch like this one by Seurat, done outdoors at four in the afternoon to capture what Monet referred to as "the impression" found an appropriate medium in oils, since they make it possible to mix shades and do any necessary touching up without sacrificing any freshness.

Chiaroscuro in Pencil

A pencil consists of a small core of a mineral known as graphite surrounded by a wood casing. Graphite can also be bought separately in the form of a bar or in powder, for the purpose of creating broader lines, or even broad areas of color if it's applied in powder form with the fingers or a rag. Graphite never produces black, since its natural color is slightly metallic gray. It is applied to uncoated paper, and it can be corrected using an eraser. An eraser can also be used to create light areas in a patch of color, although it can also smudge if there is a lot of graphite on the paper. A pencil can be used for working with lines and crosshatching as well as with shading. In both cases a pencil is always very suggestive and poetic.

Colored pencils have a lead made of pigment and a binder. If the binder is water soluble, the color is also water soluble. Colored pencils aren't a particularly satisfying medium for creating contrast, so they are not recommended when light is the central theme.

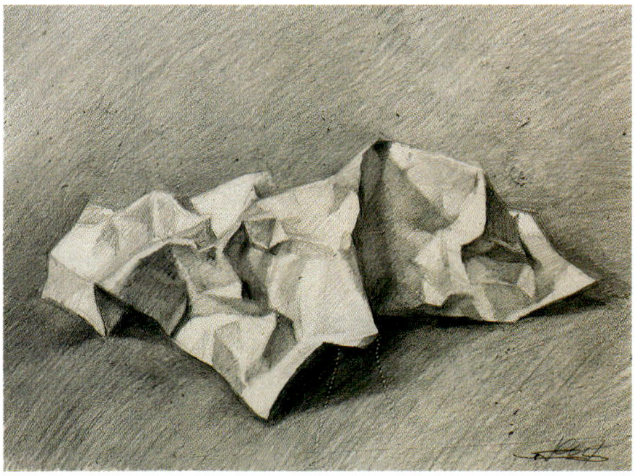

Pencil sketch of paper by Miquel Ferrón. The pressure of the pencil on the paper is another factor that influences the intensity of the line.

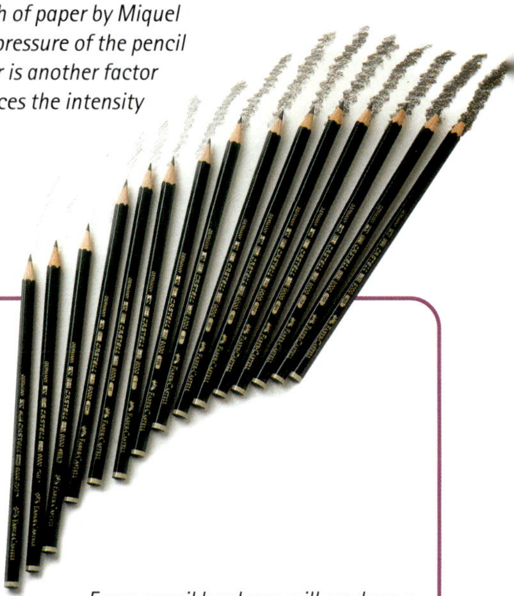

DIFFERENT HARDNESSES FOR DIFFERENT LIGHT VALUES

Graphite leads come in different hardnesses. Leads are numbered according to a standard code, from the hardest, which are identified with the letter H, to the softest, which correspond to the letter B. Some commercial brands have ranges of fifteen hardnesses, and others have up to seventeen or eighteen; in that case the pencils will go from 9H, the hardest, to the softest, 7B, by way of HB, which is the medium and the most commonly used hardness.

Every pencil hardness will produce a different gray. The hardest leads yield a very pale gray and a fine line that may even scratch the paper if enough force is applied. The softest leads produce very dark grays and make it possible to draw thick, variable lines. It's not common to use them all, but it's interesting to combine different hardnesses in a single drawing.

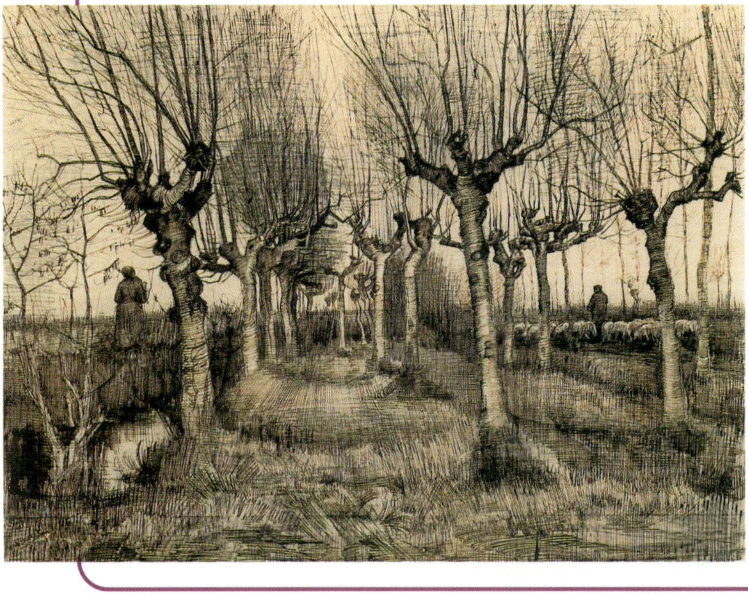

Vincent van Gogh, Pruned Willows, *1884. Rijksmuseum Vincent van Gogh (Amsterdam, Netherlands). Pencils make it possible to develop chiaroscuros using shaded areas of color and crosshatched lines. In this drawing, van Gogh created grays with very expressive linear strokes.*

Charcoal

This is the oldest medium known, since charcoal was used for painting as early as prehistoric times. Formerly, branches were burned in hermetically sealed pots, but nowadays sections of vine or willow branches are carbonized in special ovens. In addition to the charcoal sticks you will need a rag and an art eraser, fixative, and, as a support, porous or laid paper.

Customarily, charcoal has been used for preparatory sketches, but it is a valid and expressive medium unto itself. Various techniques can be used with charcoal: crosshatching with linear strokes, smoothing in with the fingers or blenders, applying powdered charcoal or using the breadth of the stick, washes with a brush and water, touches of light with white chalk, and erasing with a rag or an eraser. Charcoal can be combined perfectly with other mediums, especially with chalks—sanguine, sepia, white, or gray. The results are even richer on colored paper.

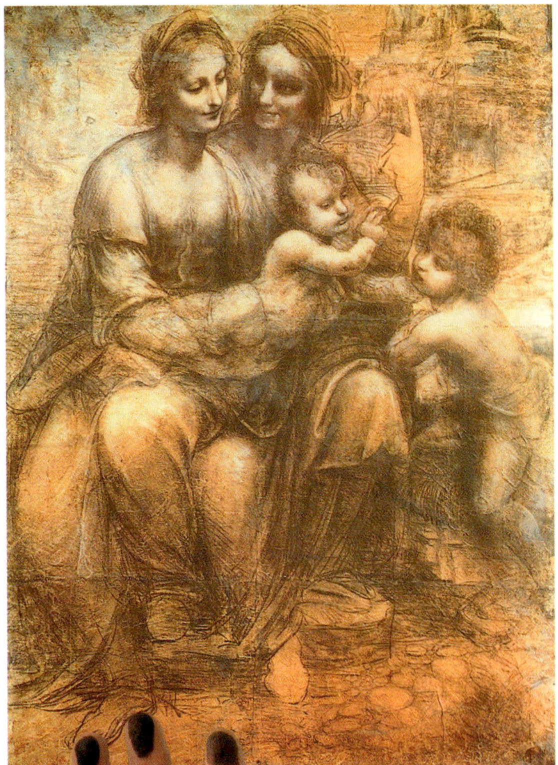

Leonardo da Vinci, The Virgin, the Child, and Saint Anne *(study), 1498. Tate Gallery (London, U.K.). A magnificent interpretation of the shapes in this preparatory sketch by Leonardo da Vinci, thanks to the versatility of charcoal and sanguine, which make it possible to blend in, draw lines, and erase with ease.*

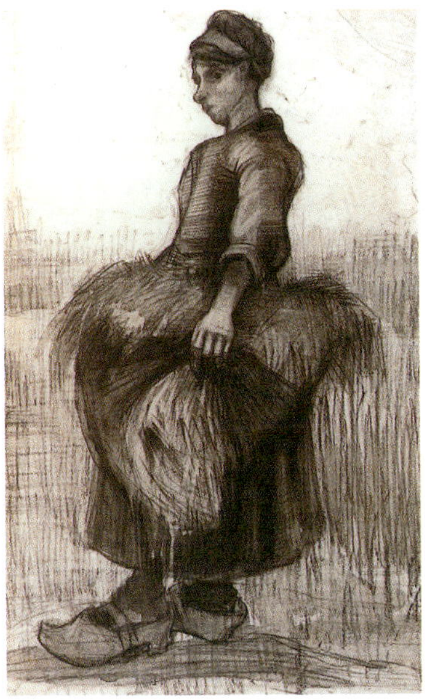

Vincent van Gogh, Peasant Woman Carrying Wheat in Her Apron, *1885. Rijksmuseum Kröller-Müller (Otterlo, Netherlands). Drawing done in black ink on laid paper. The reflections were created by erasing on dark areas.*

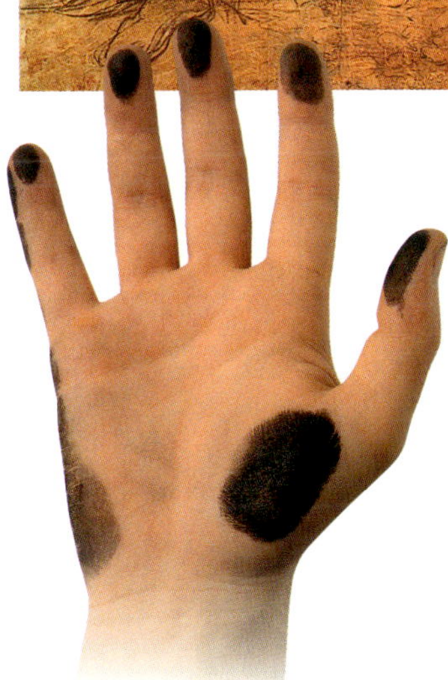

The hand is a basic tool for working in charcoal. The palm is used to blend in large areas, and the fingers are used for details.

These sticks of charcoal are nothing more than carbonized willow branches.

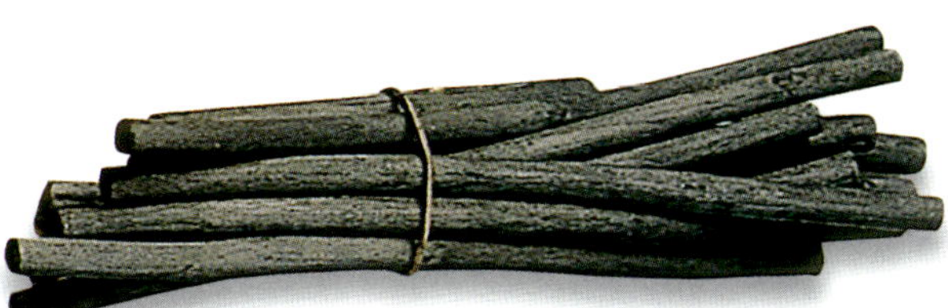

Chalk sticks and pencils. Chalks are pigments that are pressed with a little binder; they are a good complement to charcoal. The sticks make it possible to apply broad areas of color.

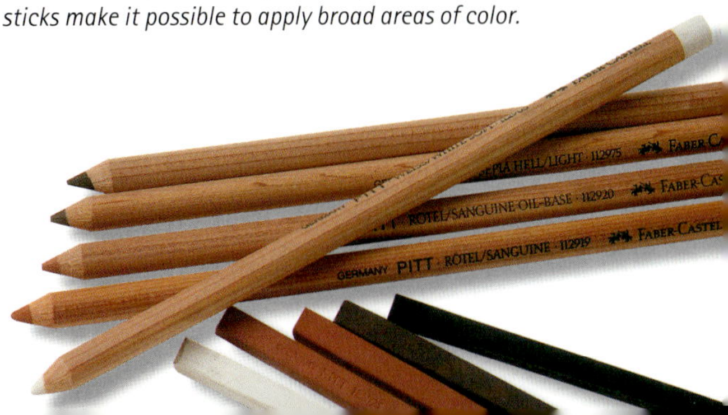

Pastels

Pastels consist of bars of paste containing pulverized, agglutinated pigments with very thin tragacanth gum. They have been in use since the eighteenth century (Rosalba Carriera, Quentin de la Tour, Chardin, etc.). In the Rococo period, many artists used them because of their freshness and spontaneity.

Pastels combine the qualities of drawing and painting. The bar makes it possible to produce lines as well as linear shading effects, plus freestanding or blended areas of color with very picturesque results. Pastels require a spontaneous and sure technique, without many corrections. The best approach is to work expeditiously and enjoy the fresh, quick work. The blending can be optical or real. The greatest danger of this technique is that of falling into an affected, bland effect, like butter, due to excessive shading.

In addition to the pastels, the equipment required for working includes colored papers, both fibrous and grainy, blenders, a soft eraser, a blade for sharpening the sticks, a brush for removing excess pigment, and fixative.

Odilon Redon, Portrait of Ari Redon, Son of the Artist, *1897. The Art Institute (Chicago, Illinois). Post-impressionists like Redon used pastels with a certain degree of smoothness and preciseness, but without falling into an affected aesthetic.*

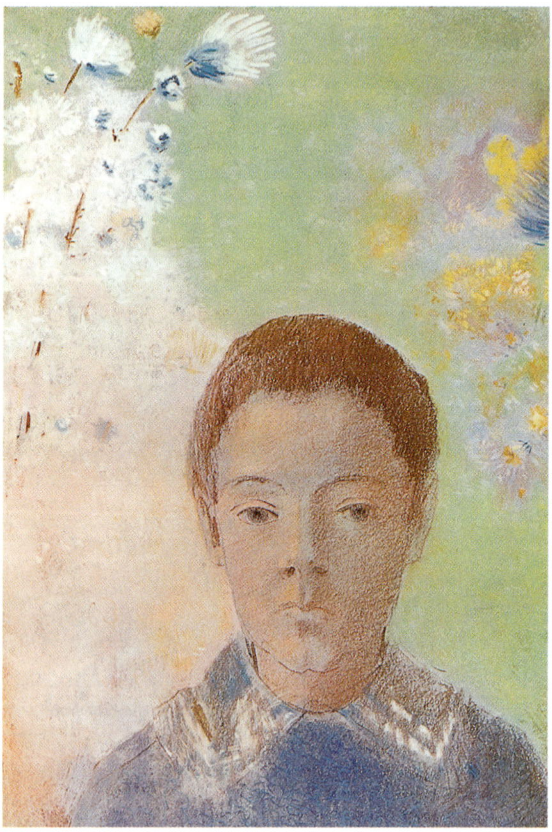

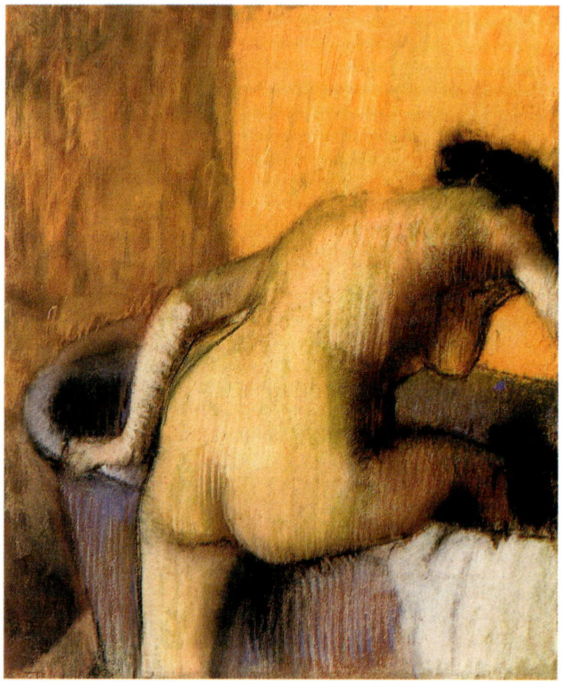

Edgar Degas, Woman Climbing into a Bathtub, *ca. 1890. Metropolitan Museum of Art (New York). Degas worked in pastels in a very picturesque way, using superimposed lines that produced great color density and a certain texture. Light is present as an explosion of vibrant color that goes beyond the limits of traditional chiaroscuro.*

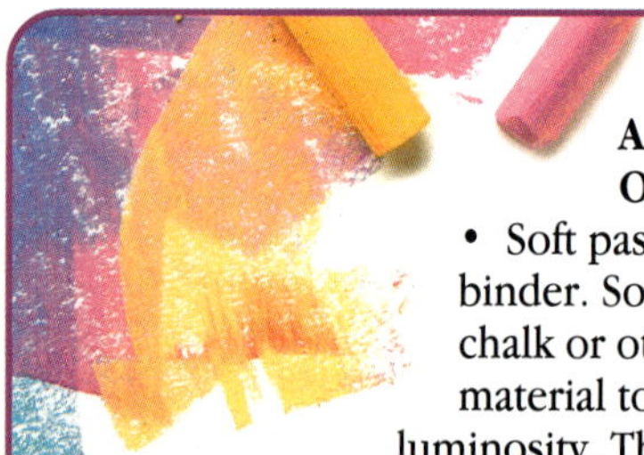

A VARIETY OF PASTELS

- Soft pastels with little binder. Some contain chalk or other white material to provide luminosity. They break easily, but they come in a full spectrum of colors.
- Hard pastels with more binder. The color range is more limited. They are used for sketches, linear details, and finishing.
- Pastel pencils, which are ideal for linear touches. The leads are of medium hardness.
- Oil pastels with a dense, greasy texture because of the binder, which is oily. It's difficult to superimpose colors, but they can be blended and spread using turpentine.
- Water pastels. These are similar to oil pastels, but they are water-soluble. They are good for uniform and semitransparent water glazes.

Working with Inks

Inks are the oldest of all the wet techniques. They originated in China around 2500 B.C. Inks are a very expressive and direct medium that make it possible to reveal the artist's temperament and character. Chiaroscuros done in ink are very violent, with scarcely any intermediate values. They are based more on the value of the line or color than on the modeling.

There are several types of ink: India ink (animal based), anilines, and stylographic. Except with India ink, bleach can be used to produce oxidation. All the inks can be diluted with water. Regarding the utensils for applying them, there are several types of pens—inkwell nibs, pens with a refillable reservoir, reeds or quills, and stylographic pens—plus soft-bristled brushes. Inks are applied to paper and support a great variety of techniques, based mainly on the value of the line: dots, stripes, crosshatching, splashes, washes, dry brush, sponges, fingers… For very precise finishes it's a good idea to do a preliminary layout in pencil. Reserves can be created using wax, since it repels the ink.

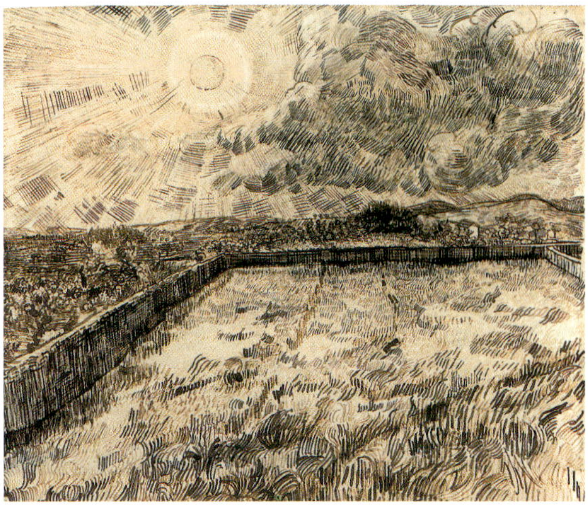

Vincent van Gogh, Wheatfield with Sun and Cloud, *1889. Rijksmuseum Kröller-Müller (Otterlo, Netherlands). The chiaroscuros were created using crosshatched lines done in pen.*

A reed can be used for very expressive lines of variable width.

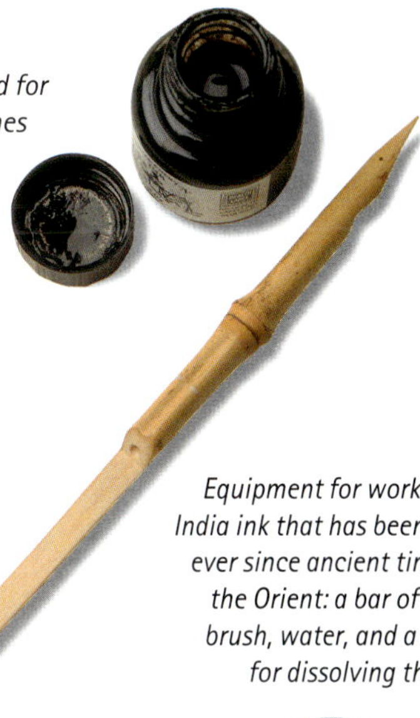

Mary Cassatt, Mother's Caress, *1891. National Gallery of Art (Washington, D.C.). This engraving, which is characterized by clean drawing and a lack of chiaroscuro, is illuminated with colored inks, creating a tender and luminous effect.*

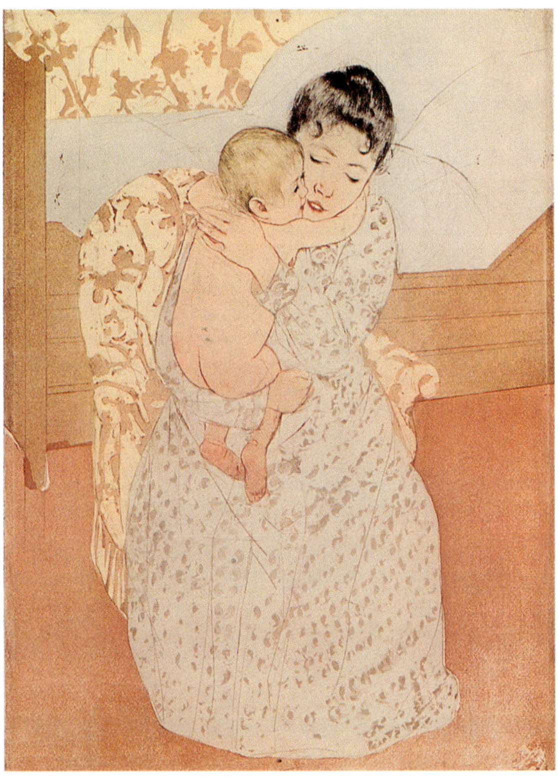

Equipment for working in India ink that has been used ever since ancient times in the Orient: a bar of ink, a brush, water, and a stone for dissolving the ink.

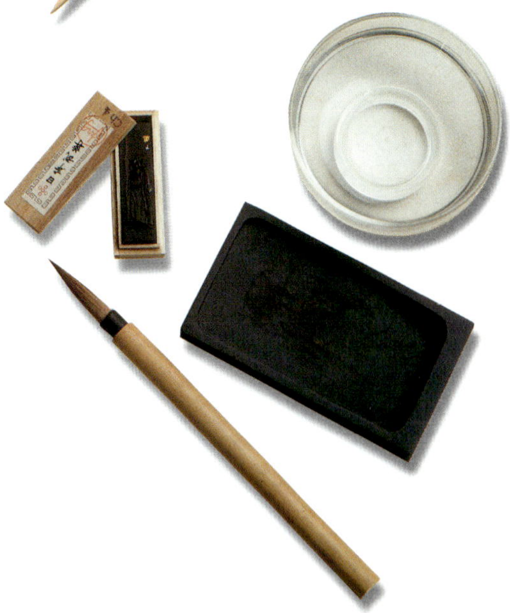

Watercolors and Light

Watercolors are a wet medium characterized by transparency. This property is due to the fact that the pigment has been bound with gum arabic and another compound that gives it plasticity (honey, glycerine . . .). Water is used for diluting. This is a difficult technique because corrections are not possible, and the artist needs to know how to control the water.

The paper is very important. It's commonly allowed to show through, since it's not just the ground but also a component of the color, to which it gives light. The paper's weight and texture determine the final finish. It is stretched for working, since the water produces stretching and buckling that will vanish as it dries. The colors are applied with soft, high-quality artist's brushes, and with sponges for broad washes.

The process always begins with the light shades, which are produced by diluting the colors, and reserves are left on the paper for pure white. The dark shades are left until the end. The most common techniques are glazes, washes, gradations of wet on wet, atomizing, dotting, scratching, reserves using wax or masking, sponges, areas of color, and velaturas.

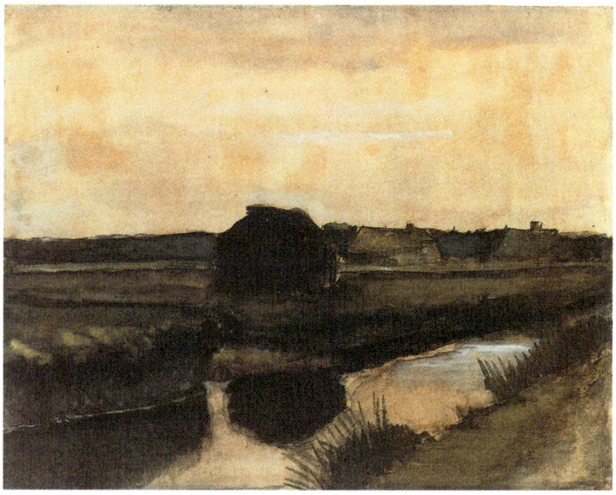

Vincent van Gogh, Landscape at Nightfall, *1883. Rikjsmuseum Vincent van Gogh (Amsterdam, Netherlands). A wonderful combination of washes, wet-on-wet work, and velaturas.*

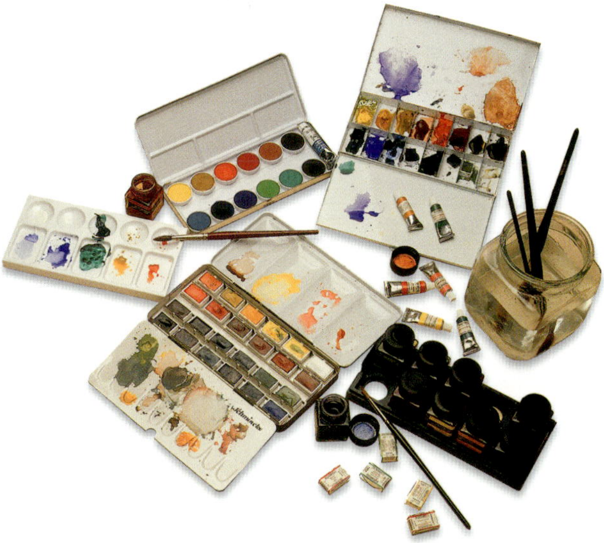

Watercolors are available in stores in the form of tubes, tablets, and bottles. Each form requires a different procedure, but without sacrificing the effect of luminosity and transparency.

Doug Lew, Big Ben in the Rain. *Private Collection. It's possible to depict a rainy and blurry landscape like this one because watercolors can be worked very wet without sacrificng their essential character.*

Oils, the Premier Technique

The origins of this technique go back to the fifteenth century, with the Van Eyck brothers, although people had previously experimented with similar techniques. Oils are a greasy medium that uses oil from linseeds, poppies, or walnuts as a binding agent; oils dry slowly and have tremendous elasticity. Essence of turpentine or regular turpentine is used for thinning. The most interesting part of this medium is the fact that the colors are bright and lively, and they lose nothing in drying. Additionally, oils remain fluid and pasty for quite a while, which makes corrections and effective blending possible.

In addition to the colors, other materials are used as driers and varnishes to speed up the drying, increase viscosity, add luster, and so forth. Oils can be used on any kind of ground—canvas, wood, metal, paper—as long as it is first prepared with a layer of primer. Oils are applied with brushes, palette knives, or scrapers, and they allow for fine layers and glazes, as well as thick impastos and fillers such as marble dust.

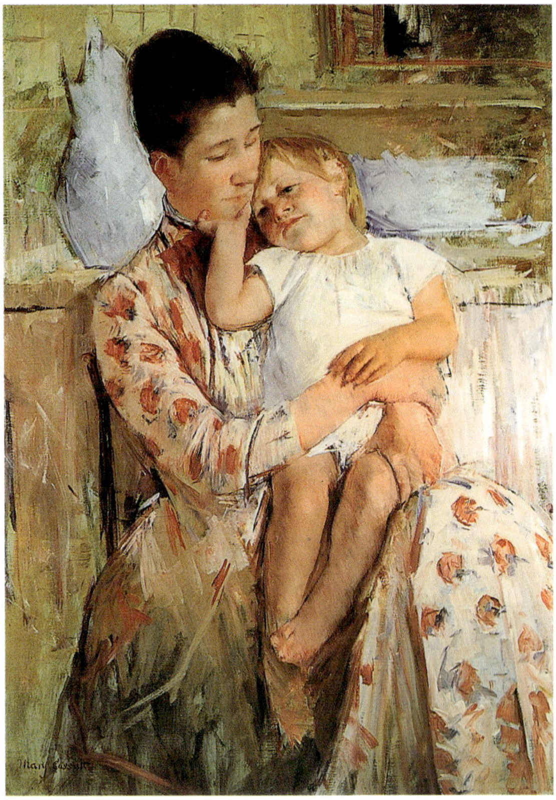

Mary Cassatt, Emmie and Her Child, *1889. Wichita Art Museum (Wichita, Kansas).*
Oils are good for very fresh, free strokes that vary the density of the painting so that the picture has an unmatched richness of textures. Note the variety of brushstrokes in this work by Cassatt.

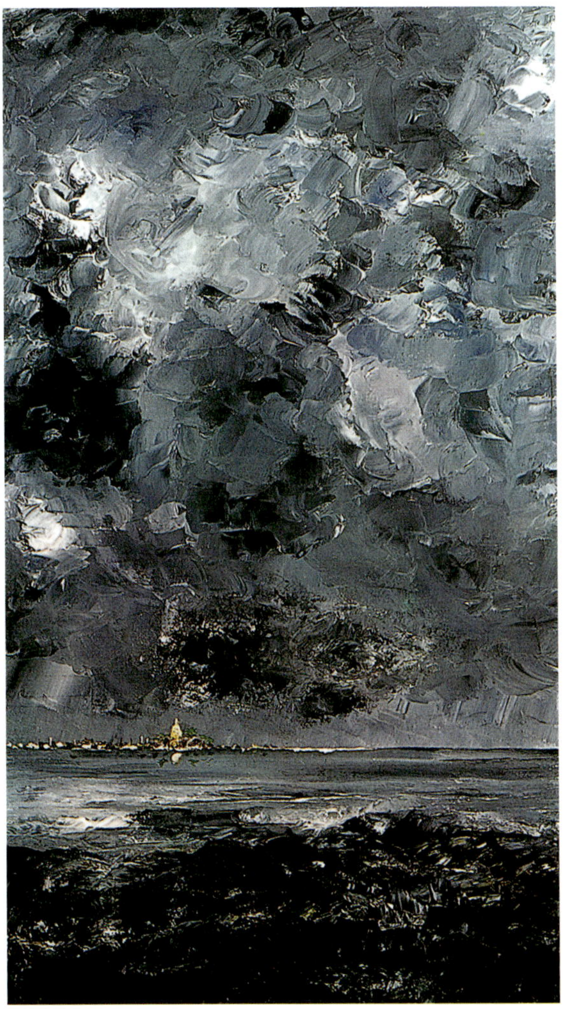

August Strindberg, The City. *National Museum (Stockholm, Sweden).*
Night view of a distant city done in oil impasto. The use of palette knives produces this type of result, which has great expressive force. The light created with impasto is denser; it seems to be inside the material itself, as a reflection rather than a source.

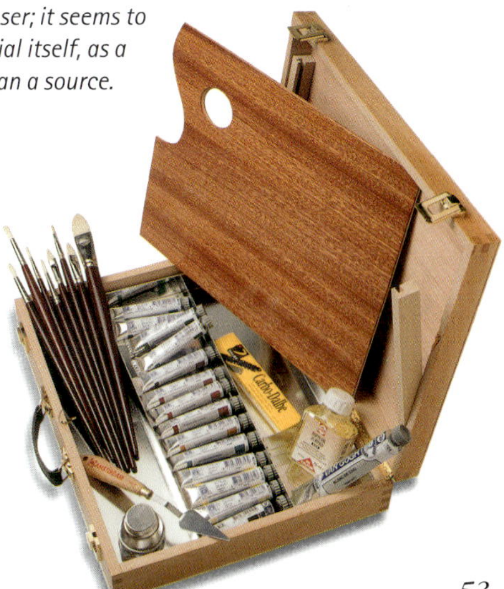

A case of oil paints with the necessary equipment.

Possibilities with Acrylics

In the middle of the twentieth century, in response to the needs of mural painters, artists experimented with a medium that would dry quickly and stand up to atmospheric agents. That resulted in acrylics, which later were applied to painting on canvas. With acrylics, the paint is agglutinated with a synthetic glue that is diluted with water. Every layer can be painted over with scarcely any delay, which allows the artist to work quickly and add velaturas, flat colors, and any necessary corrections.

It's fairly common to make the paints at home by simply combining the pigment, water, and synthetic glue, almost always latex.

Acrylic paints are applied to all kinds of non-greasy surfaces using artist's brushes, sponges, palette knives, scrapers, rags, and so forth, since they allow for a great variety of techniques: impastos, velaturas, *sfumatos*, flat inks, washes, reserves, and others.

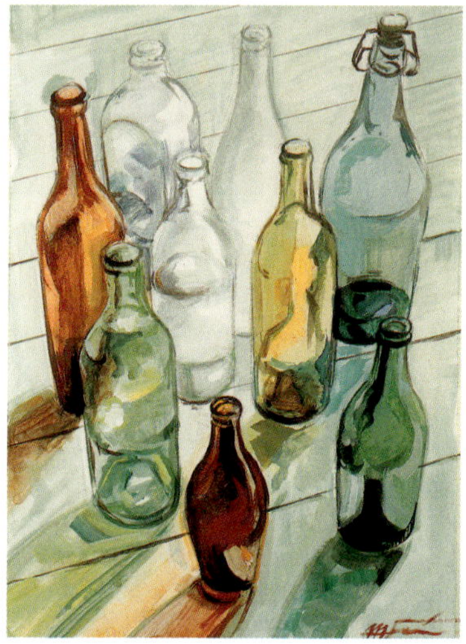

This painting by Myriam Ferrón shows a more aqueous treatment that is possible with acrylics, and more similar to watercolors than to oils.

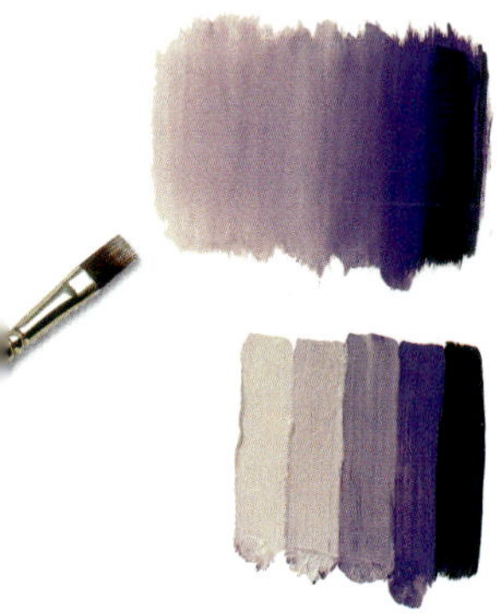

Two types of gradation: blending and contrasting. Acrylics are used in both types, using flat colors, or like oils, applying the colors in impasto and letting them mix on the canvas.

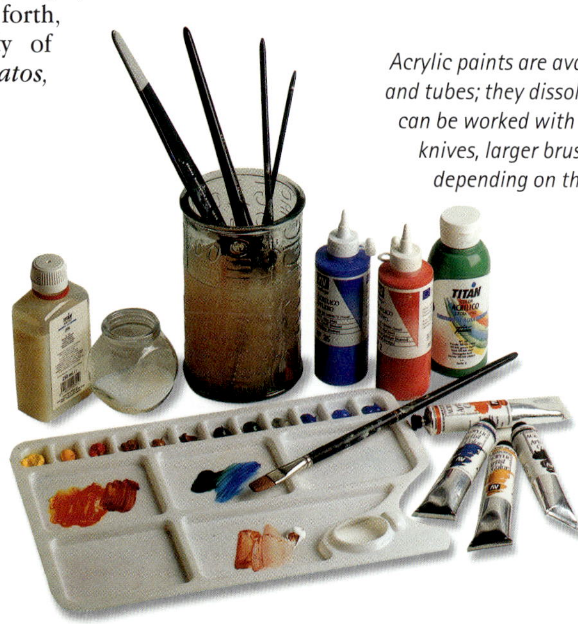

Acrylic paints are available in bottles and tubes; they dissolve in water, and can be worked with brushes, palette knives, larger brushes, or sponges, depending on the desired effect.

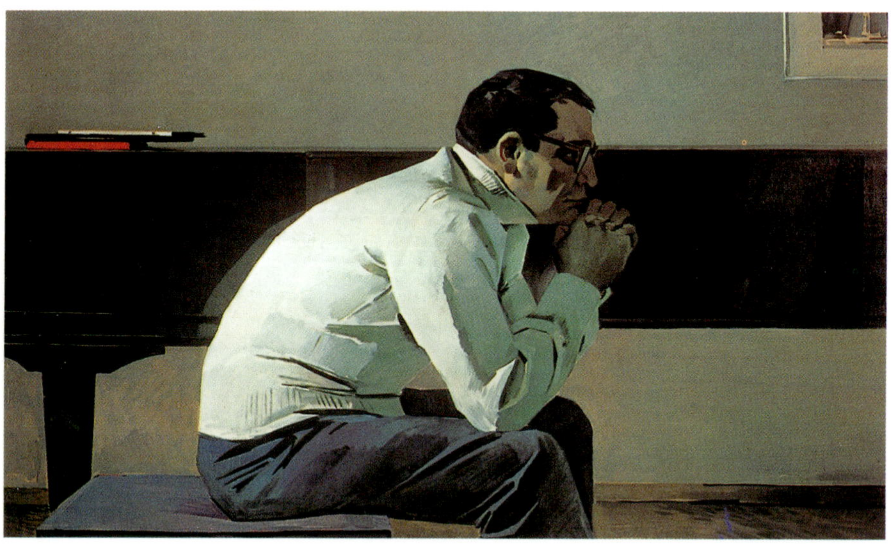

Tair Salajov, Portrait of the Composer Kara-Karayev. *Tetriakov Gallery (Moscow, Russia). Acrylics can be used to produce results similar to oils, although they dry more quickly and it's harder to blend the colors. This portrait by Salajov is an example of modeling with flat colors and no blending.*

Procedures and Techniques for Chiaroscuro of Objects

In the following pages we will work on three still lifes step by step. These are three very different projects with respect to technique and subject, but all of them involve an object and light.

So far we have examined the theoretical aspects related to the subject of light and color in painting and drawing: the history, the conceptual and expressive bases, perception, chiaroscuro, color, and technical principles. Based on this broad introduction, we will now do a series of more concrete and practical works in which each project can be followed step by step. At the outset we will do three still lifes, then three subjects involving the human figure, and finally four landscapes.

The first still life is a monochrome pencil work. We have chosen this technique because of the simplicity of the scene: a simple composition involving three vegetables on a table, in the style of the intimist still lifes of the Baroque period, with dramatic lateral illumination. Then, an indoor scene illuminated by natural light coming in through a window. We have chosen watercolors for this backlighting, since the type of color and the luminous atmosphere invite working with velaturas and fresh strokes that suggest air and light.

Each of these three exercises is a door that opens onto new projects involving an object and light.

Finally, we will do a study of clothing. The subject is unusual: a knot. This final picture should be considered more than a mere exercise in depicting fabric, since the knot itself is a very expressive and evocative conceptual theme. The illumination is artificial and from overhead, so that the tensions and folds of the cloth stand out more clearly. Each of these three exercises is a door that opens onto new projects involving an object and light. We hope that the reader will become immersed in the subject and experiment with other still lifes and types of illumination.

In doing this picture, Vicenç Ballestar has chosen to use oils, since they offer a broad spectrum of visual registers, such as blending, impasto, and deliberate lines. Every fold and tension in this knot is expressed with a force that conveys poetry.

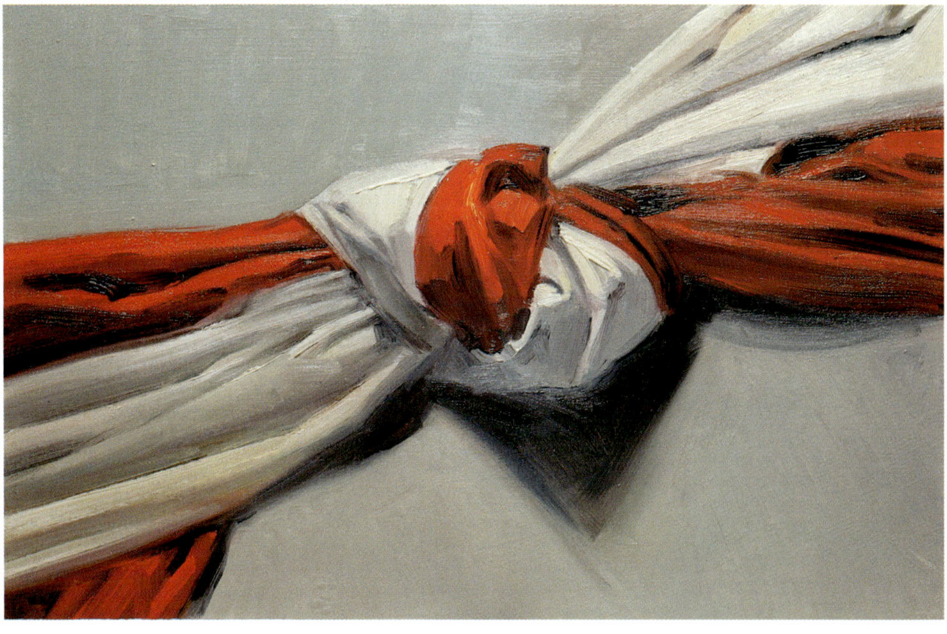

A Monochrome Still Life

The most subdued still life in existence is a monochrome one. As the name indicates, only one color is used; in this case, the black of graphite. To create values of light and darkness, we merely need to intensify to varying degrees the graphite applied to a certain area, whether using crosshatching or varying the hardness and pressure of the pencil or stick of graphite. In this still life by Josep Asunción a major contrast was desired to exaggerate the sense of luminosity and create a tenebrist atmosphere, as in the first Baroque still lifes, in which the objects seem to be bathed in a vivifying light.

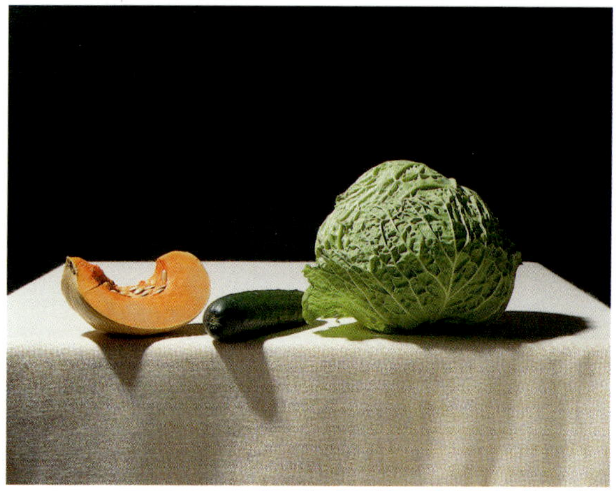

There is nothing more on the intensely illuminated table than three pieces of produce. The dark black background evokes empty space and accentuates the presence of the objects; it also brings the light to center stage, since it is the true subject of the composition.

MATERIALS

- Smooth, heavyweight drawing paper
- Pencils of different hardnesses
- Graphite stick
- Blender
- Artist's eraser

1

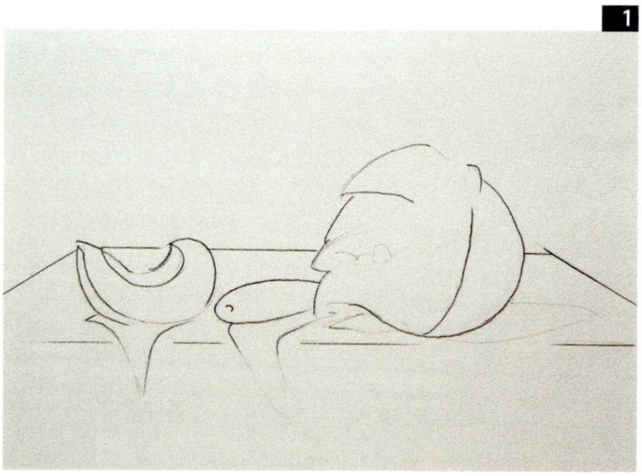

1 First, the image is outlined in a preliminary sketch. This involves structuring, creating the basic skeleton of every element. In this case, the suggested outlines and the perspective of the table are all that's needed to adjust the proportions and locate the objects on the paper.

2

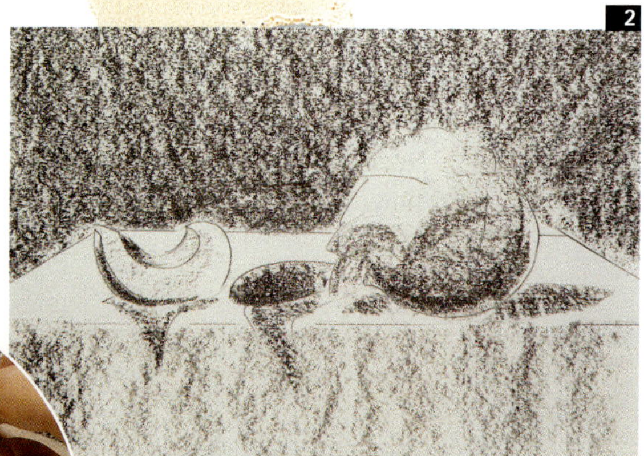

2 The values of chiaroscuro require an initial setup of the contrast and the general scale to be applied. There are very dark and very light values. A soft graphite stick (6B) is used to locate the general areas of color.

3 Since the graphite doesn't cover all the pores of the paper, it is blended in to create a denser mass. The lightest values are left white.

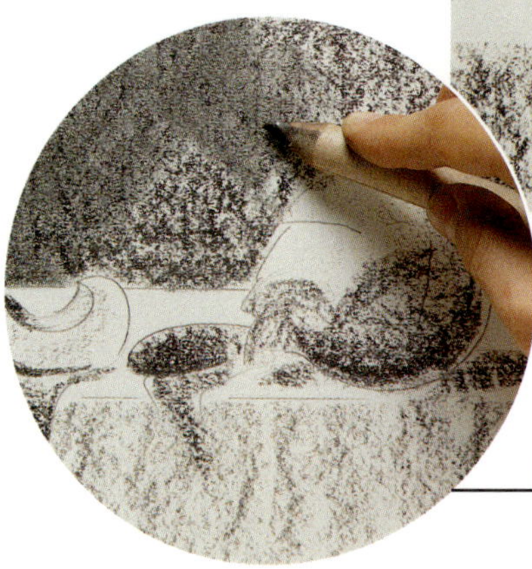

3

TECHNIQUES USED

◆ Outlining ◆
◆ Coloring ◆
◆ Blending ◆
◆ Crosshatching ◆
◆ Erasing ◆

4

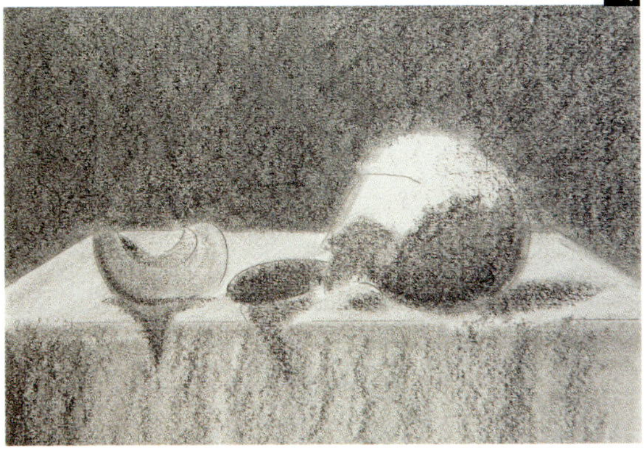

5

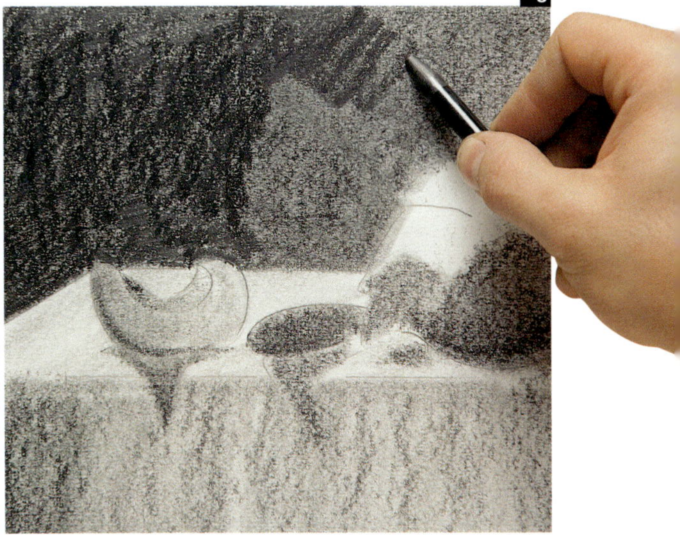

4 The general structure is completed. Now the work advances by adjusting the values to correspond to the model, since this first step doesn't take into account the richness of the grays in the scene.

5 Since the background is a very deep black, a second layer of soft graphite is needed. Applying the graphite with the stick held at an angle produces a broader and softer stroke. A third layer may be needed near the end, since the background still isn't totally black.

6

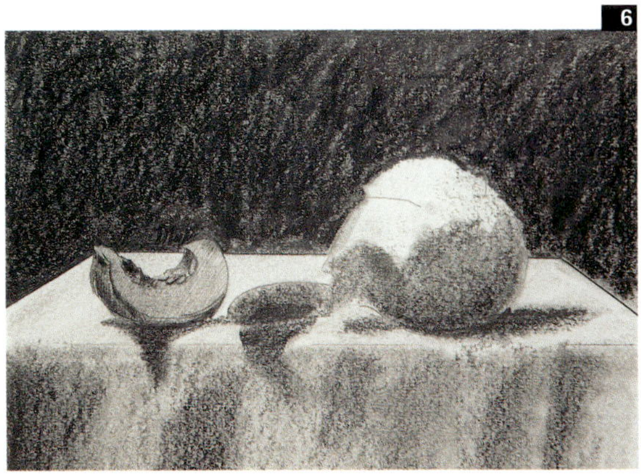

6 Next, each element is worked with care to highlight the shapes and details. The only way to adjust the values of gray is to compare them to one another. In this case, the scale is very broad and the contrasts are strong, but that doesn't mean that there can't also be small differences in the grays between one area and another. Let's start with the squash.

7 The cucumber gains presence as it takes on the dark color it needs. An eraser has been used to create the luster. The linear crosshatching on the blended background makes it possible to show the artist's style.

8 Before finalizing the details, you need to do an overall evaluation and adjust the values. We have determined that the background in fact needs a third layer of graphite, and that layer has been applied. The entire tablecloth has also been worked on, using crosshatching with pencils of different hardnesses: HB for the dark areas and 2H for the light ones.

7

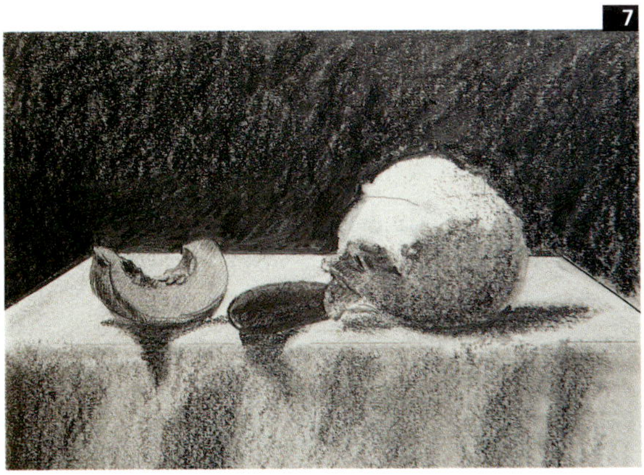

8

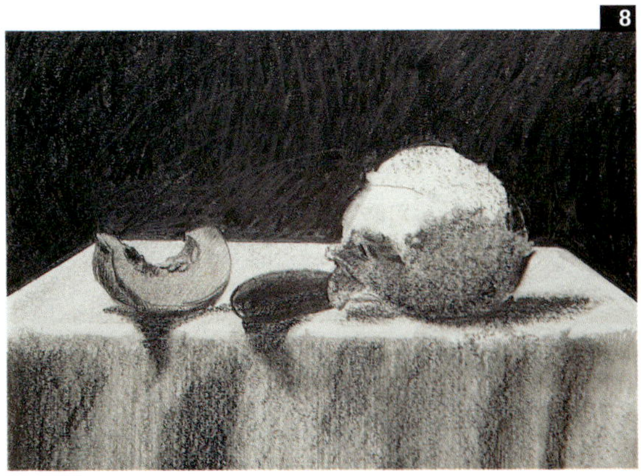

The Final Details

The route to follow in any extremely realistic figurative representation involves proceeding from the general to the specific. The veracity of a work of this type depends in large measure on the final details of the drawing, but these can be finalized only at the end of the entire process, when the proportions and the general light values are in perfect balance. For doing the details in pencil, it's appropriate to change hardness, since you can't produce very precise lines with soft pencils, or very intense darkness with hard ones.

THE VALUE OF THE PENCIL STROKE
Part of the richness of using pencils involves combining lines and areas of color. The lines can be very expressive or poetic, depending on the pressure and the speed used in drawing them. Too much shading will give the drawing a bland and impersonal aesthetic; however, a combination of the two effects creates a perfect balance between veracity and expressiveness.

9

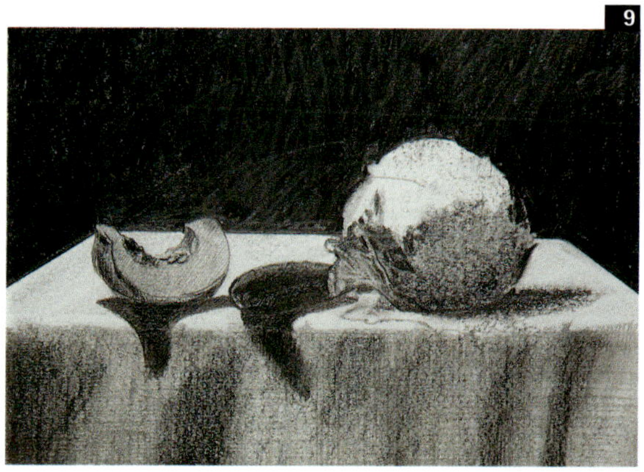

9 In this step the shadows cast onto the tablecloth have been improved, defining their limits and intensity more effectively. The cabbage is starting to take on more presence since its texture is becoming visible.

10 In drawing the cabbage, pencils of different hardness have been used, depending on the desired grays. The luster of the cucumber has also been improved by spreading out the light through application of the eraser. When the textures have been completed, the drawing can be considered finished; it has taken a sharp turn in the direction of accurate depiction.

10

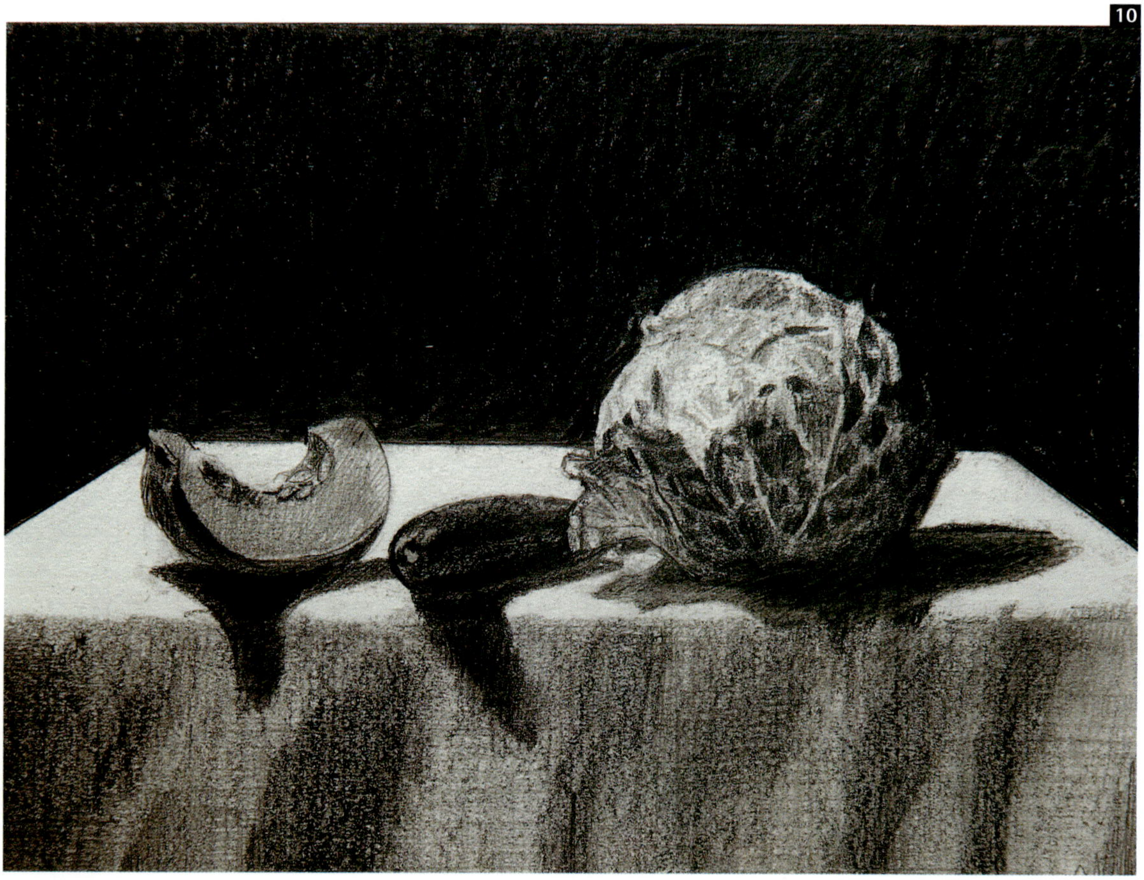

Natural Light Indoors

Painting indoor scenes involves spaces and objects in a scene, so there is a connection to still life. The treatment of light is basic to creating the pictorial climate. In the watercolor that we are about to see, done by Mercedes Gaspar, a formal dialog is established between the indoors and the outdoors by means of a balcony. Balconies, doors, and windows, which are common parts of indoor scenes, act as surfaces for the passage of light and reinforce the idea of intimacy, since they confirm that the observer's location, like the scope of the scene, is inside rather than outside. Watercolors are the technique that offers a more ethereal and immaterial sensation, due to the fluidity of the medium, which is entirely liquid.

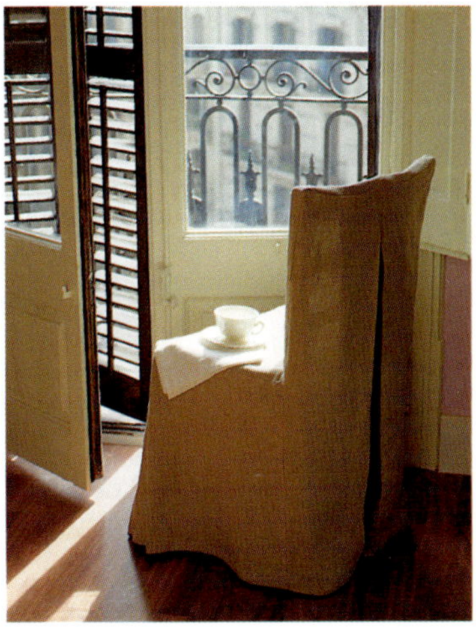

This model presents an everyday moment, but one that's filled with magic: the passage of light into an indoor scene. This is backlighting, a fairly common type of illumination in the painting of indoor subjects, and which is very theatrical.

MATERIALS

- Paper for watercolors
- Watercolors
- Round artist's brushes with soft bristles
- Sash brush or other flat brush
- Masking tape
- Reserve pencil

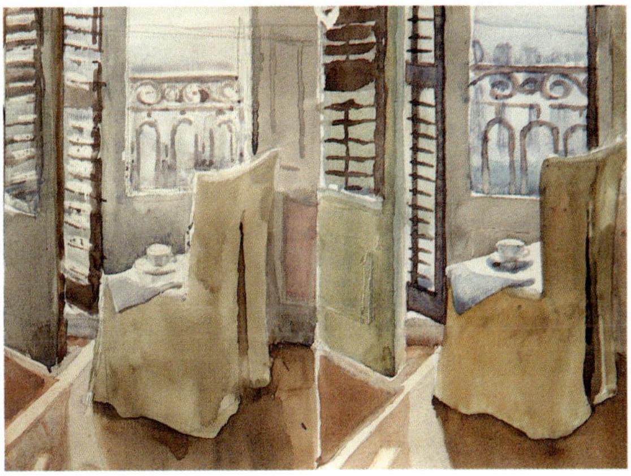

Before starting this work, the artist has done a couple of preliminary studies to experiment with the level of contrast and the range of colors.

1 The layout of a watercolor begins with a pencil sketch. The artist has chosen a pencil with a medium lead. A very hard lead is not a good choice, since it may damage the paper; nor is a very soft one, since it could smudge.

1

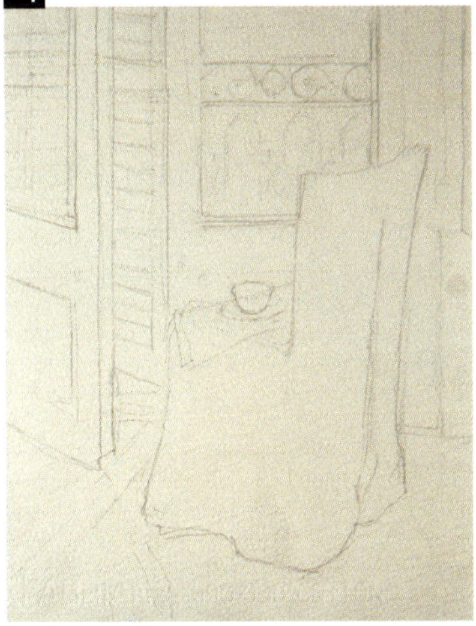

2 Before applying the watercolors, the paper has to be attached to the easel by taping it all along the edges to keep the page from distorting. In order to keep the watercolors from soaking into certain areas of the image, some masking has been applied by painting it on with a grease pencil designed for the purpose.

TECHNIQUES USED

◆ Preliminary studies ◆
◆ Initial sketch ◆
◆ Reserves ◆
◆ Applying colors ◆

2

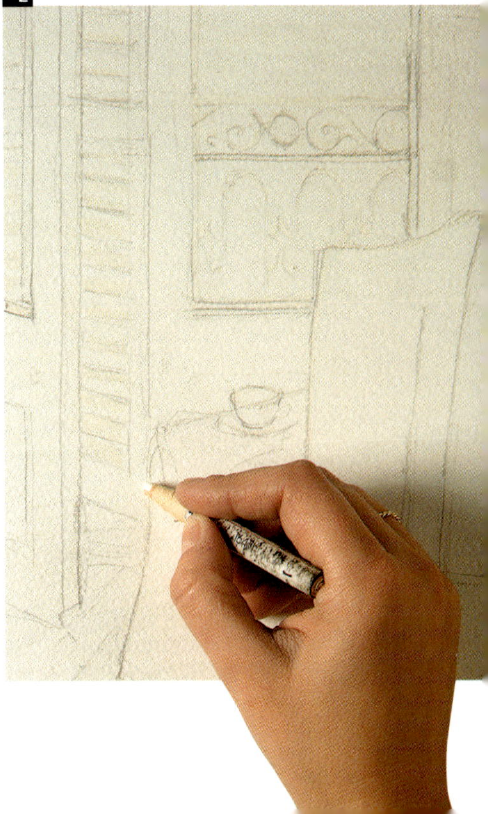

3

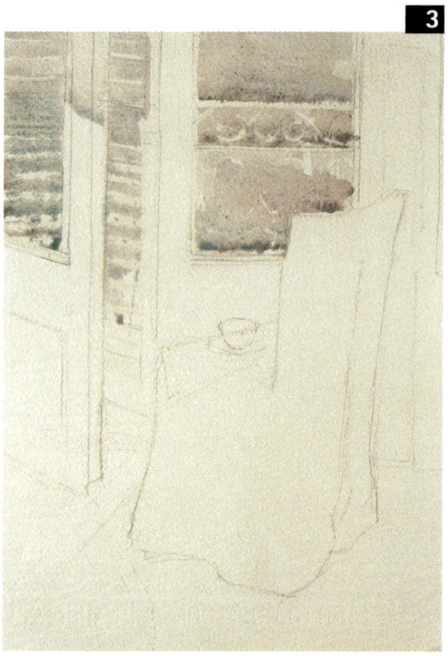

ORDER AND PRUDENCE IN APPLYING COLOR

The first application of colors in a watercolor usually is gentler than subsequent ones. This is due to the prudence factor, since within this technique it is difficult to lighten a color, but it's always possible to darken it. In determining the desired shade, it's always a good idea to try every color on a separate piece of paper, since unwanted colors are hard to adjust once they have been applied to the definitive paper.

With watercolors, light is in the white of the paper, and it is never applied a posteriori, so the risk of smothering the painting in a saturation of color is very high. Therefore, the artist has to envision from the outset what areas will be allowed to breathe the pure white of the paper in order to accentuate the light to the maximum.

3 The first brushstrokes with watercolor are applied with a view toward the brushstrokes that will follow, keeping the colors within their appointed boundaries so that there are no unwanted velaturas later on. When two colors overlap, they create a third color and darken the area at the same time.

4

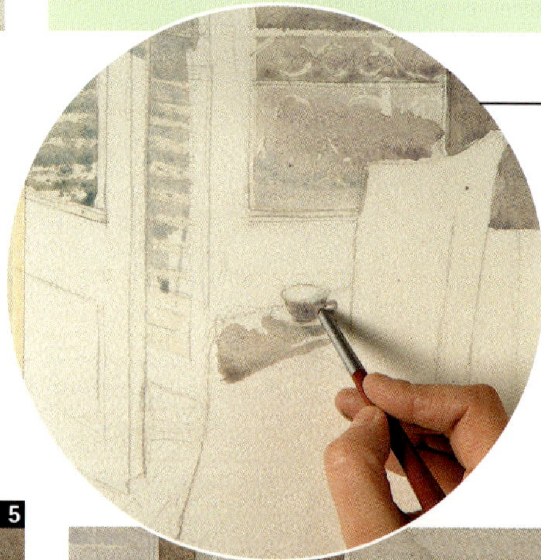

4 The colors interact with one another in such a way that the same shade is present in several places. In this case, a mauve shade indicates shadow or depth.

5

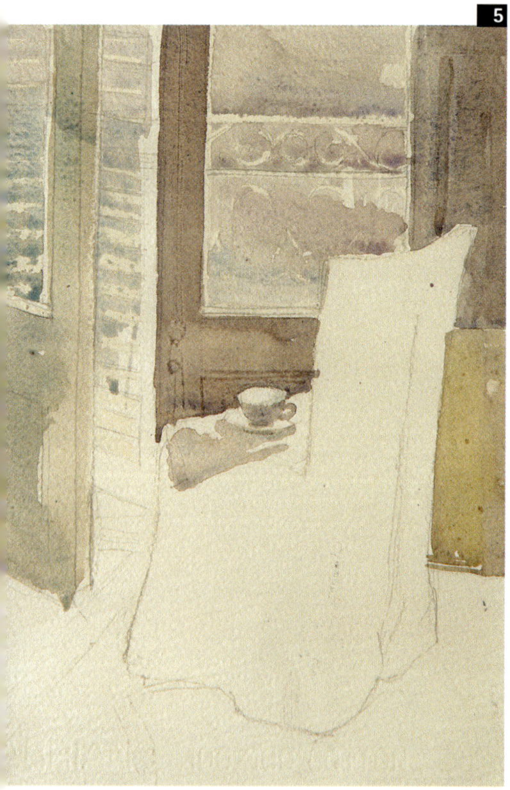

6

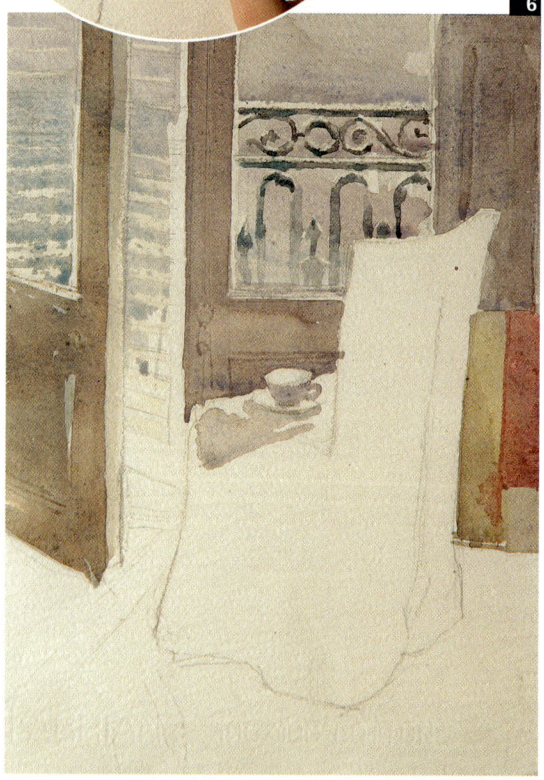

5 Two greenish grays have been chosen for the door to the balcony and the wall; they will serve as the base for subsequent colors.

6 Once the top colors have been applied, we can see that the base colors have an effect on the later ones, but no white appears among the colored areas.

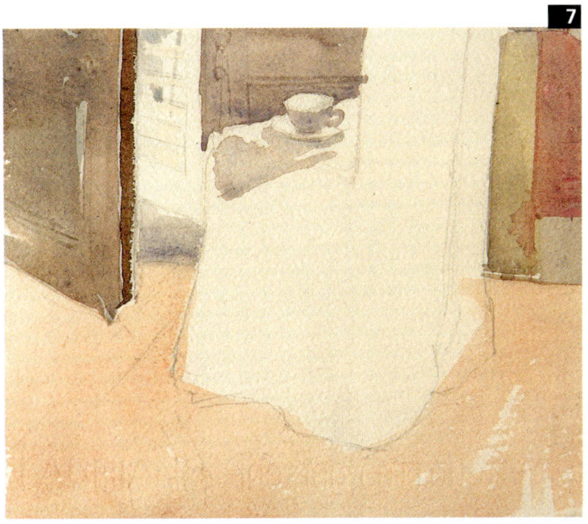

7 In an indoor scene, the floor is one of the most important color masses because of its extent, and because it is the space on which reflections and shadows fall. In this case a neutral tone is the starting point; it corresponds to the highest light level.

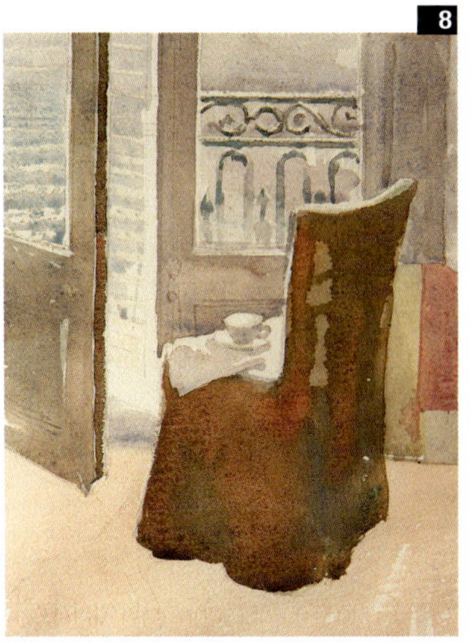

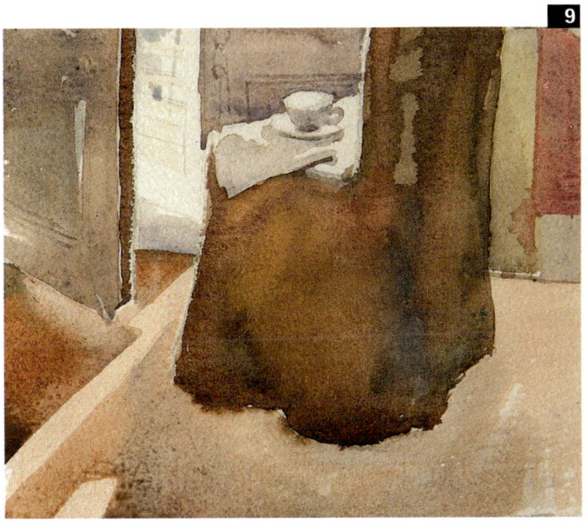

8 The fabric on the chair is the last large colored area. Once it has been painted, the scene can be appreciated with all its chromatic and luminous potential. From this point on, everything involves developing the shadows and contrasts, and adjusting the shades.

9 Because of the perspective, the shadows on the floor create a sense of spatial depth. By using a neutral color on the entire floor, the artist has created a chromatic unity that makes it possible to perceive the shadows as part of the same floor deprived of light.

10 Backlighting requires substantial contrast, so the shadowy area on the floor is darkened further.

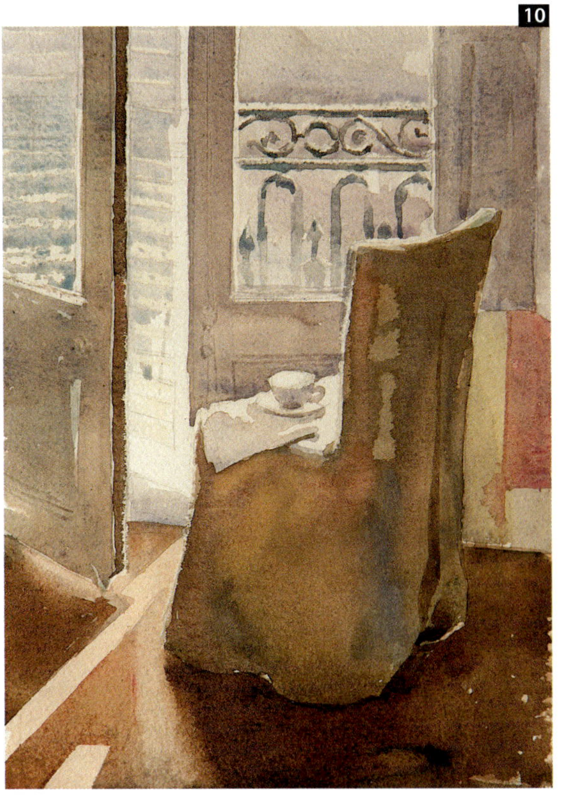

PERSONALIZING THE COLOR SCALE

When we are presented with a scene like the one in this watercolor, where there is no single dominant color to distinguish it, nor very pure or crucial colors, a door to creativity and expressiveness is opened for us. There is no single correct vision of color, but rather many visions, as many as there are gazes or artists. Neutral or muted colors like most of the ones in this model allow for a great variety of hues: greenish, mauve, bluish, and reddish. The artist's interpretation creates a personal color scale charged with expression and poetry.

CONTRAST FROM BACKLIGHTING

When we intend to represent maximum light, even in our imagination, we almost always come up with a totally white image. This is useful as an evocation of an experience similar to an explosion, but it's entirely useless if you want to apply it to a painting to illustrate light. As we have already seen, contrast is the tool that meets the needs of perception, and the perceived effect of light in this painting is produced only through contrast, or backlighting in this case.

11

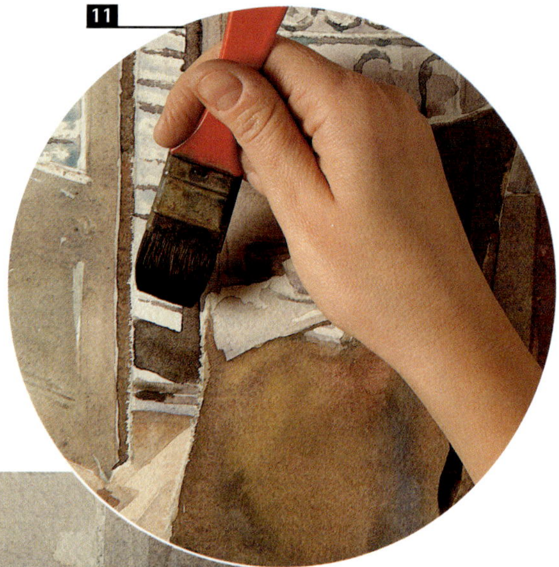

12

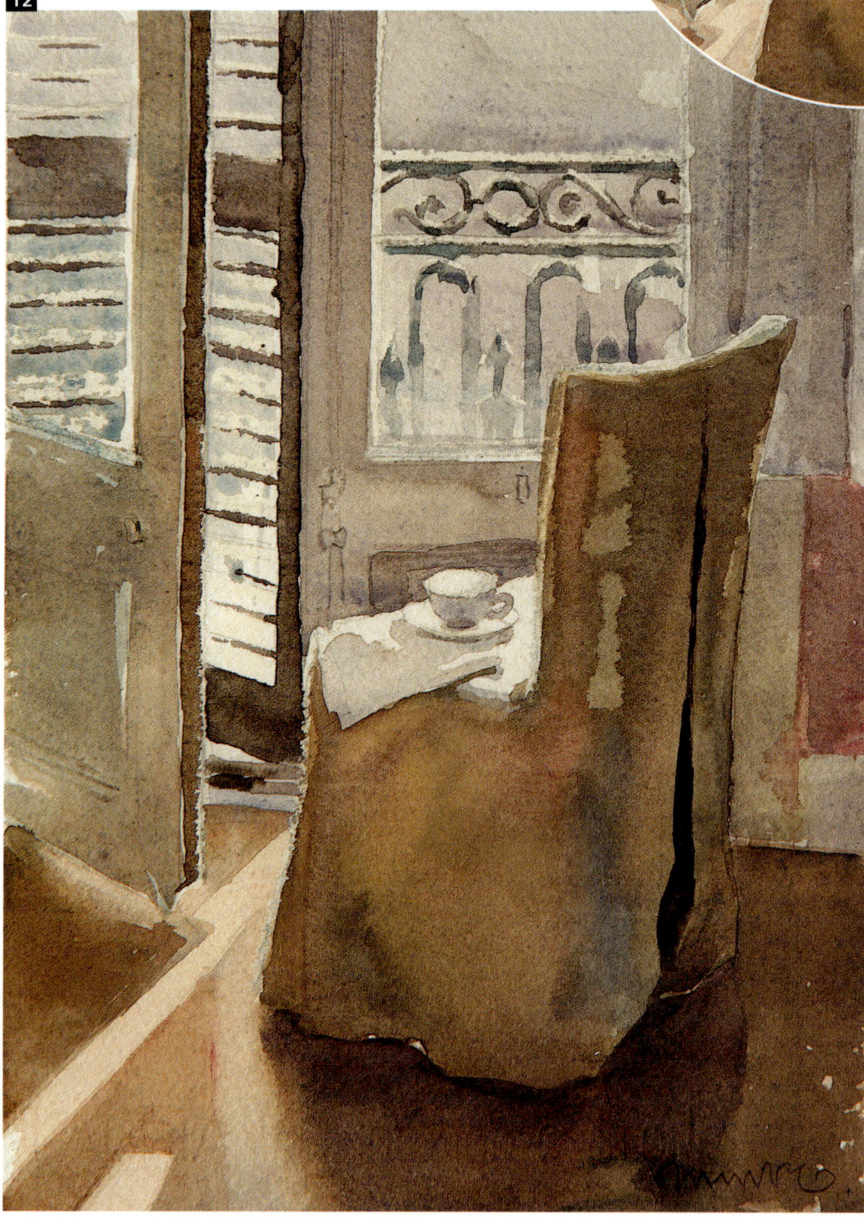

11 A sash brush can be used to create horizontal lines with a single stroke. The dark values of the shutters are a final note that the scene requires for setting up greater light contrast, thereby creating a heightened sense of light.

12 Here is the final result. Note that the contrast is the decisive element in conveying the direct light.

Modeling Fabrics

For most painters throughout the history of painting, depicting the shapes, folds, and tensions that exist in fabrics has been excellent training for learning to paint many other things. In recognition of this, many art schools include studies of clothing in their training courses. In this next exercise, done by Vicenç Ballestar, all the lessons of modeling and chiaroscuro are summed up marvelously. A simple knot moves the fabric from its usual secondary role as an accessory to center stage in such a way that the wrinkles and folds become the narrative theme and the catalysts of the visual emotion.

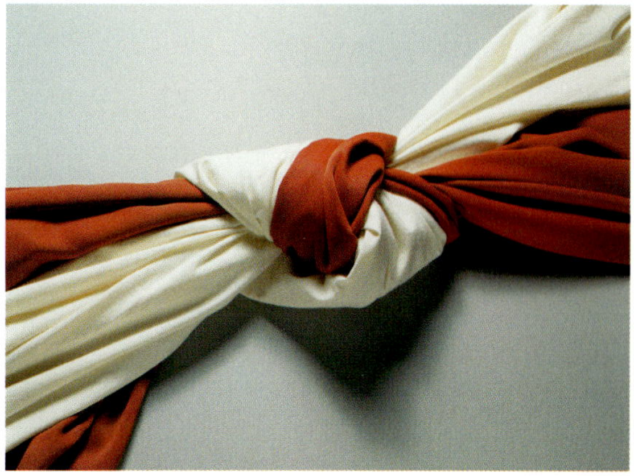

The chosen shape has great expressive force, so it needs a neutral background.
The diagonal composition contributes a dynamic quality, and the low overhead light produces a shadow that increases the sense of volume in the knot.

MATERIALS
- Board prepared with gesso
- Charcoal
- Oil paints
- Flat boar's bristle brushes

TECHNIQUES USED

◆ Preliminary sketch ◆
◆ Chiaroscuro modeling ◆

1 The first strokes in charcoal serve to lay out the composition. This preliminary sketch sets up the main lines of tension, which coincide with the folds.

1

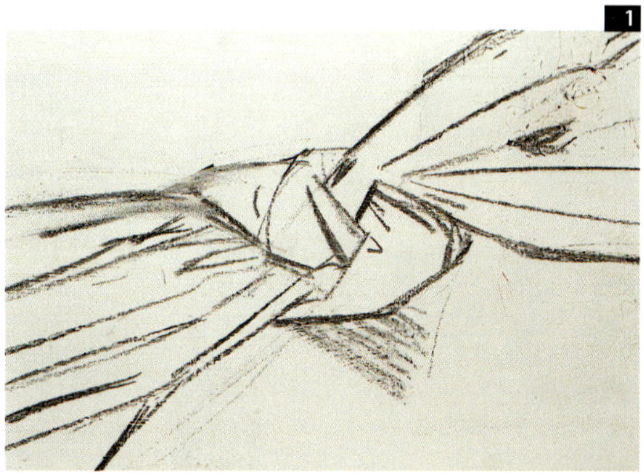

2

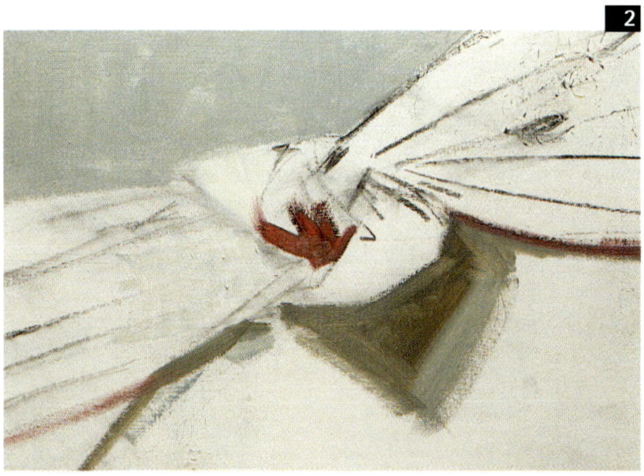

3

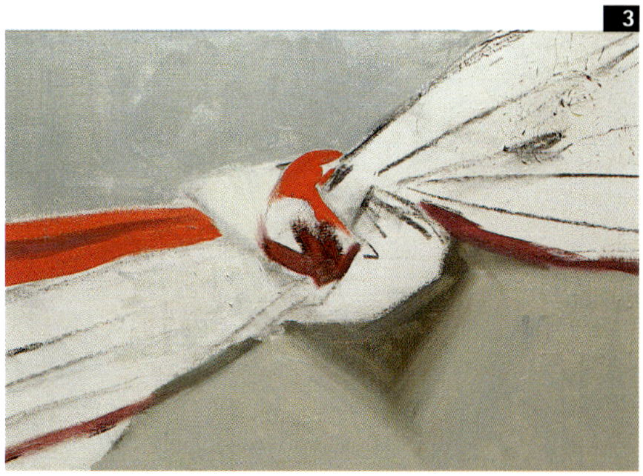

2 When the drawing is considered acceptable, it's erased with a rag so that the charcoal doesn't taint the colors. This erasure is not complete; rather, a trace of the lines remains to help orient the subsequent application of colors.

3 The background is as important as the knot. Therefore, it's not a good idea to devote too much energy to the figure and leave the background for later, since the values of light and shade get their meaning in relation to one another rather than separately.

SHOULD WE START WITH LIGHT OR SHADOW?

When it comes to modeling the shape with chiaroscuro, a question always arises about where to begin. It's a good idea to start with the extremes and work toward moderate shades. If the background is white, first locate the main shadows, withholding paint from the light areas; next paint the most neutral color, and then on the basis of these three general shades you can work toward the secondary ones. If the background is dark, the first strokes will be for the lightest shades, and then, holding the dark areas in reserve, you proceed in a similar fashion.

4 The direction of the stroke marks the lay of the fabric. Imagine a brushstroke in a direction perpendicular to this one and you will see right away that it goes against the natural movement of the fold.

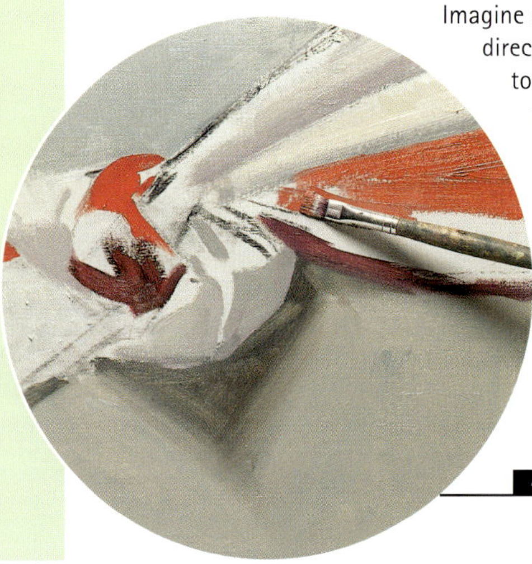

4

5

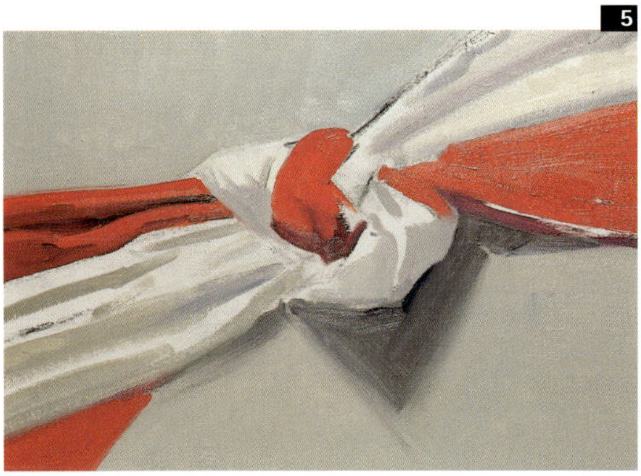

6

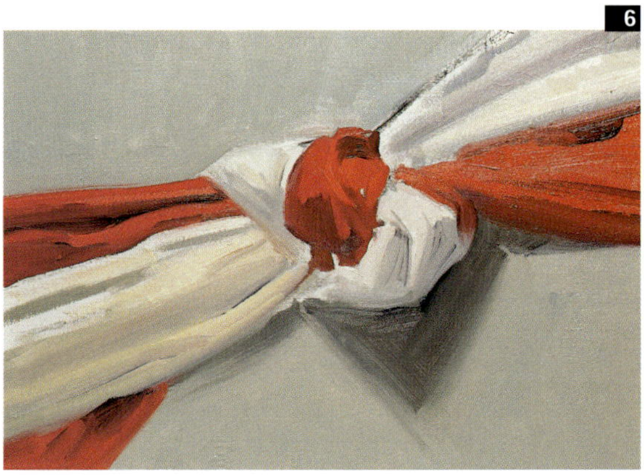

7

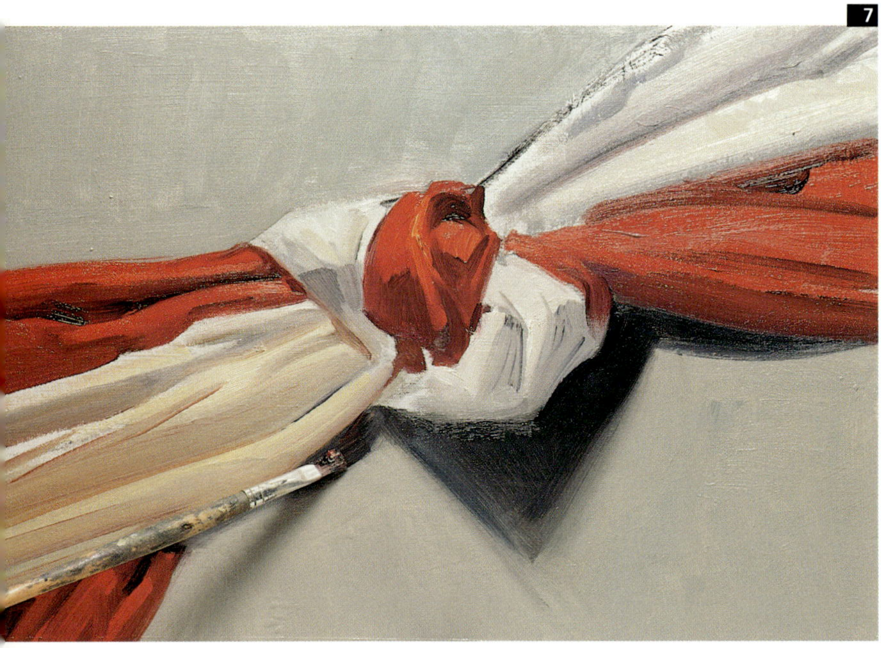

5 In this phase, the main values of light and shadow are already in place, although in only a very general way.

6 Here we can see the lay of the fabric fairly well. In addition, we have added some color, providing more of an ivory hue to the white fabric and establishing the principal shades of red.

7 The shadows have been strengthened by darkening them further. Note that the brushstrokes follow the same direction as the projected shadow.

Direction and Intensity of Line

In representing fabric the artist needs a basic mastery of line, with respect to both direction and intensity. The direction must always follow the lay of the fabric. Sometimes the fabric falls in smooth, sinuous folds; at other times, in a straight, tense line. It may even form an irregular line with convolutions, but in every case the brushstrokes must follow the same direction as the cloth. With dry techniques such as pencils, charcoal, and pastels, the intensity of the lines is controlled by the pressure exerted; with wet or oil techniques such as oil paints, watercolors, and acrylics, it's a function of the amount of paint. This factor is used to communicate the type of fabric. A filmy silk is conveyed more effectively through the lightness of a wash or a *sfumato,* whereas a canvas invites the use of blending and impastos.

8

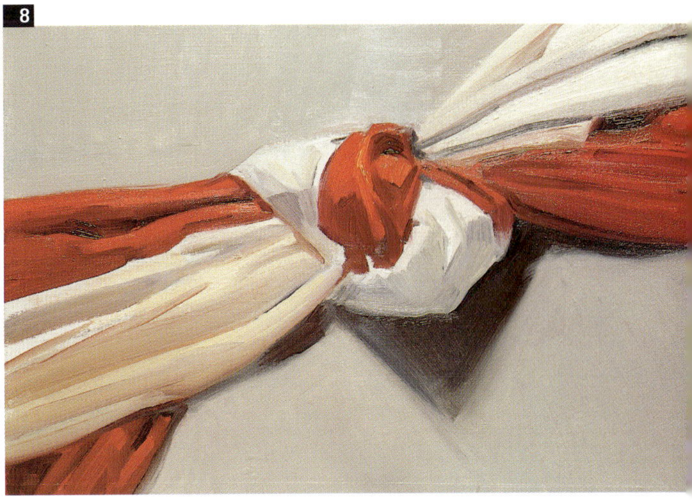

9

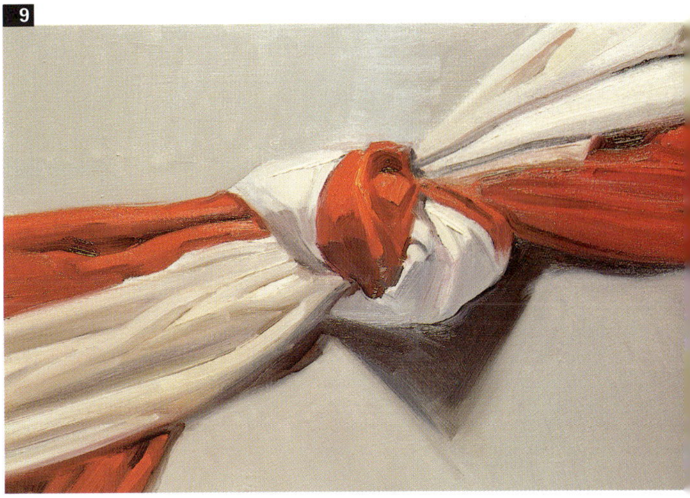

8 The shadows in the folds have been highlighted so that the contrast will heighten the perception of the shape.

9 Since the color of the light fabric was too yellow, it has been adjusted and neutralized so that the color appears as a reflection of the warm light rather than the color of the fabric itself.

10 The shadows in the fold of the red are deepened, and the purple in the shadow from the knot is softened to keep it from being overly theatrical.

10

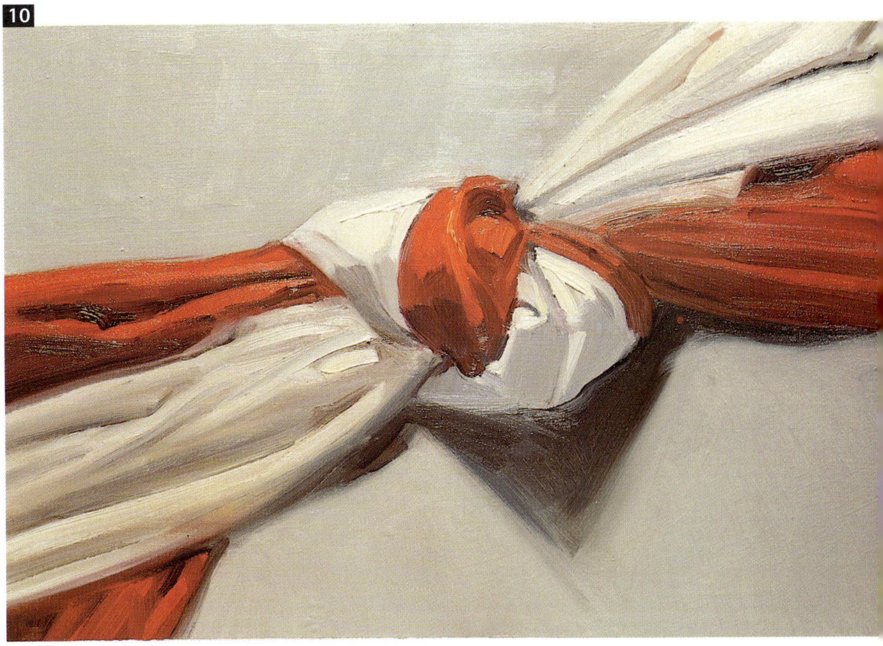

COMPLEMENTARY COLORS IN SHADOW
The presence of an object's complementary color in its shadow opens a door to chromatic enrichment of the chiaroscuro. Impressionist painters applied this principle to their paintings. The relationship between two complementary colors produces a visual effect of shock and estrangement, so a slight presence of the complement in the shadow exaggerates the difference in tonal value.

11

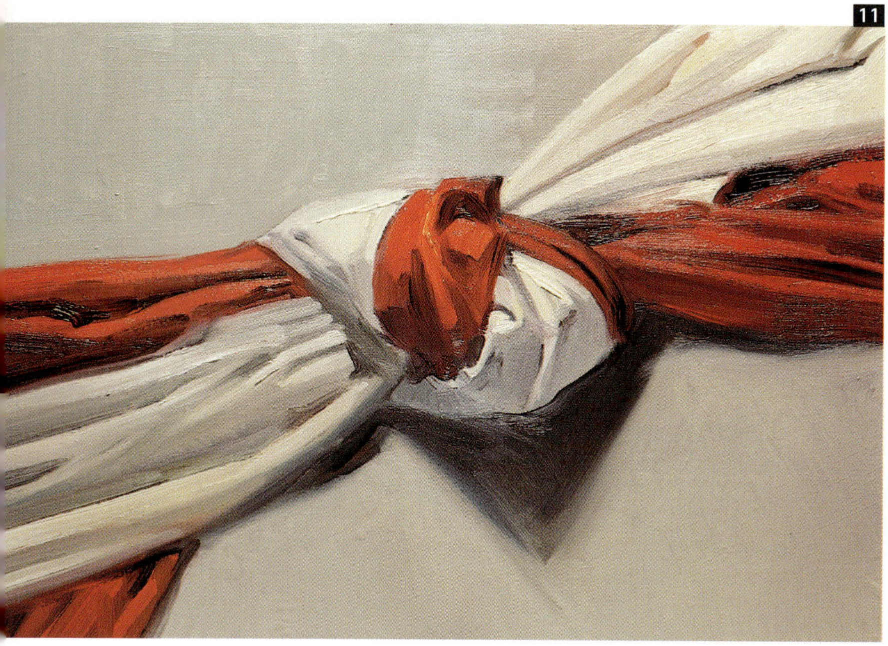

11 Now that the work is nearly done, note how greater expressiveness is achieved by strengthening the contrast in the folds.

12 Here is the finished product. In a work of this nature it's not crucial to achieve a photographic match with the model. There's no problem at all if you leave out or add a wrinkle or fold; the main thing is to capture the attitude of the fabric and its character.

IMPASTOS AND BLENDING

Painting in oils makes gentle velaturas and blending possible, and, at the same time, impastos and heavy brushstrokes. This broad gamut of effects makes oils the ideal technique for depicting all types of fabrics, from felts and silks to the coarsest sack cloths.

12

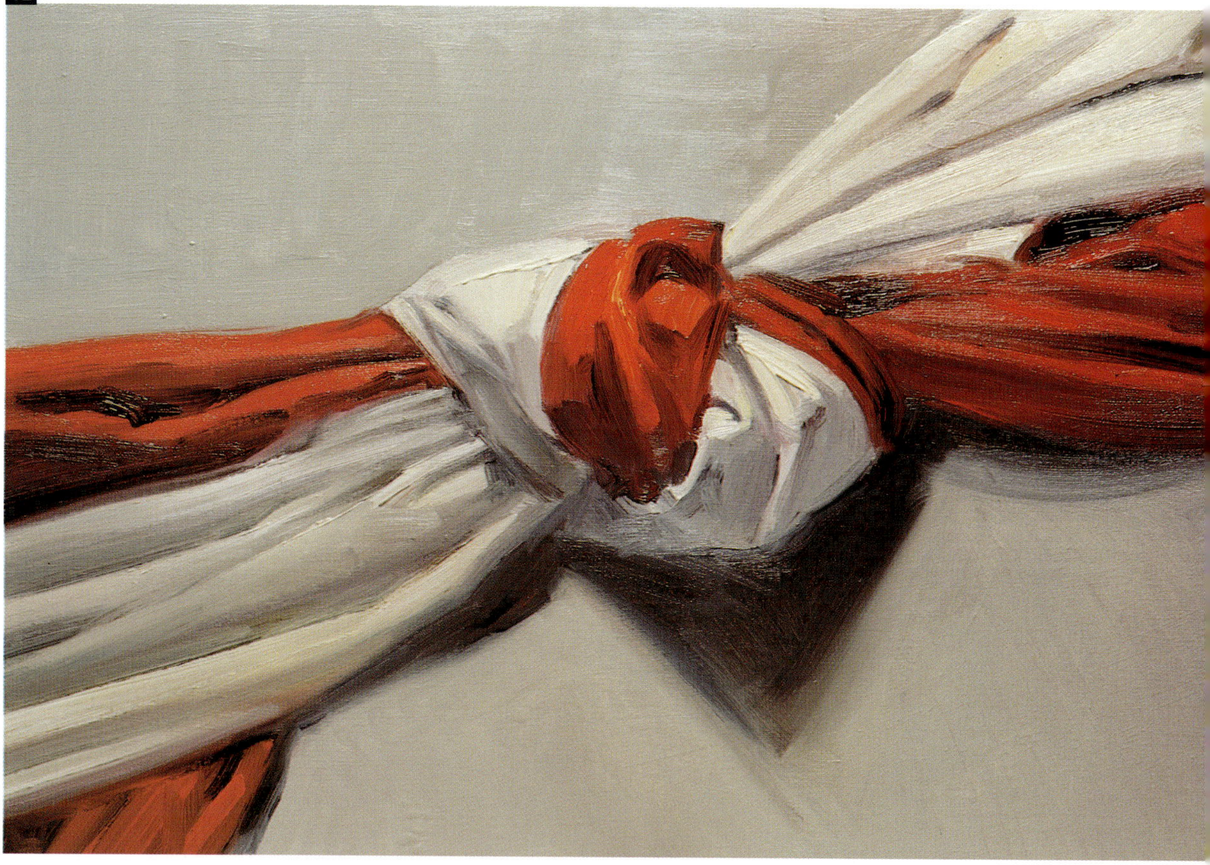

Procedures and Techniques for the Human Figure

A study of light and the human figure is not much different from what we have already seen with respect to objects; in both cases the main concern is to depict the shapes according to the light conditions.

The artist's most difficult task and major challenge is to succeed in capturing the life that animates the model. For that purpose there are three major subjects that require special attention: conveying the shapes and forms, the flesh tones, and the relationship between the figure and the surroundings. The first of these great topics is based on the study of light, considering the human body as a form that can be modeled using either classical chiaroscuro or color valuation; in any case it must be given values and modeled with consideration of the same factors as for objects: the direction and intensity of the brush strokes and the tonal valuations.

With regard to the second topic, the flesh tones, we have to discard all the existing clichés, especially the ones that indicate a single route, like a recipe, that are sometimes dogmatic, that indicate what the true flesh color is and how to achieve values of light and shadow. Finally, we must insist on the importance of the third topic, the integration of the figure and the background into a single unit that is the image. We mustn't simply review the word *background,* which denotes division and a thematic break, but also the concept, for when a figure is "on a background" the result is aseptic and cold, and that's disappointing unless that effect is sought intentionally. Instead of backgrounds, we should be speaking in terms of space, surroundings, shape, depth, and scene, concepts that are much richer and more integrative.

◆

The shapes and forms, the flesh tones, and the relationship between the figure and the background are the great topics connected to the human figure.

◆

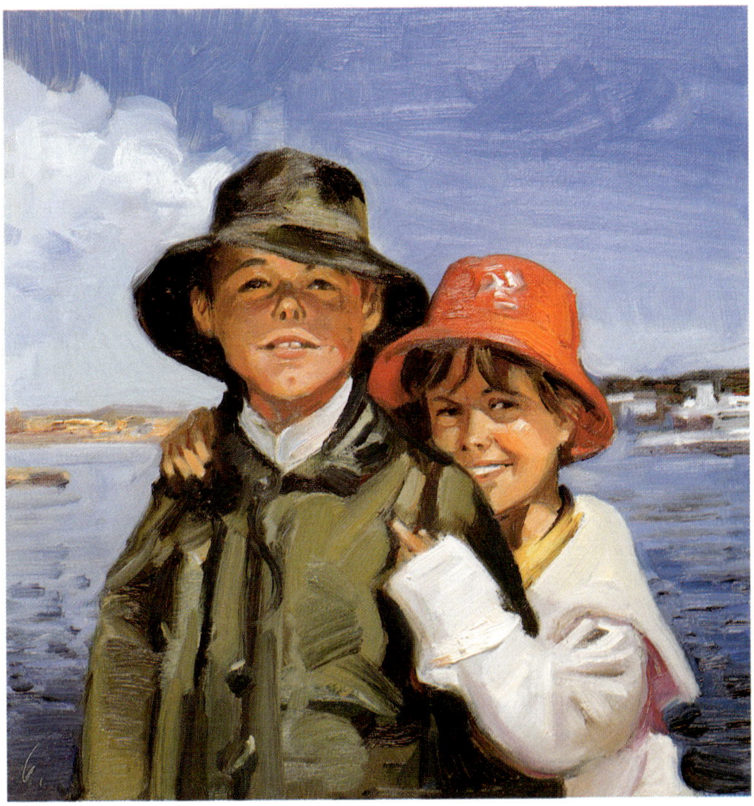

In painting the human figure we produce an encounter between two distinct realities: the personality of the model and the personality of the artist. All artists, in searching for the expression of the model, are also involved in a search for the purest expression of themselves.

Drawing a Torso Using Artificial Light

In order to render the human body pictorially, it's almost a necessity to begin by sketching it. The drawing is the foundation on which apprenticeship as an artist is built, since it is the primary, the most elementary, tool for understanding the form, the shapes, and the space. Next we will explain step by step how to do a drawing from life. We have chosen a male nude as a model, specifically, a torso. Little by little, using lines and areas of color, the form will take shape, of course with consideration for light values. For that purpose, the artist, Ramon Massana, will proceed from the general to the specific, in other words, to the details. That is the general rule to follow.

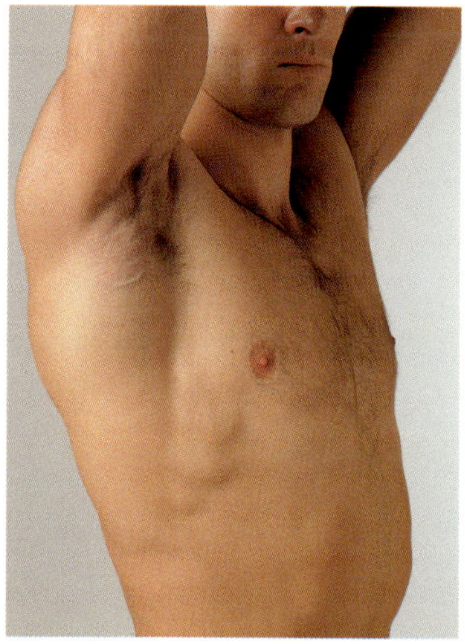

Every pose can express something different. In this case, when the model raises his arms and frames his face and waist, the entire theme is centered in the shape of the thoracic cage.

MATERIALS

- Ivory colored Ingres paper
- Charcoal
- Sanguine and white chalk
- Fixative

1

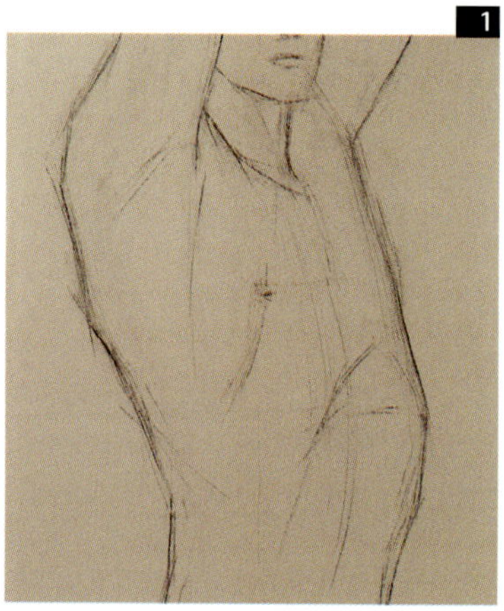

2

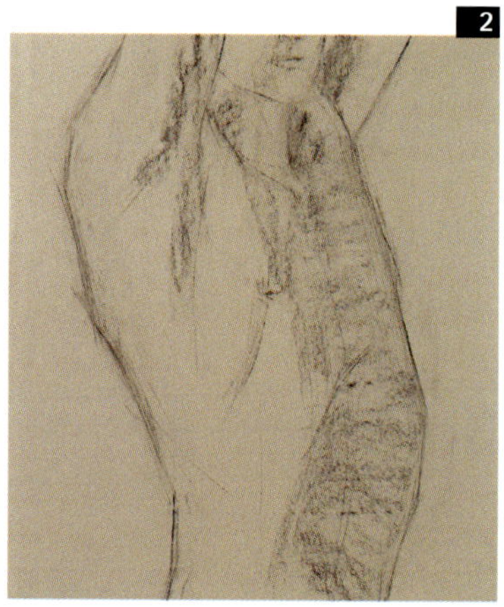

3

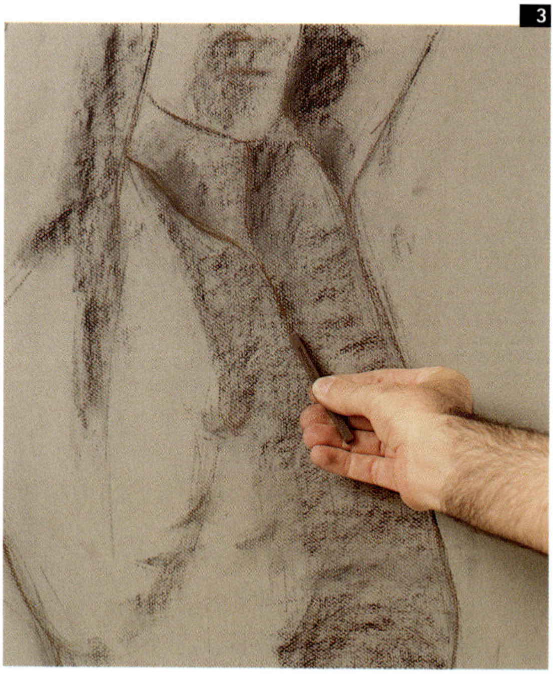

1 The layout is done in lines, sketching the outlines and some inner areas such as the solar plexus, the neck, and the chin. It's important to situate the torso properly on the paper and arrange all the parts with care, revising the layout as often as necessary.

2 Once the layout is acceptable, the shaping begins by using the charcoal to shade the darkest areas on the torso.

3 The neck area is where the greatest variety of shapes and tensions are located.

TECHNIQUES USED

◆ Layout ◆
◆ Shading with charcoal ◆
◆ Combination of charcoal and chalks ◆
◆ Blending ◆
◆ Applying fixative ◆

4

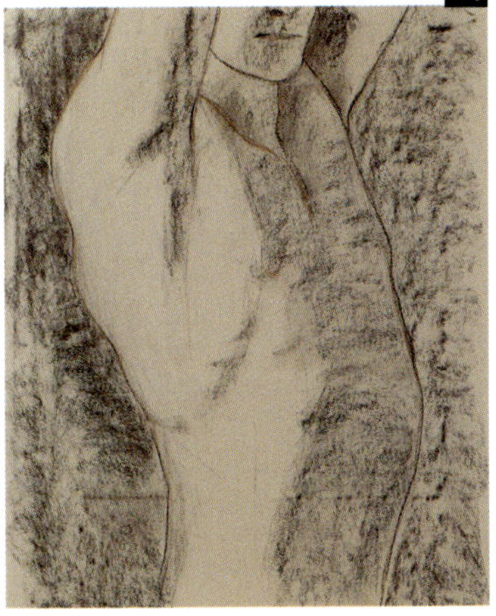

BLENDING
Some dry techniques, such as charcoal, pastels, and chalks, are applied to papers that have some grain, or to laid papers, for the pigment wouldn't adhere well if they were applied to very smooth papers. This means that you have to blend the pigment to distribute it thoroughly on the surface and create darker areas. This blending can be done with the hands, with a rag, with cotton balls, or with blenders. When the paper can take no more pigment and you still want to create a darker mass, you apply fixative to that area and subsequently darken it by adding successive layers.

4 It's time to fill in the background. Although the figure is against a nondescript background, it establishes a dialogue with the space that surrounds it, and you cannot continue with the drawing of the figure without addressing that space.

5 Since the charcoal may leave many pores of the paper unfilled, it's a good idea to use your hand to blend it in using smooth motions.

5

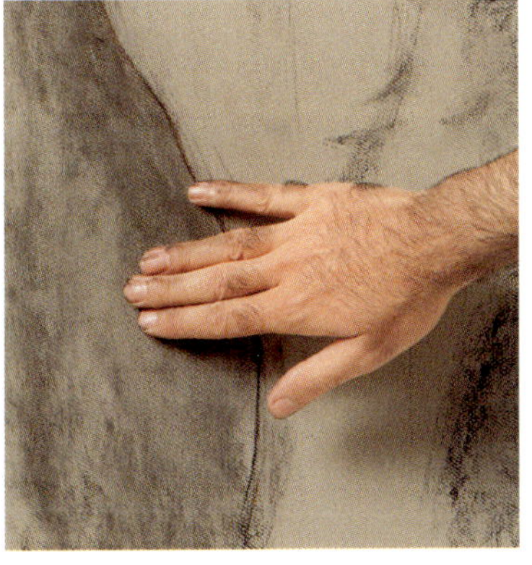

6

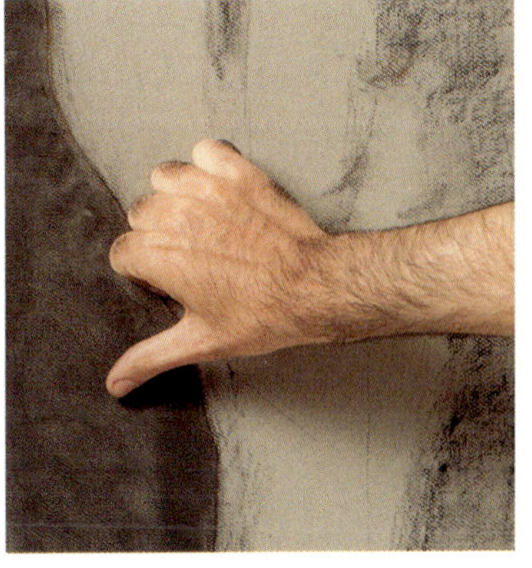

6 In order to cover smaller areas we must apply charcoal with the fingers quite covered with charcoal, for if the fingers are clean, the natural oils in the skin will act like an eraser and remove the charcoal from the paper.

7 Now the more analytical work begins; this involves studying the light in greater detail. To begin with, the shadows of both the surroundings and the figure are darkened.

7

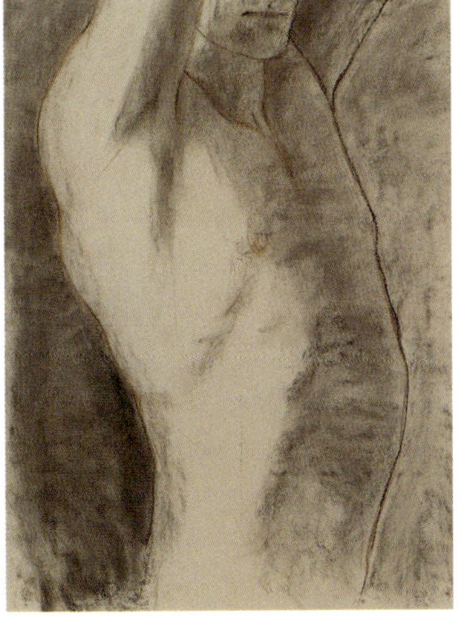

8 In this phase, in order to enrich the drawing, we introduce the chalks; when they combine with the charcoal, they bring new color shades. The medium grays of the skin and the smooth relief of the thorax are adjusted by mixing sanguine with the charcoal.

8

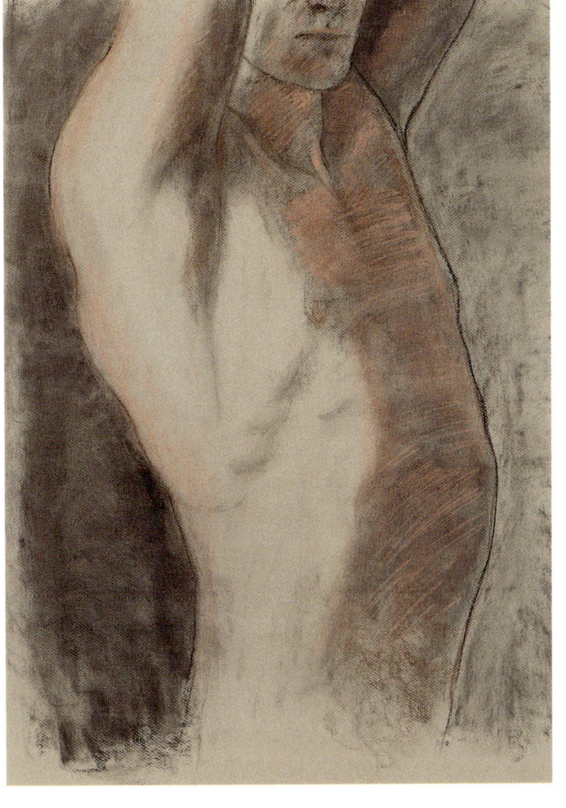

AVOIDING AFFECTED FINISHES

In many beginners' paintings and drawings, the most common defect is an excessive finish, especially if the shape and form are blended or defined in such a way that the artist's style is completely nullified. This type of finish, commonly referred to as "affected," can be avoided by stopping the work in time and placing more emphasis on the strokes.

REPRESENTATIONS OF HUMAN SKIN

In contrast to what is commonly believed, it's not the color that creates the impression of human skin, but rather the proper representation of the shapes. When the body presents a coherent distribution of light and shadow, the observer deduces the skin. Another factor to keep in mind, although no less important, is the texture. The skin of a baby is not the same as that of an adult or an old person. Blending, shading, and harsh coloring are used in resolving these textural features, depending on the intended results.

9 White is used for the touches that indicate maximum illumination. At this point, you have to be careful not to mix the white with the charcoal or the sanguine, since that would create new shades of gray and orange that are very different from the ones used up to this point.

9

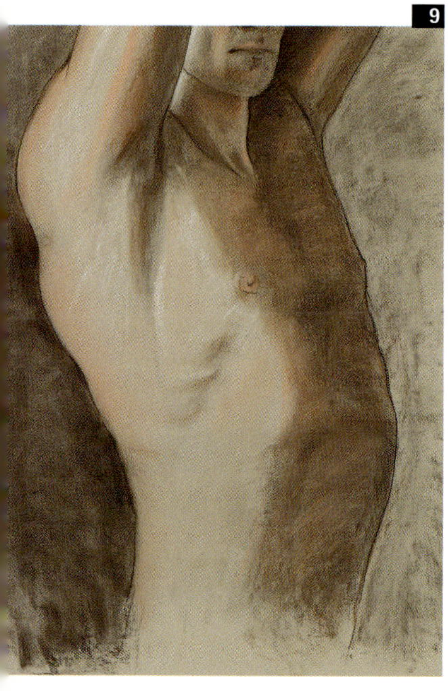

10

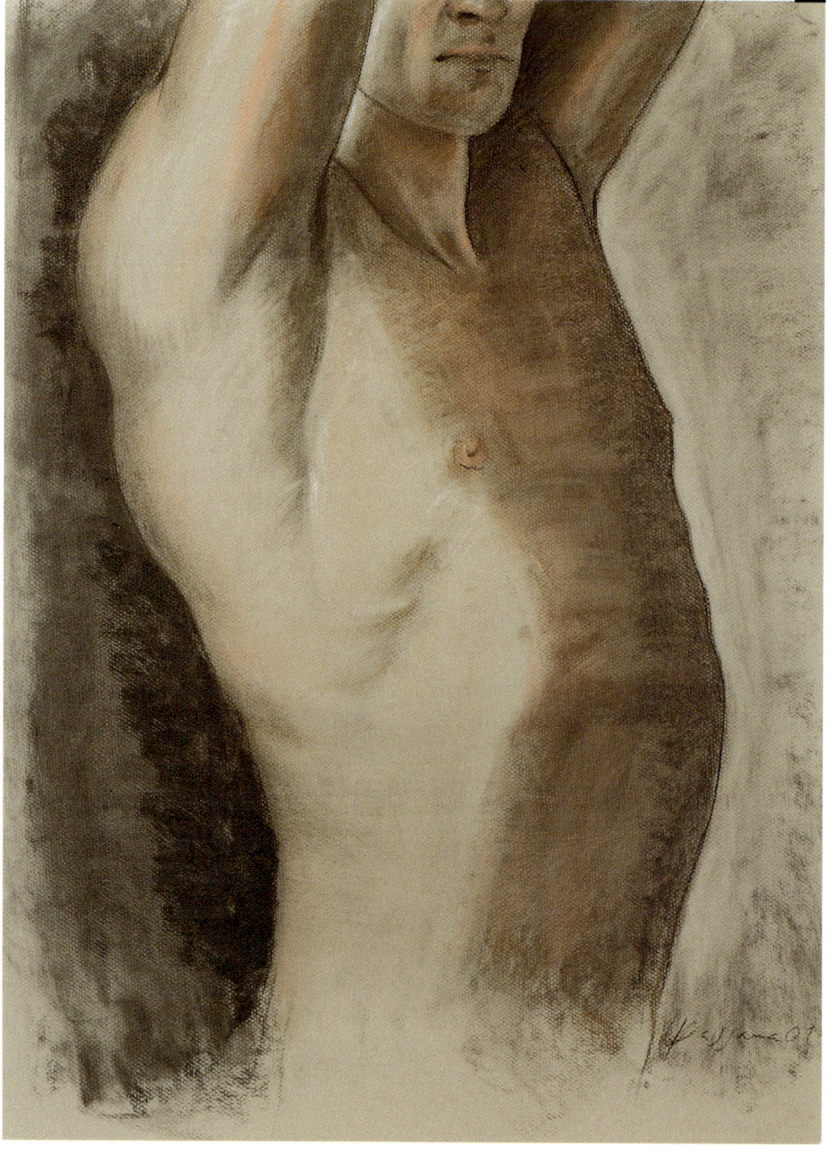

10 Here is the finished drawing, with a fairly advanced level of realism and detail, but without falling into the realm of the affected. Note the prudence with which the white and the sanguine were applied, as well as the play of lights from the surrounding space: dark for the illuminated side of the figure, and light for the shaded side, a very dynamic effect that reinforces the rhythm of the pose.

Figures in Full Sunlight

One of the most appealing features of painting is color. When light enlivens the entire chromatic potential of a landscape or a figure, the end result is fascinating. Impressionist painters experimented with this fascination on an experiential level, visiting landscapes and painting *en plein air*, that is, outdoors, the impressions of that light on nature. The following exercise by Vicenç Ballestar is a hymn to light and color in all their splendor. The human figure is integrated into nature bathed by the same light, clear and fresh, of a noonday next to the sea. Rendering the figure in oils allows for a great chromatic vibrancy and a fluidity of strokes that recall the scenes involving children on the beach by Joaquín Sorolla and some characters by Mary Cassatt, two great impressionists.

TECHNIQUES USED

◆ Preliminary sketch ◆
◆ Bold coloration ◆
◆ Blending ◆

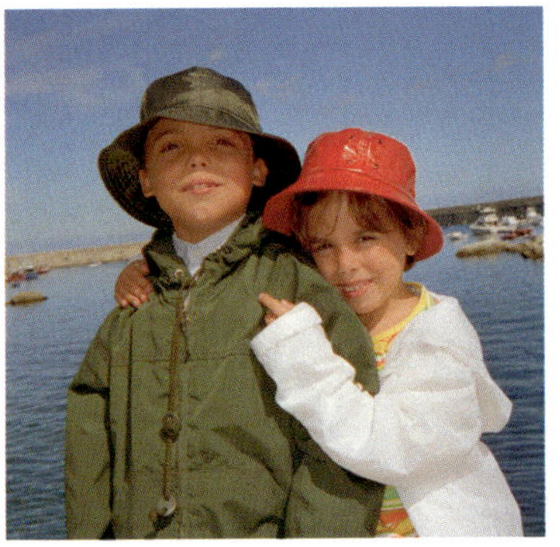

The true subject of this painting is the natural light and the color. The interplay of light and shadow that is set up on the children's faces by the hat brims is somewhat difficult, since it requires a modeling of the faces that's very different from modeling involving classical lighting from the side.

MATERIALS

- A board prepared with gesso
- Oil paints
- Flat sable brushes

1 The initial layout consists of a drawing done in graphite to indicate the main areas of shading. You have to set the drawing up properly and get the proportions right to avoid problems when painting.

2 Following the advice of Sisley when he said, "I always begin a picture by painting the sky," the artist Ballestar has first tackled the marine environment, which sets up the framework of the clear light through the deep blue and the fresh, luminous whites.

3 A fairly orange shade is used for the flesh tones. Orange and blue are complementary colors, and that reinforces the chromatic vibrancy.

1

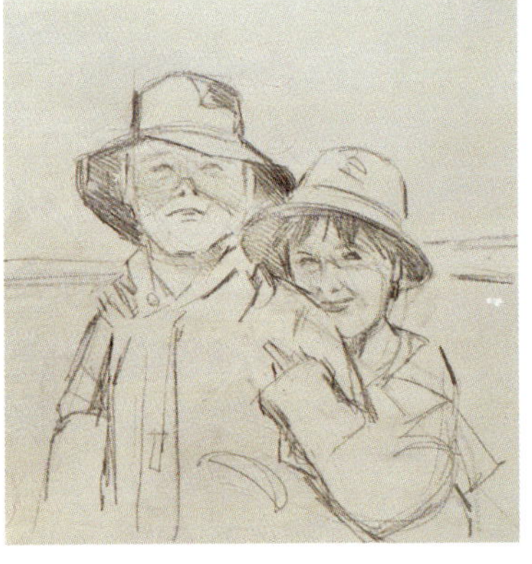

2

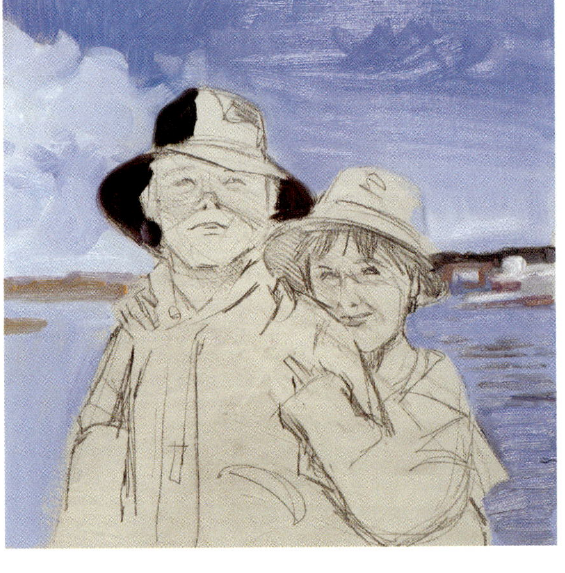

3

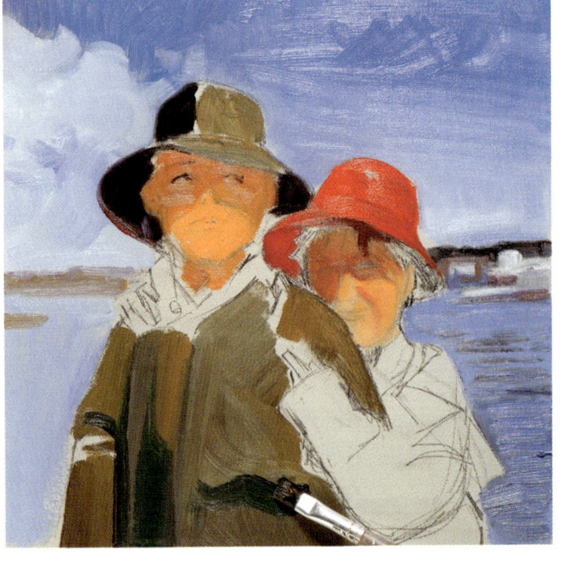

4

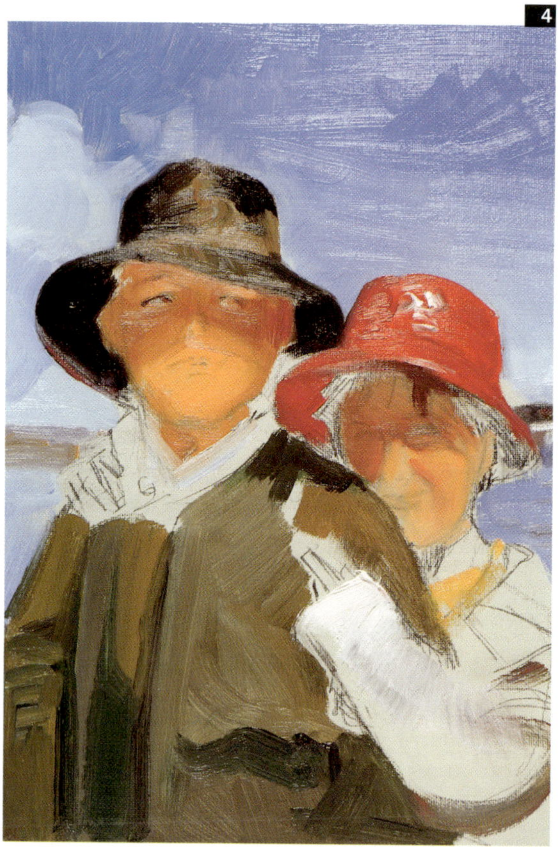

5

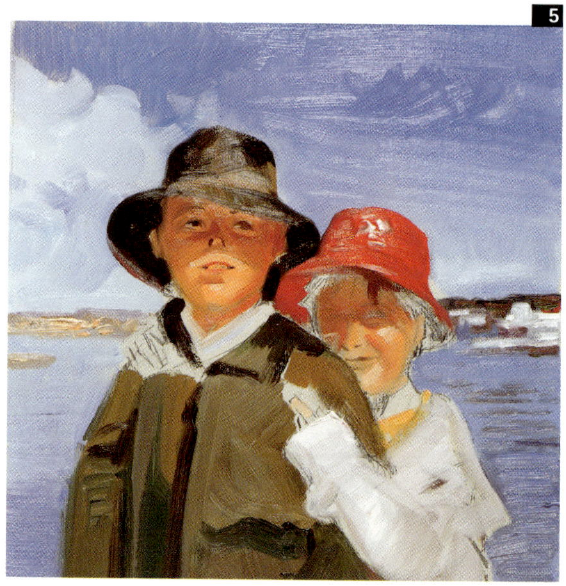

4 In establishing the general shades of the clothing and the faces, two general values of light are set up from the beginning in order to create a basic shape.

5 As the work advances, new values are added to define the features little by little: the facial features, more folds in the clothing, the background landscape, and so forth.

6

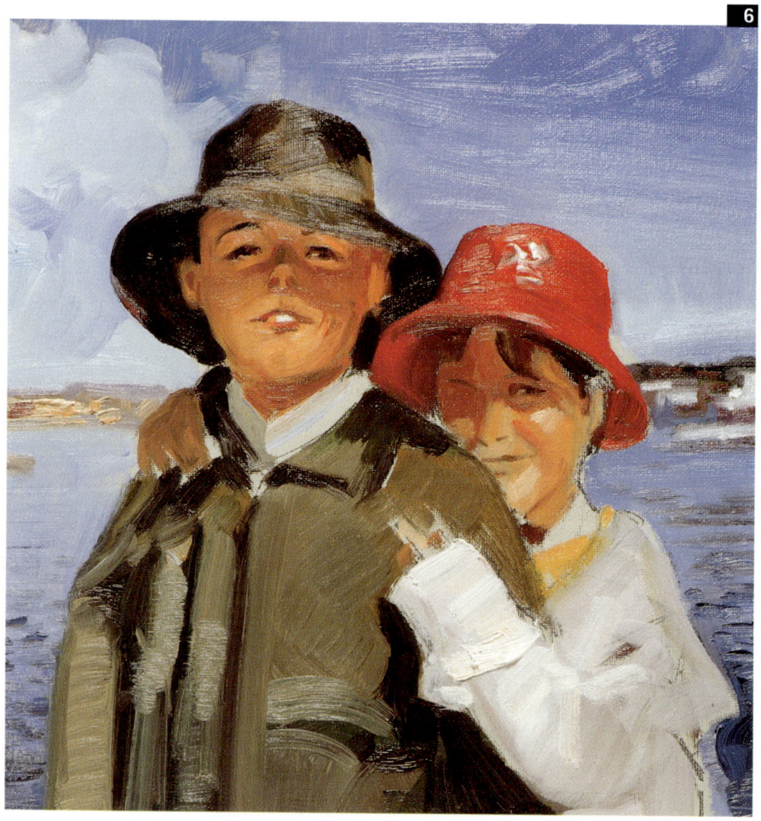

PURE COLORS

In this instance the colors have hardly been modified, thereby avoiding any neutralization that doesn't correspond to the greens and the shadows of the raincoats. Even the shadows on the faces have been darkened using bright, earthy colors to avoid losing the light of the colors.

6 The sea also has to be worked in the same fashion. The waves impart a sense of movement and water to the depth of gradation. Note that additions to the figures alternate with those to the surroundings.

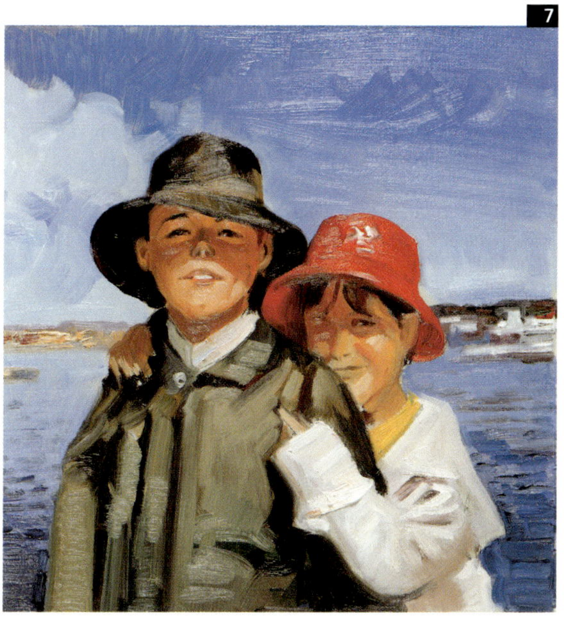

7 In the following steps, the work is more detailed; it involves an attempt to adjust every intervention to the vision of the model, relative to both the definition of the faces and the clothing.

8 The girl's face takes on shape much like the boy's did. The reflections on the hats suggest the materials of which they are made: waterproof duck for the green one, and plastic for the red. Both of them are subjected to the same light, but they reflect it differently.

9 At this stage the painting is nearly done. The details of the raincoats give the scene a good deal of veracity.

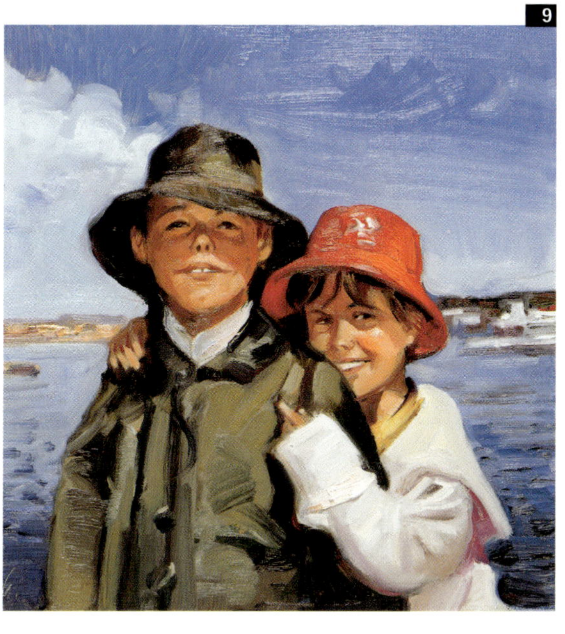

DEFINING THE FEATURES

People often believe that in order to define the facial features or any other element (e.g., the buttons or the folds of an article of clothing or the windows of a building), it's necessary to do a nearly photographic rendition. But that's not the way it is in painting. In learning this difficult art of synthesis, it's important to do sketches in which the painter deliberately works with few resources and measured intervention.

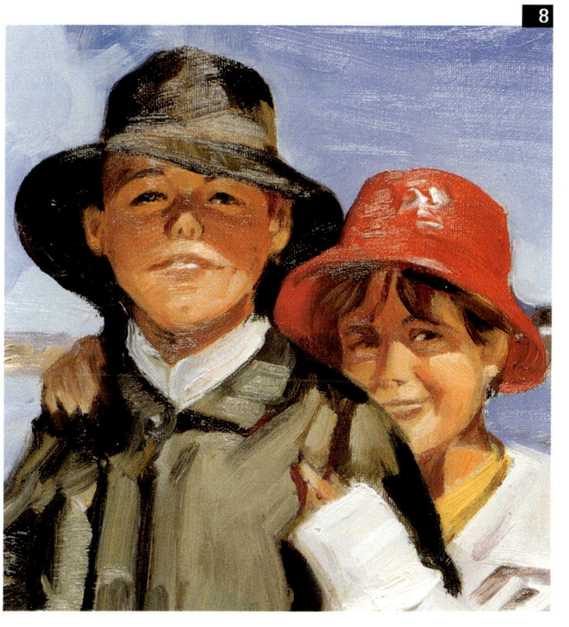

THE GENERAL LIGHTING OF THE SURROUNDINGS

The presence of water in the scene being painted is basic to reinforcing the clarity of the ambient light. The clouds reflect white light from their vaporous density, much like cotton flowers, and the sea maintains a light surface and a very pure blue that suggest cleanliness. This is the light after a summer storm, and even though the children's clothing communicates the moment, it's really revealed through the purity of the colors.

The intent of every impressionist painter at any given moment is to capture this impression of light, and the surrounding light is the key to making this painting work.

10 In order to exaggerate the dazzling effect on the boy's face and the difference between the two areas of light and shadow, the mouth was initially modeled using too much contrast. The final step in this work involves softening this part of the face to return it to a softer and more childlike expression.

11 Now the finished product has a more pleasant appearance. The teeth have been reduced in size and the lips have been softened. Also the cloud that appears behind the figures has been shaded off a little to further lighten that part of the sky.

10

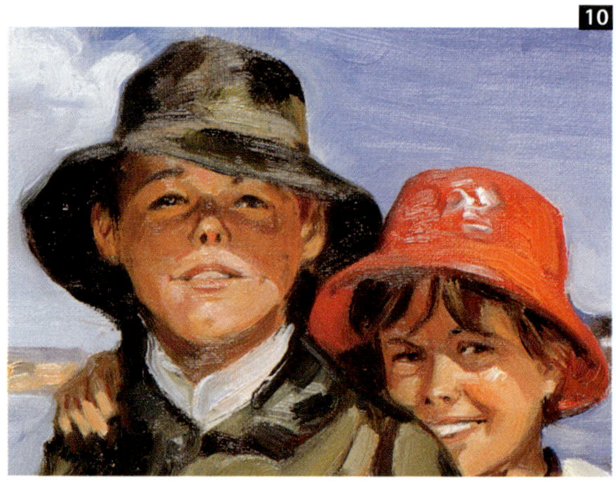

11

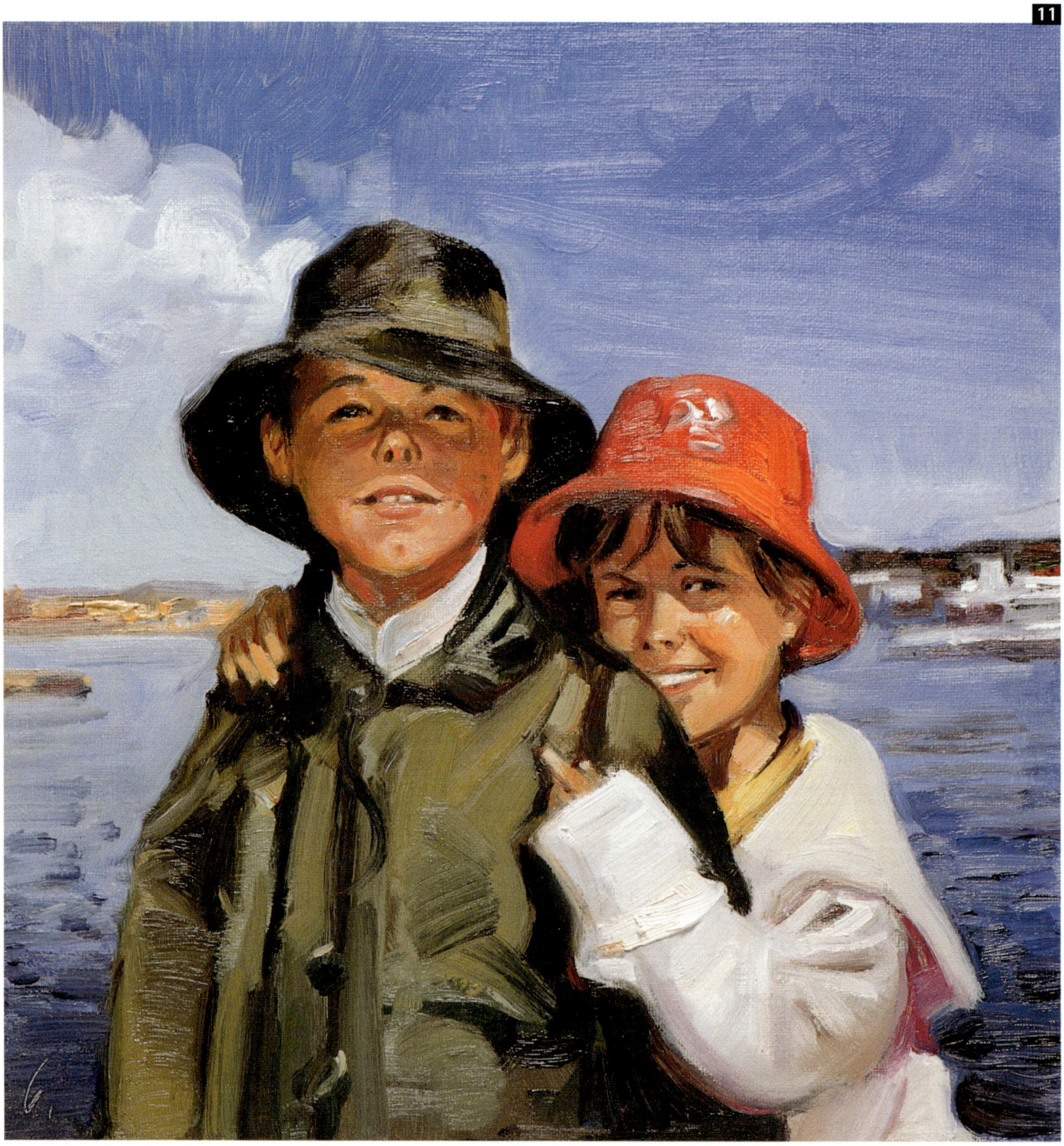

A Self-portrait in Natural Light

Portraiture is a specialty within painting the human figure; its goal is to express accurately the artist's perceptions of the model. This accuracy is the result of the resemblance that makes it possible to identify the subject based on the portrait. In the next exercise we will see how a painter who has focused his work on this genre, Josep Maria Cabané, does his self-portrait. This exercise will allow us to follow step by step and in detail the modeling of a face illuminated by natural light with no excesses or special effects. This is an invitation to experiment by using your own face as a model and the mirror as a master, an exercise nearly all painters have done with very satisfying results.

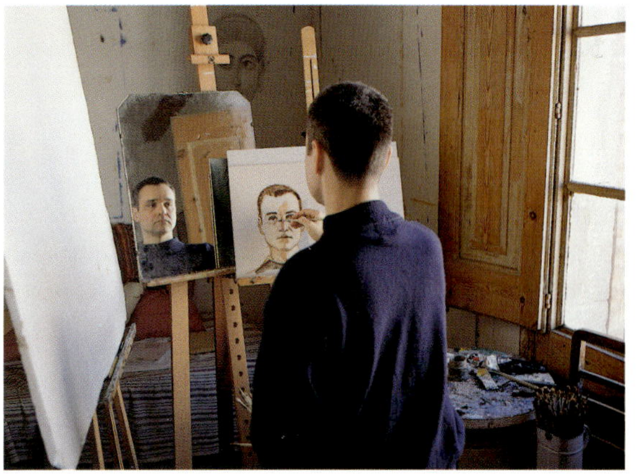

Natural, lateral light is used in doing this self-portrait. In order to compensate for its dramatic effect, a reflective panel has been placed opposite the light source (the window) to soften the shadows and create a gentle dark line at the center of the face.

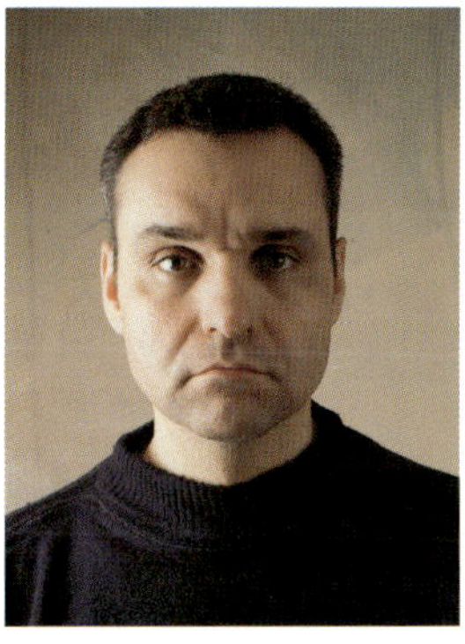

Here is the artist's face as it was photographed at the start of the session. It's what any observer sees in looking at the model.

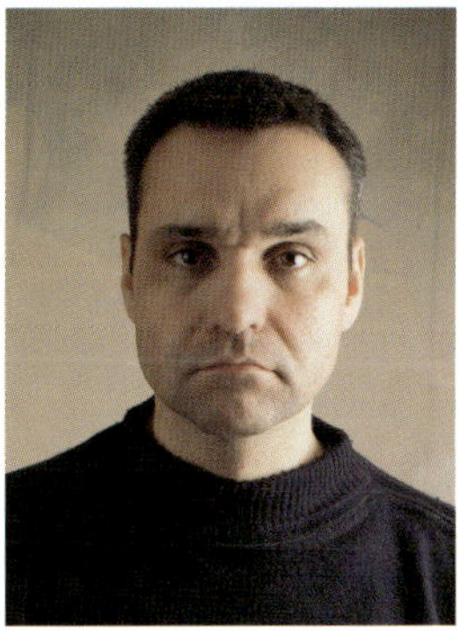

Here is the same face as seen by the artist. The effect of the mirror reverses right and left of each half of the face. This is the logical position to use in doing the self-portrait, since it's what the artist sees in the mirror.

MATERIALS

- A board prepared with gesso
- Oil paints
- Round sable brushes

1

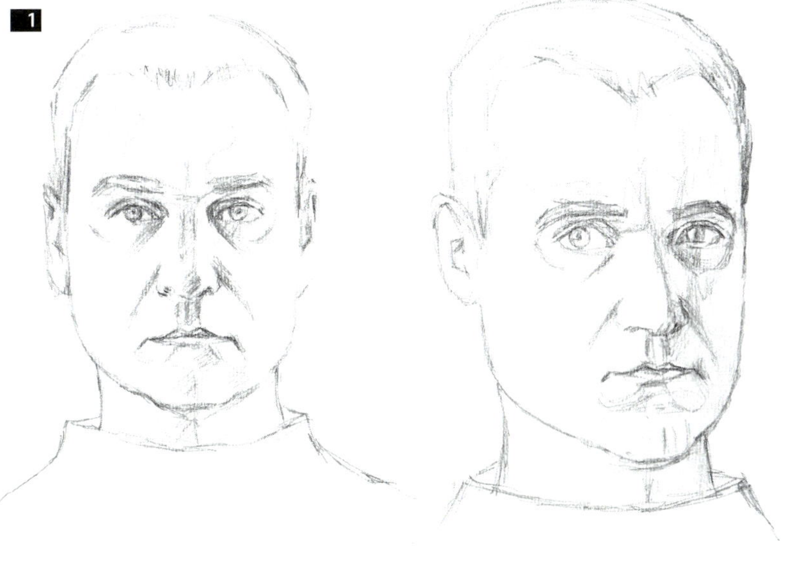

1 The first steps by the artist involve a few pencil sketches to study the viewpoint and the light. In the end he has opted for a totally frontal view with lateral light compensated in such a way that a certain dark axis of symmetry is created in the center of the face.

TECHNIQUES USED

◆ Preliminary sketches ◆
◆ Layout of the drawing ◆
◆ Shading ◆

BACKGROUND
We have started with a board prepared with gesso on both faces to avoid distortion of the wood. The base color is not white, but rather a soft gray on which the lights and shadows will stand out. The presence of features located behind or around the figure adds symbolic or narrative meaning to the pictorial discourse. Here a totally neutral background has been chosen. This neutrality avoids inferences and helps intensify the expressiveness and the emotional charge of the face.

2

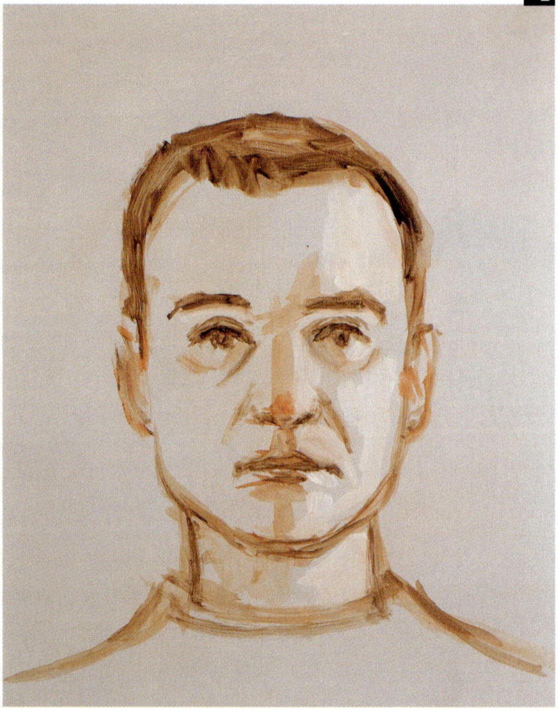

2 Using a brush, trace around the preparatory drawing. Since the drawing set up everything relative to the viewpoint and the proportions, it's now possible to proceed with greater certainty, establishing the oval of the face and the three major elements it contains—the eyes, nose, and mouth—by means of shading that suggests the initial light and shadows.

3 The next step continues to define the shapes and the space. The dark areas are intensified, and at the same time, they are adapted to the shapes. The background and the jersey have been given minimal treatment in order to focus on the chromatic and luminous relationships between the background and the figure.

4 The coloring of the face has been created with just burnt sienna and blue, plus white for the reflections. Of course the hair has been darkened.

3

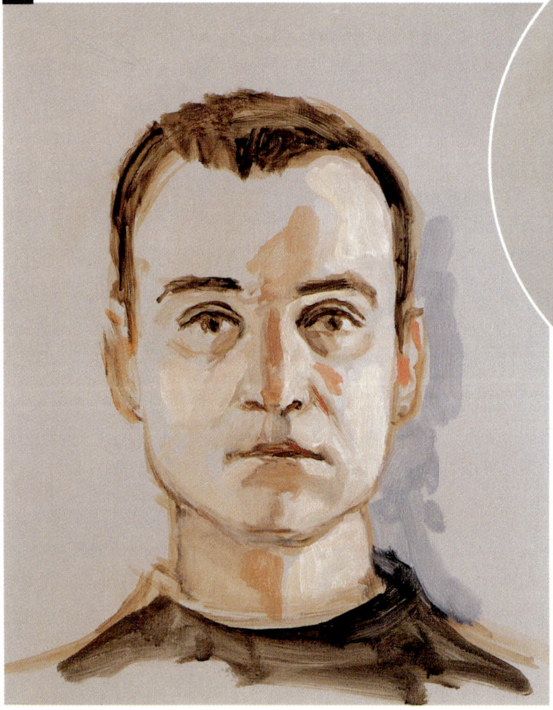

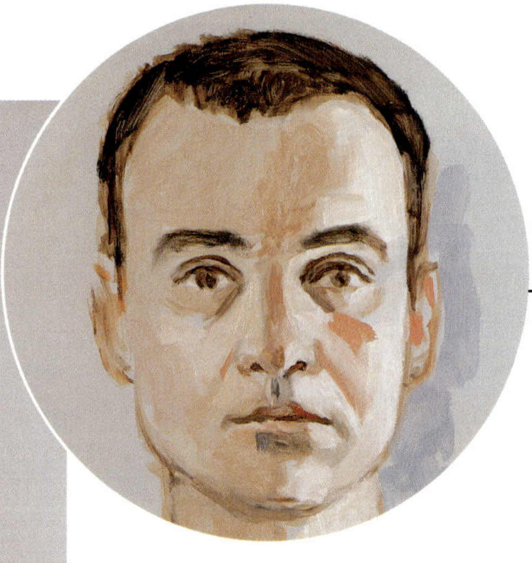

4

USING THE MIRROR AS A MASTER
In correcting a portrait, it's a good idea to occasionally look at the painting reflected in a mirror. The human face is not perfectly symmetrical, and in inverting the image, the mirror allows us to gain a more complete view of each side with respect to both the model and the painting itself.

5

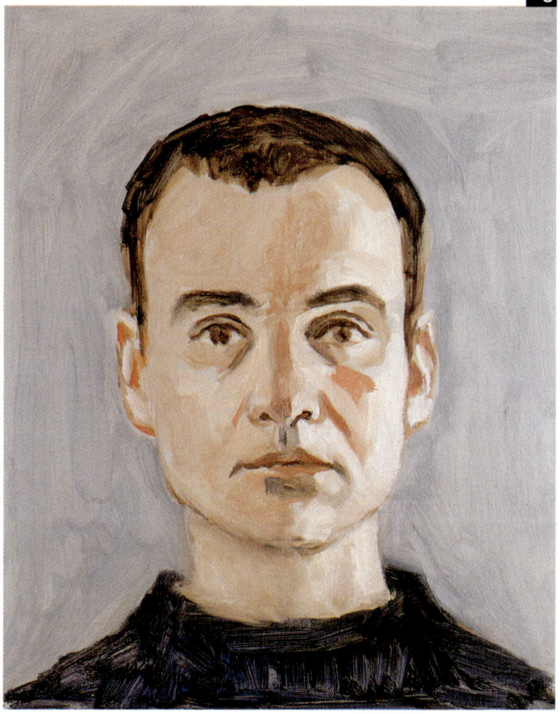

A SUBDUED PALETTE
A palette of naturalist colors has been selected for this portrait; they consist of a base color for the flesh tones, burnt sienna, which with white, ultramarine, and Payne gray can be used for lightening or darkening as required.

The mixture of sienna and blue produces moderated dark shades that, when mixed with white, create very subdued grays that are still suggestive and delicate. The colors neutralized in this way create a sensation of veracity and naturalness more effectively than saturated colors could.

5 In this step the artist has decided to emphasize the slope of the shoulders a little in order to highlight the head. Also the ears have been sculpted and the background has been colored in. Finally, the shadows have been cooled with blue and Payne gray, thereby setting up a connection to the color of the shirt.

6

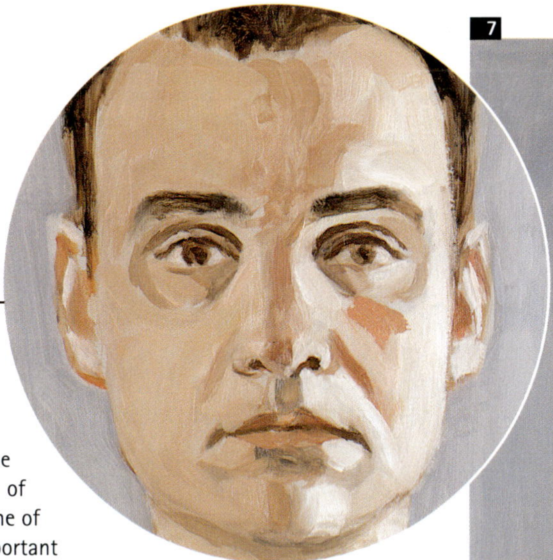

6 Clearly the definition of the eyes is one of the most important parts of any portrait, since the gaze contributes life and expression. In addition to the eyes, including the pupils and the eyelids, the eyebrows and the brow are part of the gaze.

7

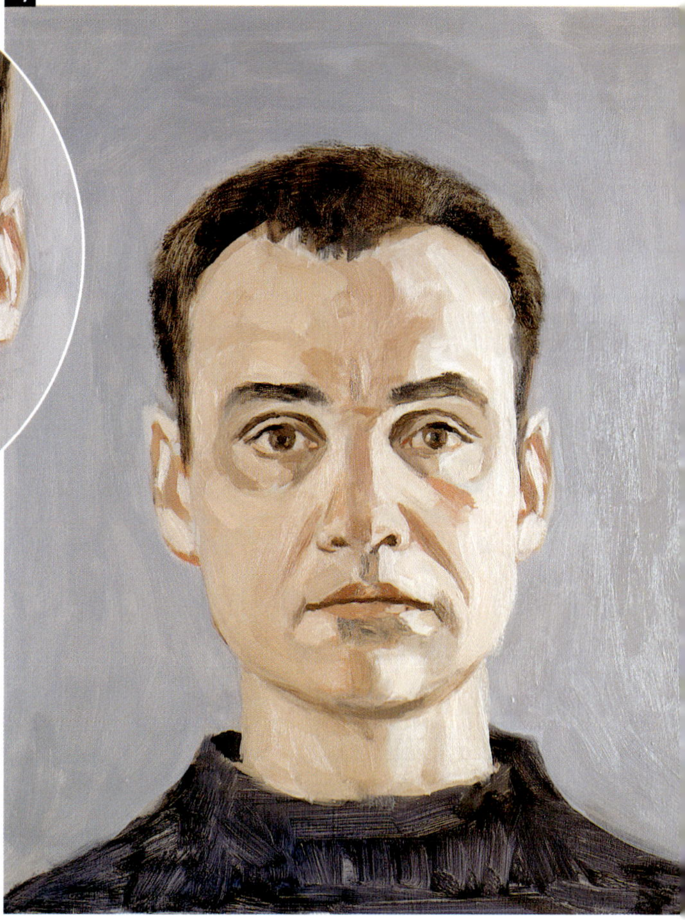

7 The expressiveness of the gaze is now well defined through the complete sculpting of the eyes, including tear ducts and circles under the eyes, plus the shaping of the brow and the forehead, which will be perfected shortly. The breadth of the face has been corrected by filling it out, and the shape of the hair has been modified, contributing to an appearance of greater relaxation and maturity.

RESEMBLANCE IN PORTRAITURE
In portraiture, the resemblance to the subject should be not only physical but, more important, psychological. However, the psychological aspects are a bit more difficult to capture and express; they require not only astute observation of every facial feature, but also a subjective interpretation. By highlighting or attenuating a wrinkle to a greater or lesser degree the artist may experience success or failure in communicating any given characteristic. The sum of the decisions on this level is what determines the aura or the presence contained in a portrait.

8

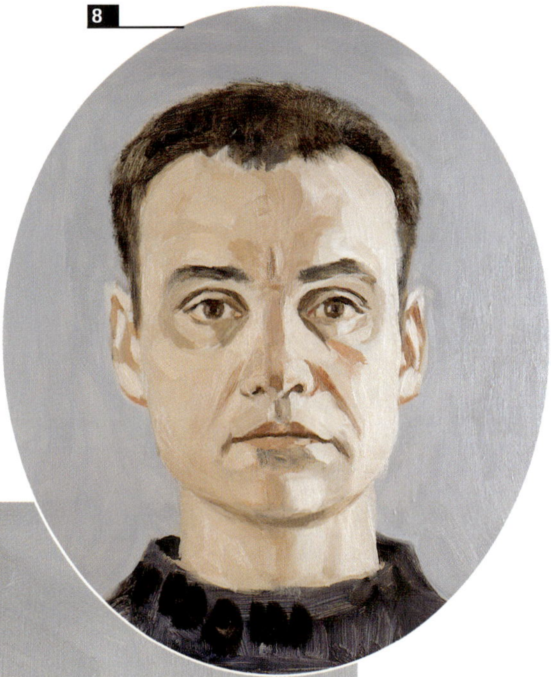

9

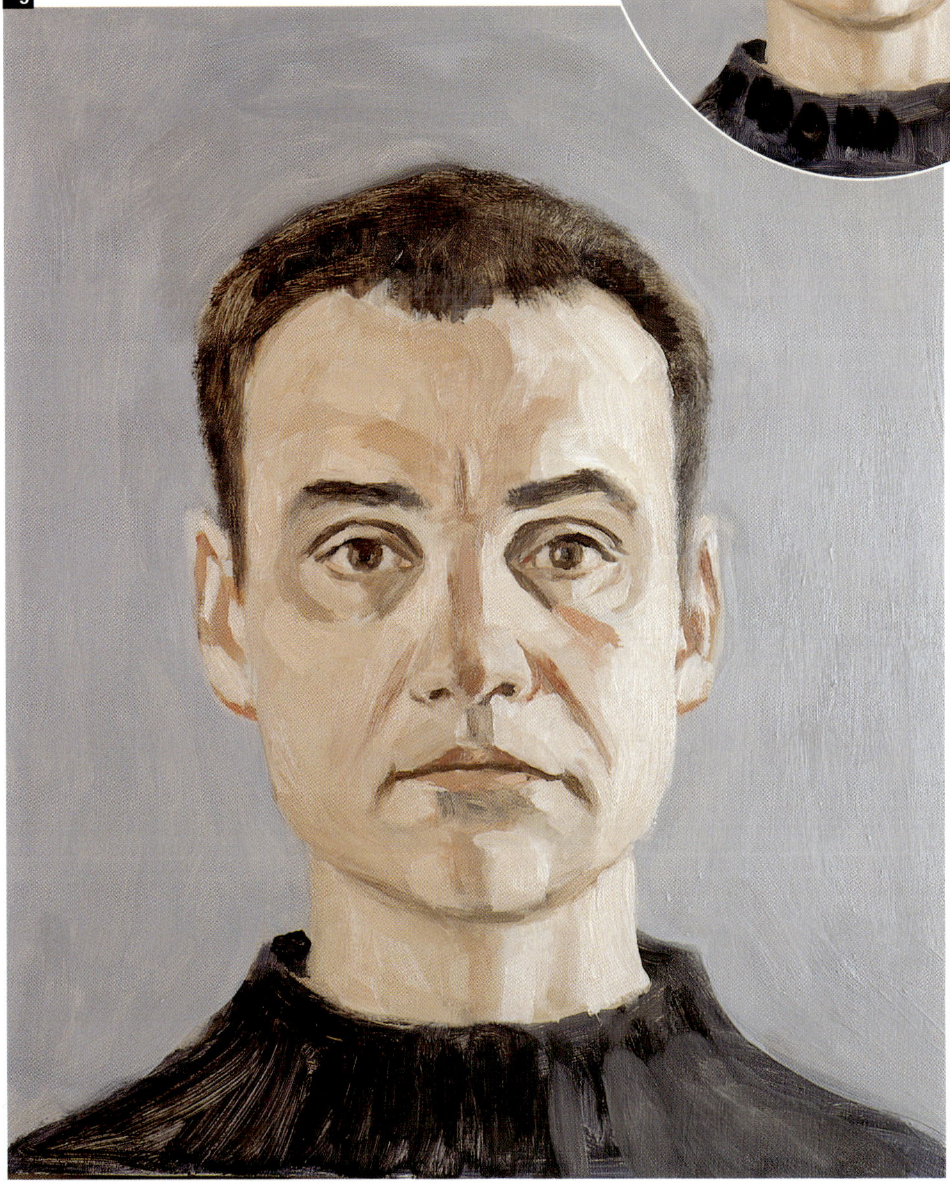

8 In order to further adjust the portrait to the model the cheeks and the jaw have been softened, since they initially were too harsh, and the frown has been intensified to increase the intensity of the gaze.

9 Finally the shirt is defined in greater detail, and the corners of the mouth and the nose have been accentuated a little more. This excellent self-portrait has great presence, thanks to the emphasis on the shapes, which is a characteristic of the artist's style.

Procedures and Techniques Applied to Landscape

In dealing with light and color, the last major subject is landscape. Painting landscapes involves painting space. The connection among all the elements involved is the atmosphere.

In the following pages, you will be able to follow step by step four works that deal with landscape. The first two involve traditional rural spaces; in the first, the depth of some agricultural fields, and in the second, the waters of a river flowing among mountains. In both cases there is one common element: the creation of the climate or atmosphere of light. Light is the real crafter of the magical moment in which the landscape envelops and captivates us; in this case, it's the light of dusk.

The last two landscapes are very different from the foregoing ones. The third is a very special city landscape. The work was done from a photograph taken from a car as it crossed a highway bridge on the way to the city. The dynamism of the bridge structure, the cables, and the skyscrapers in the background give the scene plenty of character, with its notable perspective. In this case the scene takes in the mid-morning light. Even though it is slight, a certain neutralization of the light through the urban fog remains an important element.

Finally, the last and most creative of the works involves a subjective interpretation of a floral theme, specifically aquatic flowers in a pond. In this case, three pictures have been painted at the same time, that is, a triptych. The three paintings are united thematically and stylistically. In this work, the color is more important than the light, and it brings us close to the edges between imagination and abstraction, which will seem very familiar if we think of the analogy to Claude Monet in Giverny, France.

◆

Light is the real crafter of the magical moment in which the landscape envelops and captivates us.

◆

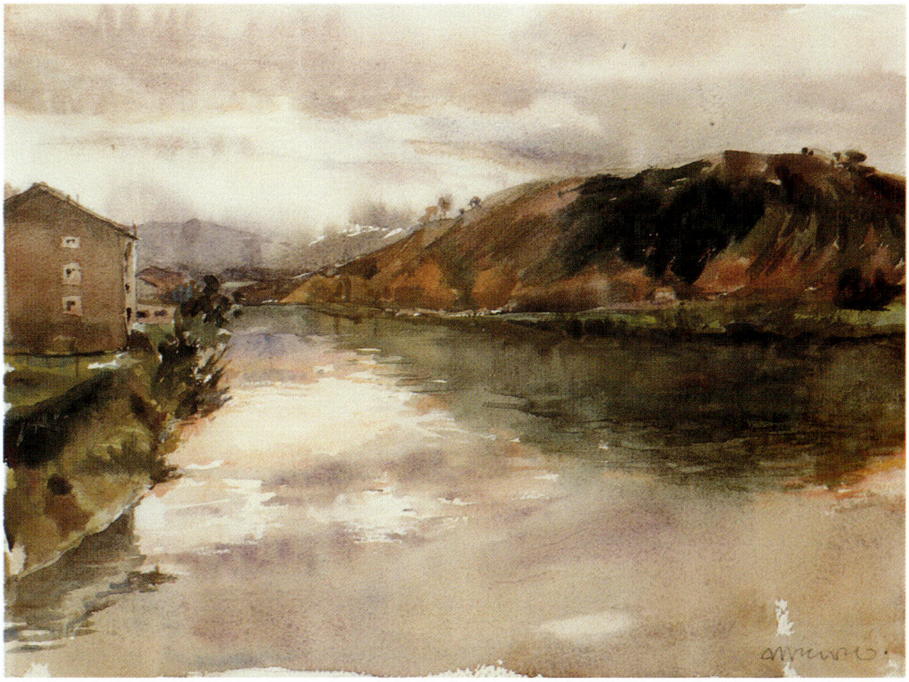

A romantic vision of landscape such as this one invites the observer to experience nature on an emotional level. The spectator is not limited to observing, but rather passes into contemplation and rapture before the sublime spectacle of light.

An Expressionistic Sunset

The relationship established between the painter and the landscape is essential for understanding this genre. In landscape painting, when the artist selects a specific time of day for painting, the motivation is the available interplay of lights and colors. This extremely variable factor is what catalyzes the connection between the human and nature, awakening emotions that subsequently are transferred to the painting. Expressionistic landscapes always have a strong character, charged with chromatic energy and rich in contrasts. In the work that we will now demonstrate, Josep Asunción has attempted to capture the visual impact of the landscape with a painting done quickly and spontaneously by taking advantage of the brief time that a sunset lasts. He has chosen to use acrylics, since they dry quickly and allow the use of layers and velaturas with very short waiting times.

The painting of skies (skyscapes) is a specialty within landscape painting that deals with the luminous and chromatic effects that the atmosphere and light produce in the sky. Clouds, clearings, fogs, and storms are wonderful subjects for great expressiveness. A foggy sunset such as the one in this study is a perfect opportunity to paint a dense and highly contrasted sky.

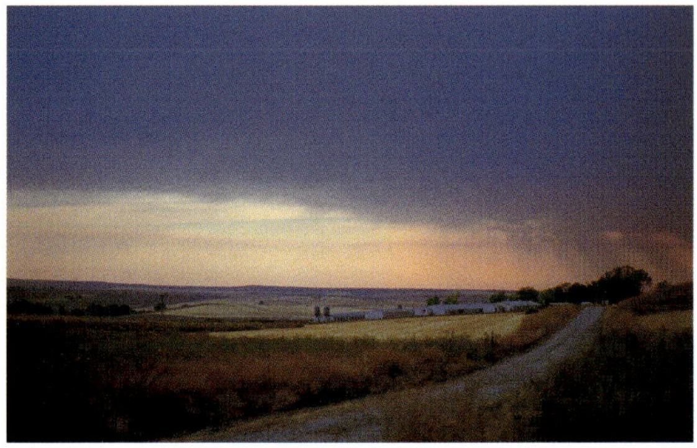

To pictorially capture an artistic moment such as this, you will have little time available, barely one hour, because light is changing and gradually disappears.

MATERIALS
- Canvas
- Acrylic Paints
- Broad flat and round boar's bristle brushes

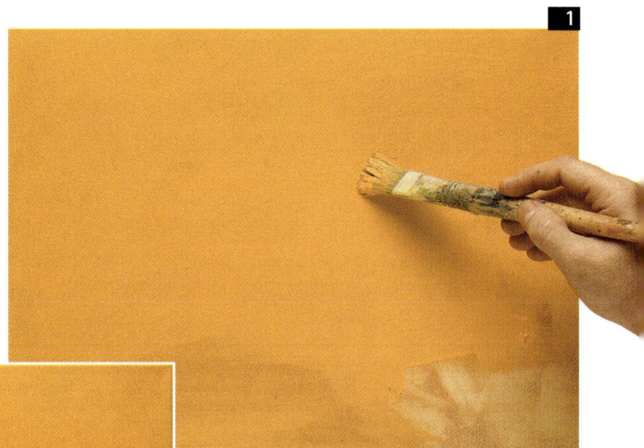

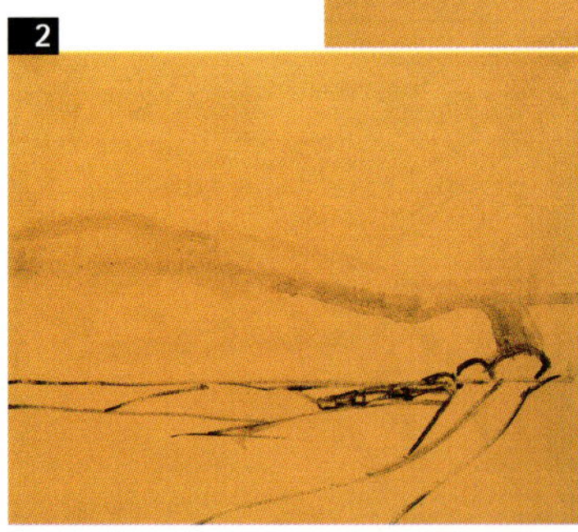

TECHNIQUES USED

◆ Chromatic background ◆
◆ Preliminary sketch ◆
◆ Quick coloring ◆

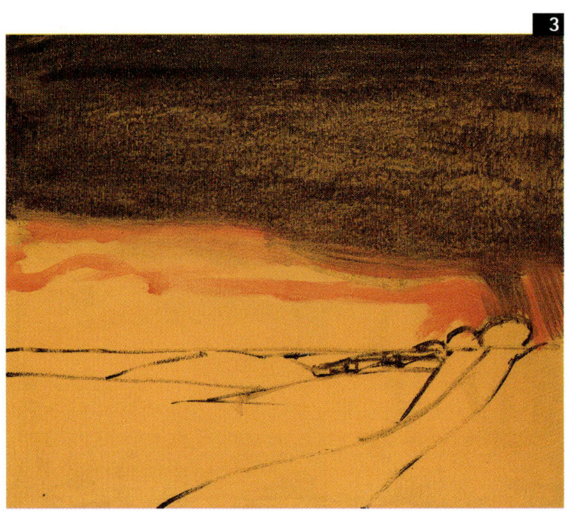

1 To begin with, create a yellow background as a chromatic base that will set up the guidelines for the subsequent touches. The acrylic paint will dry very quickly and we won't waste any time waiting for a chance to work over it.

2 The layout of the work is very simple: the horizon, the trees in the distance, the highway, and the division between light and dark in the sky.

3 The first coloring uses fairly diluted paints to avoid getting into impastos and to create a luminous valuation that's not too highly contrasted.

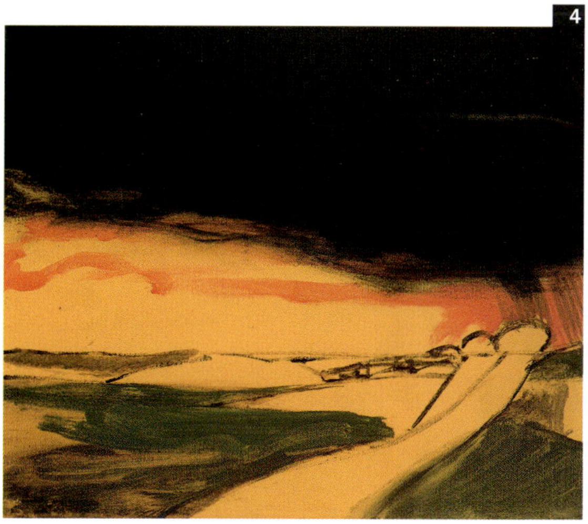

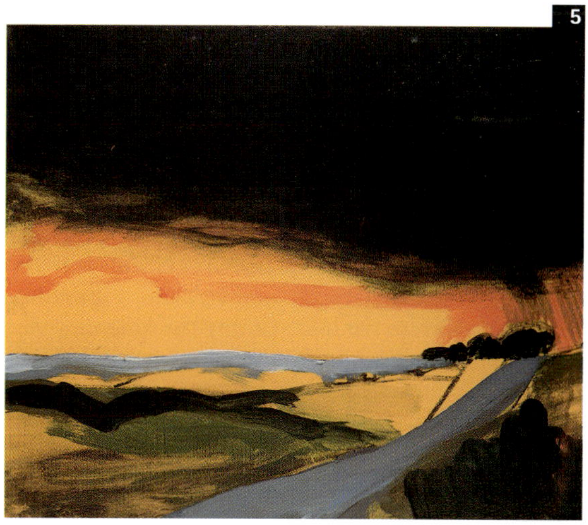

4 Next, the initial colors of the field are established, greens and blues, which let the orange beneath them breathe, creating tension and new dark, neutral shades.

5 The sky has been darkened with more blue—a blue darkened with bright orange, which suggests the arrival of night.

6 The fields that are closer to the horizon, in the distance, receive light from the sun, which still bathes them under the clouds with its orange light. The colors there are brighter.

7 Here the color of the fields has been adjusted, shading them further toward orange, and the sky has been touched up to give it more density and body and suggest the clouds and the fog of that time of day.

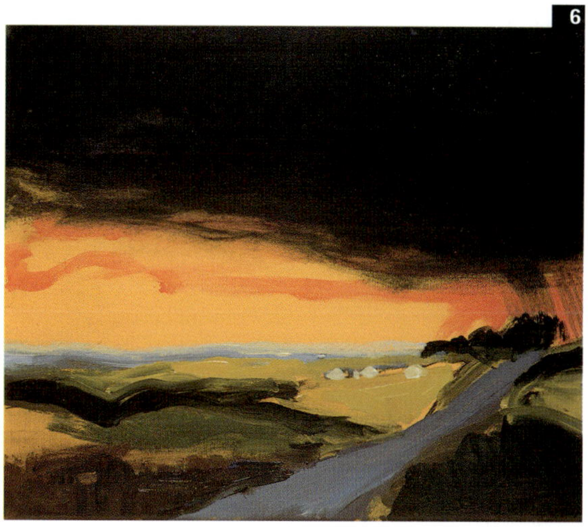

DOUBLE CONTRAST: CHROMATIC AND LUMINOUS

The color is vital to this landscape, but in contrast to impressionistic or fauvist colorist landscapes, there is a presence of black and other dark colors that helps to accentuate the light and add dramatic tension to the scene. Luminous contrast is added to chromatic contrast. In this instance there is a chromatic harmonization of complementary colors (blue and orange) to set up an intense vibrancy.

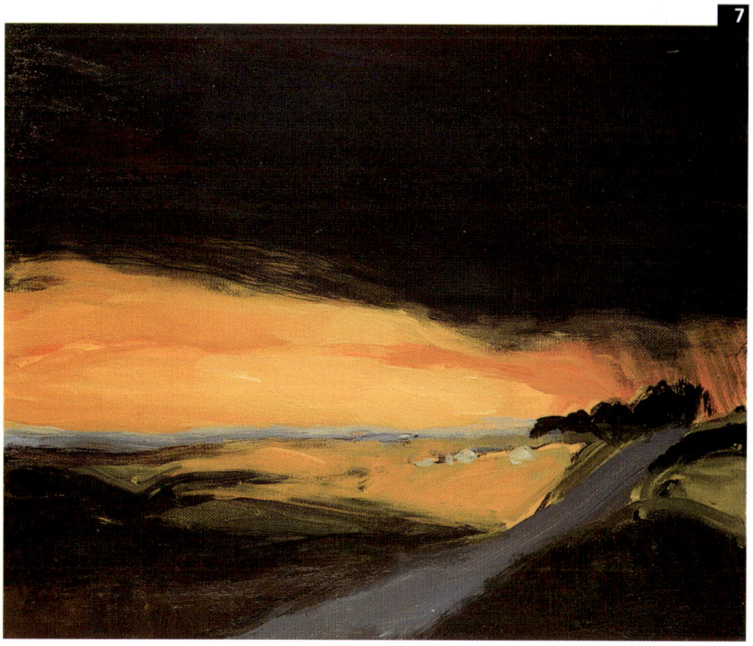

The Aesthetic Experience

There's a story that relates that on one occasion toward the middle of the nineteenth century a lady was traveling by coach on a twisting mountain road in the midst of an intense and terrible storm. An elderly stranger who was traveling with her suddenly opened the window and leaned half his body outside. The lady, perplexed by that action, remained immobile and didn't know what to do during the long time that the situation continued. When the stranger returned to his place entirely soaked and with his face lit up by joy, he kept repeating, "This is extraordinary, sublime, fantastic . . . ," and he invited the lady to repeat his experience. At first the lady hesitated, but finally she decided to abandon decorum, and despite her misgivings, she imitated her traveling companion. When they reached their destination, the two departed, but the lady always remembered that strange experience, which she scarcely knew how to categorize. Years later, she visited an exhibit of the great painter William Turner in London, and she was able to recognize in the paintings the experience she had had on that earlier trip. She was introduced to the painter, and when they shook hands, she remembered him: the gentleman from the coach.

8 In this phase of the process, an important adjustment has been made; it involves painting the dark part of the sky with a darker and more luminous blue. The painting, which is expressionistic in nature, has quickly captured the painter's emotion before the vanishing daylight at that brief moment of the day.

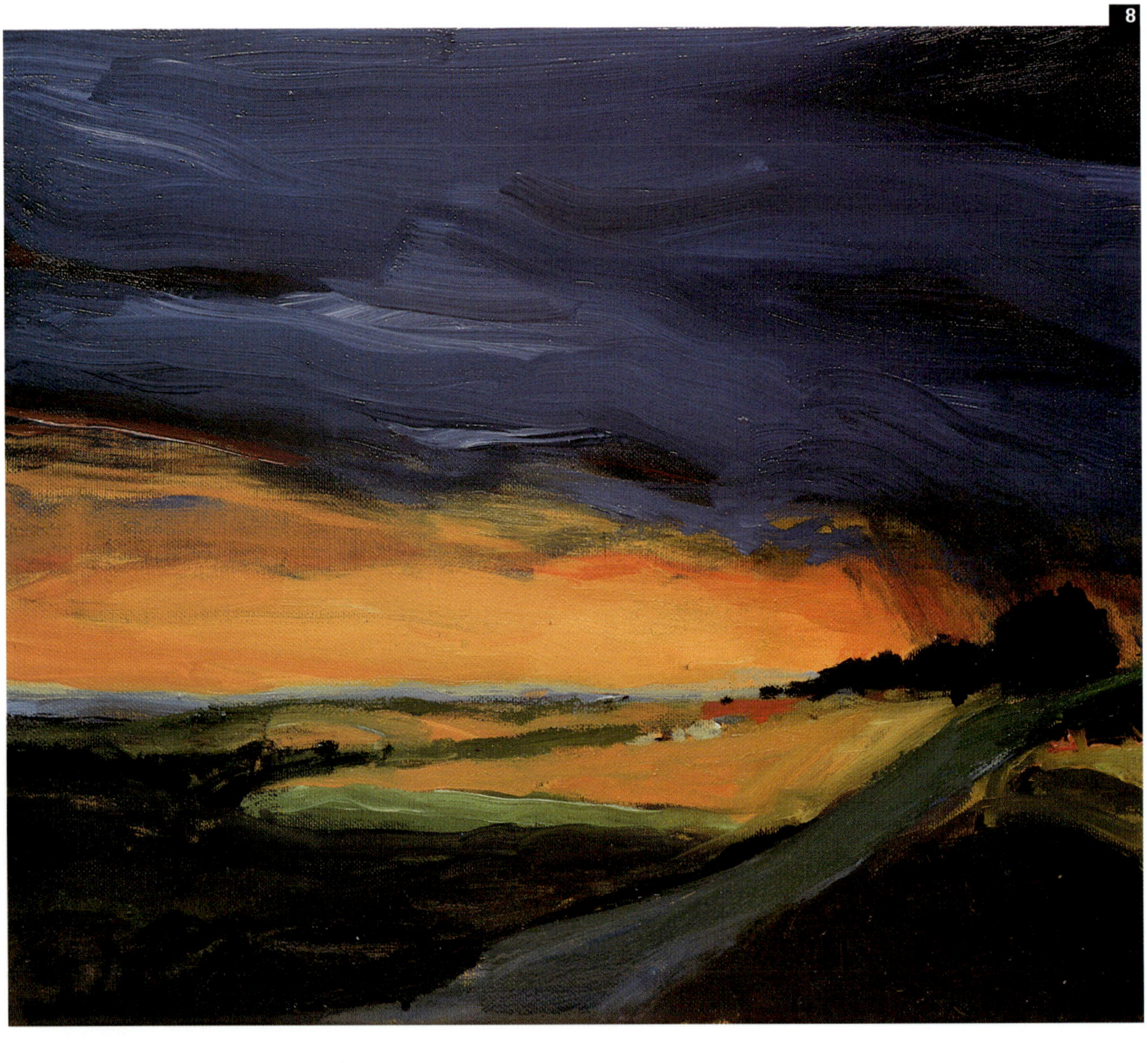

A River Landscape

Landscapes in which water plays a major role, such as the following watercolor, always present an interesting interplay of lights, since water acts like a mirror, reflecting with varying degrees of accuracy any luminous phenomenon. In the river landscape done next by Mercedes Gaspar, we explain step by step how to treat this atmosphere using watercolors, a technique that also involves the medium of water and is ideal for this type of pictorial effect. The chromatic harmonization of this work is a subdued scale that conveys the shades of half-light.

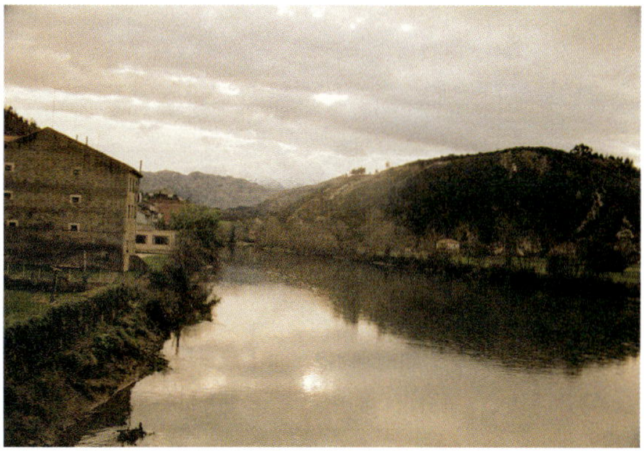

This wonderful scene of great serenity and intimacy, which takes place in a natural half-light, with scarcely any color and light, is the model for a watercolor. This is a damp and melancholy, yet truly captivating atmosphere.

MATERIALS
- Watercolor paper
- Watercolors
- Round, soft-haired brushes
- Masking tape

1

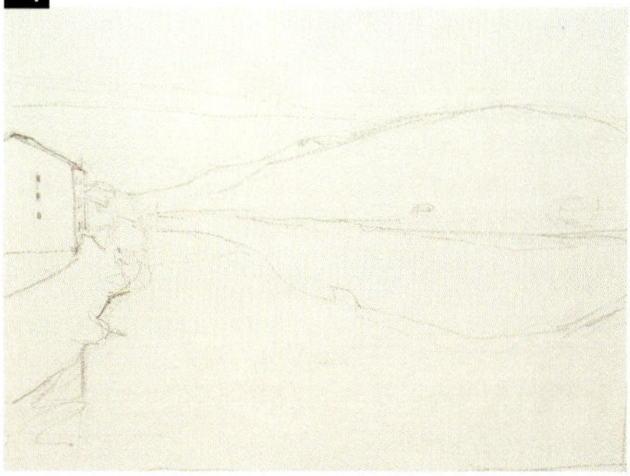

2

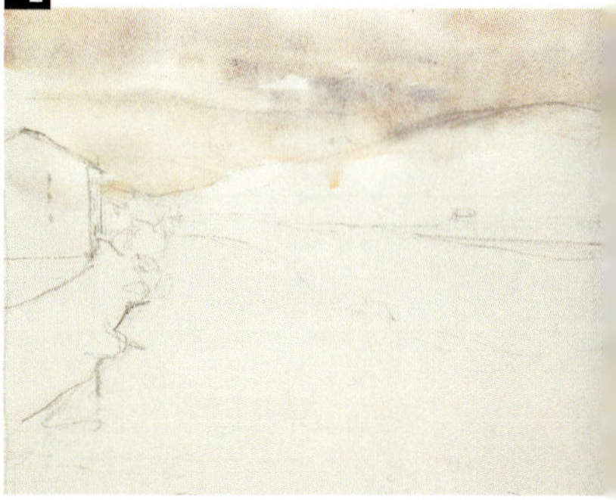

1 As with all watercolors, we have to lay out the work with a pencil sketch and attach the paper to a backer with tape.

2 The first of the fields in a general color is the sky, with its vaporous quality and warm tones. A significant amount of water is first spread over the surface so that the paint thins on the paper.

3 Applying the color more intensely onto a very damp surface creates very ethereal washes and shadings.

4 The soft orange hues of the water are produced by mixing highly diluted yellow and red, and the purples of the sky by mixing red, violet, and yellow.

3

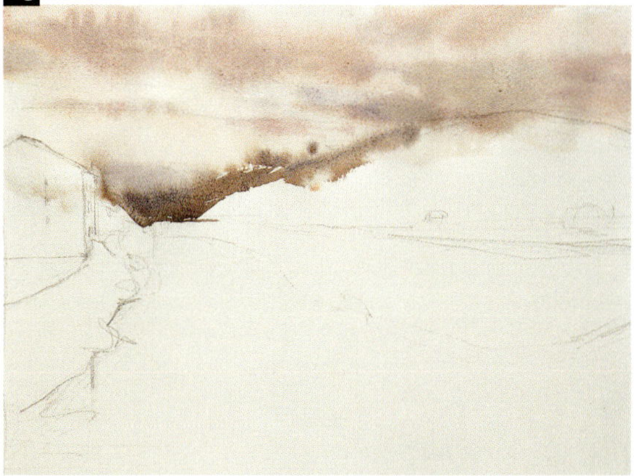

TECHNIQUES USED

◆ Preliminary sketch ◆
◆ Coloring ◆
◆ Washes ◆

4

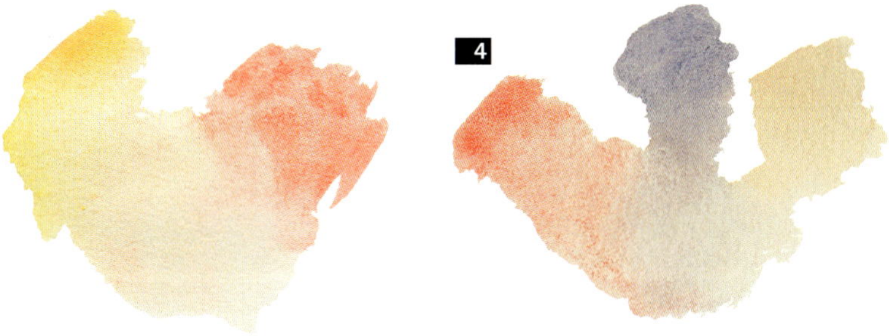

THE SUBDUED HUES OF HALF-LIGHT

Even though everything seems to be of the same color in half-light, that's not really the case. In a scene such as the one in this painting, if you pay attention and enjoy every corner, you can identify greenish, purple, brownish, bluish, orange, and even metallic grays. This is due to the effect of the light through the clouds and on the water in the waning hours of the day. In shading the grays, it's essential to work with neutralizations by mixing complementary colors. If this were done with black, the result would be a gray but dirty watercolor with no chromatic vibrancy.

5

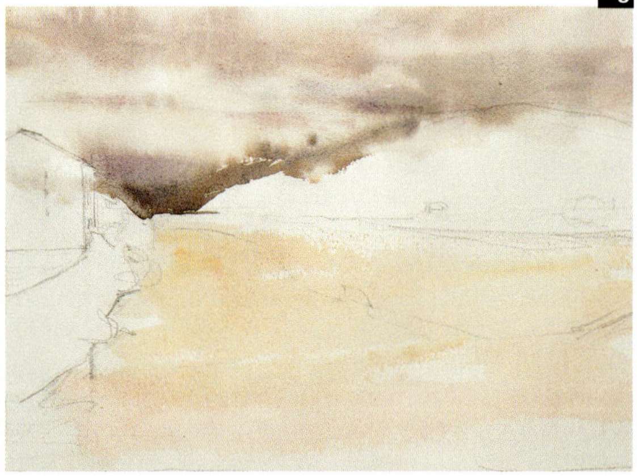

5 The second color field is the water, the real subject of this painting. As with the sky, the color is applied in a light, general, and very liquid shade.

6

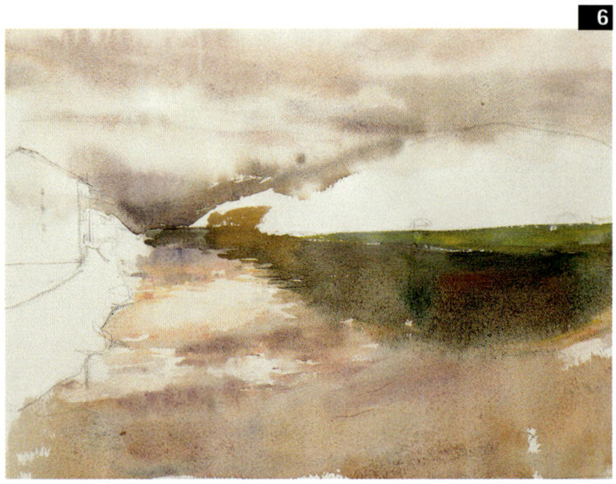

6 When darker colors are applied, they melt softly into the dampness of the colors underneath them. Having arrived at this point, we have to set aside the reserves for the reflections of light, making sure that we don't cover up these tiny sparkles with the brushstrokes.

7 In this stage we set up the area of the left bank of the river, first in fairly light shades, since there is always time to darken them, but it's impossible to go in the other direction. The mixtures of color can be done on the palette or on the paper itself if you are working wet on wet, quickly and with plenty of water.

8 In order to produce the special attenuated colors of this landscape, browns, purples, and deep greens, we have to work with mixtures of complementary colors (green and red) or with adjacent complements (violet and orange).

7

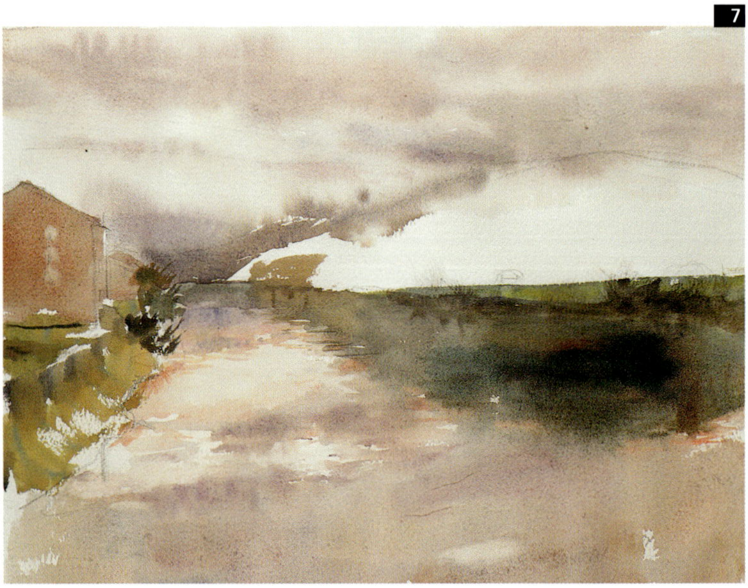

8

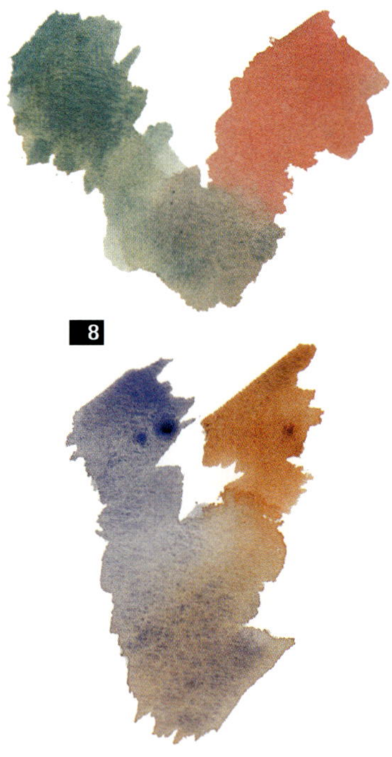

The Pictorial Atmosphere

In order to create the pictorial atmosphere of a landscape like this one, we need a general color to unify the whole. In this case, we can speak of a certain purple color that is present in a convincing way in the sky and the water, the two major subjects of the painting, but also indirectly, in the brown colors in the rest of the composition. A second factor that arises here is that there is great thematic unity: this is a landscape in a warm color scale, for even the greens are warm due to their brownish appearance. A light that is not white, but rather of an ivory hue, blends perfectly into this wonderful harmony.

9

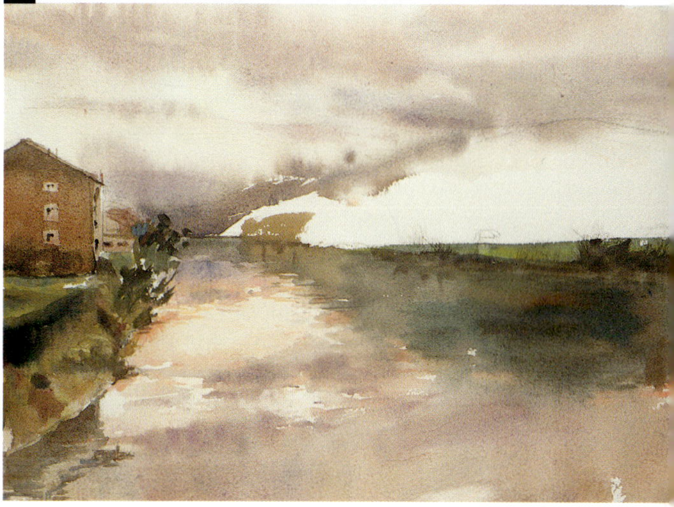

9 The details of the left bank are produced by introducing several values of light, and that creates volume.

10 In laying out the entire watercolor, the only remaining step is to cover the last large area of the landscape, the right bank. Proceed in the same way, using a light, moist base.

11 The mountain on this bank is depicted with darker areas in greenish hues by creating velaturas.

12 The dark brown shades are created by darkening the brown, earthy colors with blue, in this case, Prussian blue.

10

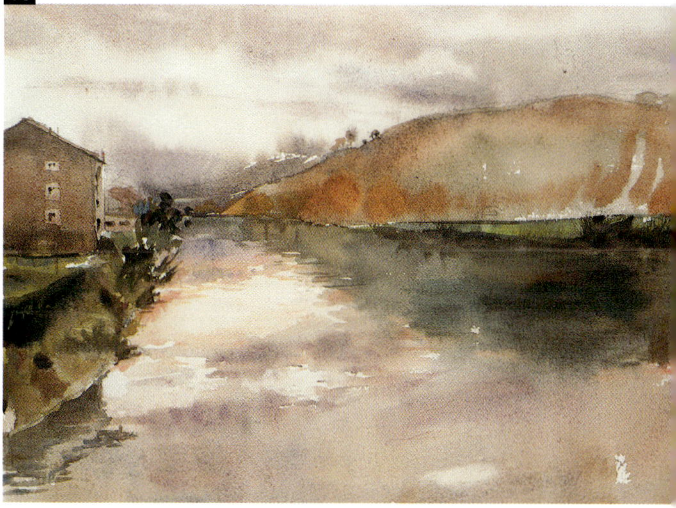

11

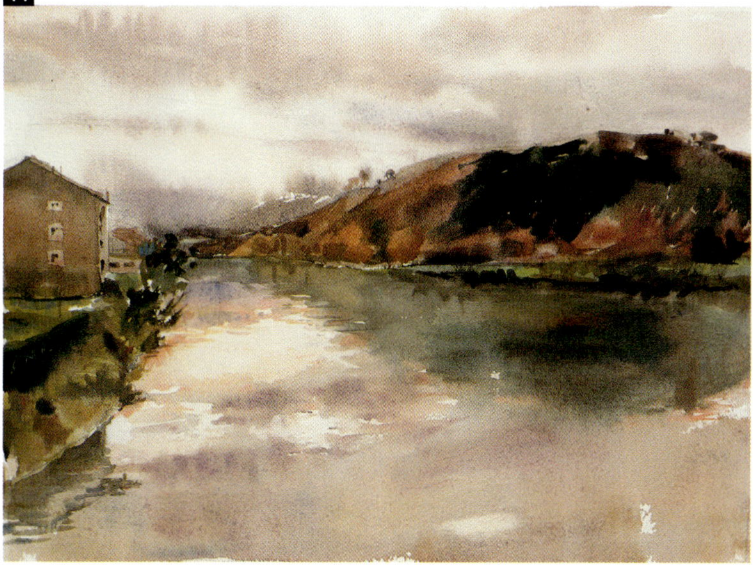

12

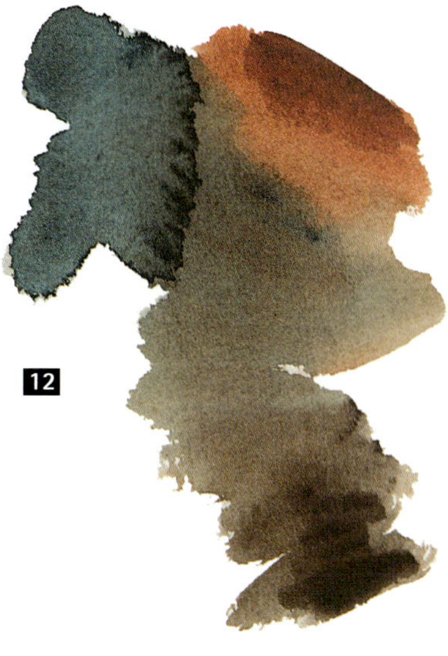

CHROMATIC VIBRANCY

When every color is foreseeable (green fields, blue sky, white clouds, white houses, etc.) it's like a movie that lets you know right at the beginning what the plot is and what the ending will be. In these cases, the result is stereotypical and mediocre, or it lacks life, or is boring or insipid. To avoid this awful effect, we have to work with vibrancy and contrast; the work needs to contain some surprises. The logical color for a feature may contain other colors that are not so logical, like reflections or shades of the same brushstroke.

WASHES AND REFLECTIONS

Washes are used to create effects of depth in water, working wet on wet and letting the colors dilute on the paper. For effects of reflection on the surface, leave reserves in white, or depending on the prevailing light, in some other luminous color.

13

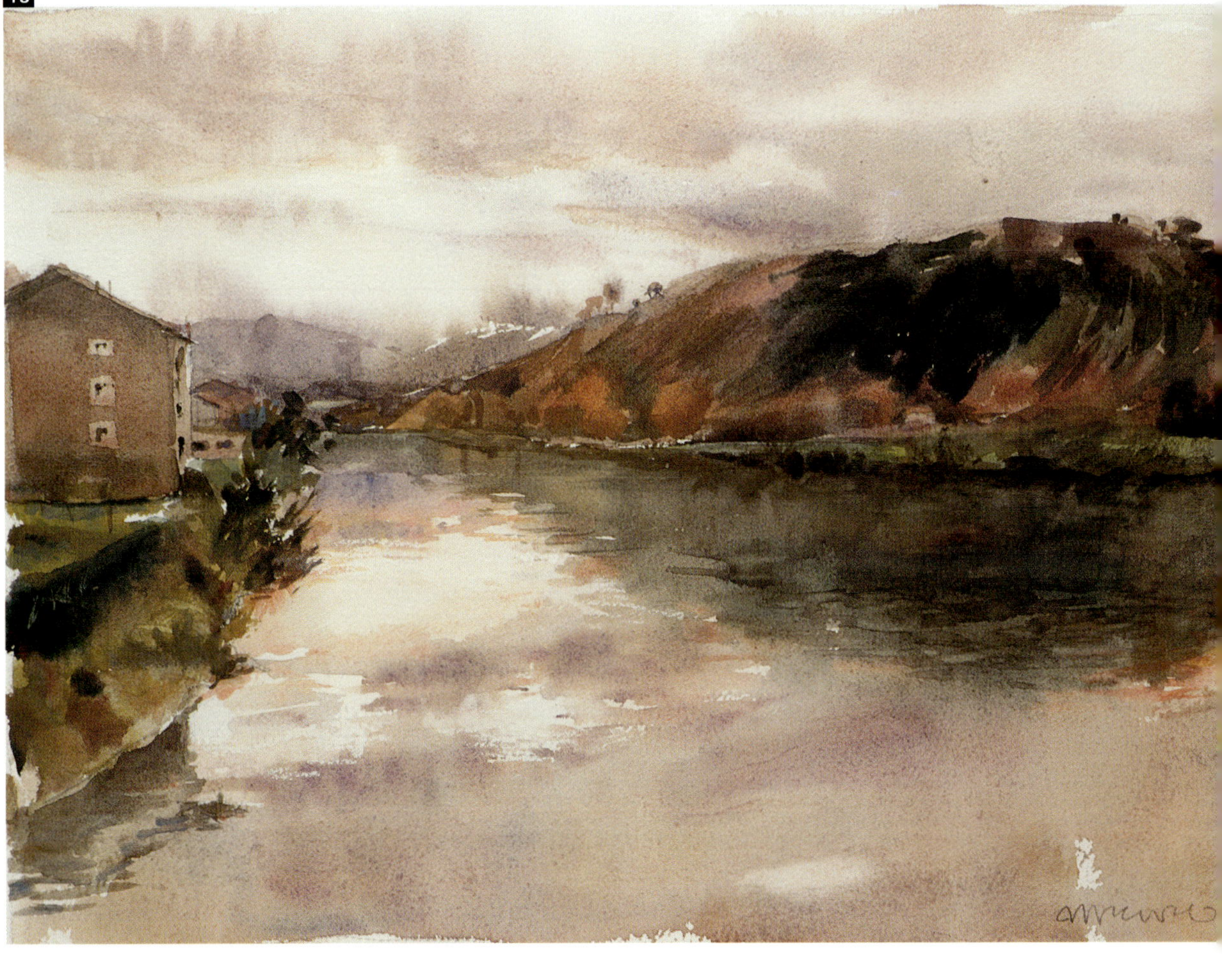

13 The only things not yet resolved were the reflections on the water in the darkest area, the shadow of the mountain. Now the final result of the watercolor is this excellent combination of washes, reserves, and velaturas.

Light in an Urban Landscape

In the following landscape we will get into the sculptural expression of light in an urban setting, which is somewhat removed from an ocean or mountain landscape. When light floods a rural or marine landscape, it defines it on the basis of textures and contrasts, according to the laws of aerial perspective. However, when light defines the features of an urban landscape, it does so based on the variations in the colors of the many planes of the buildings and the interplay of the volumetric chiaroscuro of lights and shadows, both on the objects and projected by them. In the next exercise, the artist Josep Asunción works with a different technique than in the previous ones: artist's inks. Inks are very well adapted to the type of light that prevails in a city, since they make it possible to create hazes and atmosphere, and at the same time, they allow for corrections using bleach, which is useful in creating reflections with a clearly artificial accent.

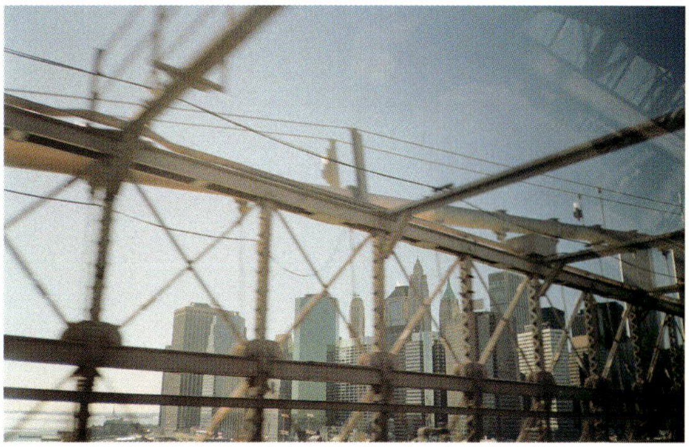

To capture an urban view as dynamic as this one, we have used a photographic model. In the upper left corner of the image, a clear feeling of movement can be appreciated, because the photograph was taken from a moving vehicle crossing a bridge and going toward the city.

MATERIALS
- Smooth paper for watercolors
- Artist's inks
- Round-tipped ox-hair brushes
- Sponge and rag
- Bleach

1 Linear perspective is applied to the first lines of the preliminary sketch, locating the vanishing points on the right for the lateral structure of the bridge, and toward the left for the upper part. The uprights exhibit a slight convergence toward the top, and they get closer together as they approach the vanishing point on the right.

2 From the basic perspective it's possible to trace the remaining features, seeking the proper proportions. This drawing was done with a nib.

1

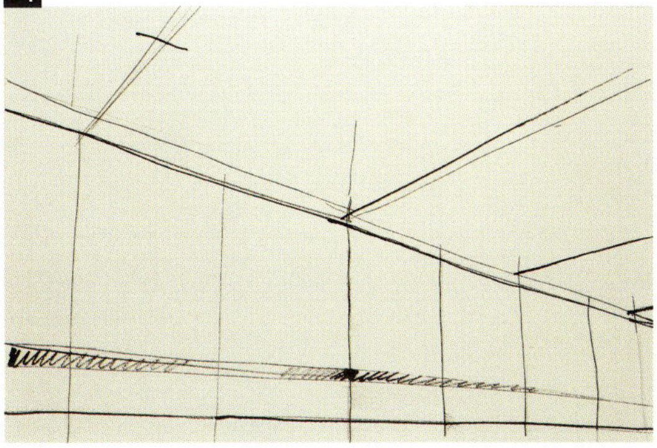

2

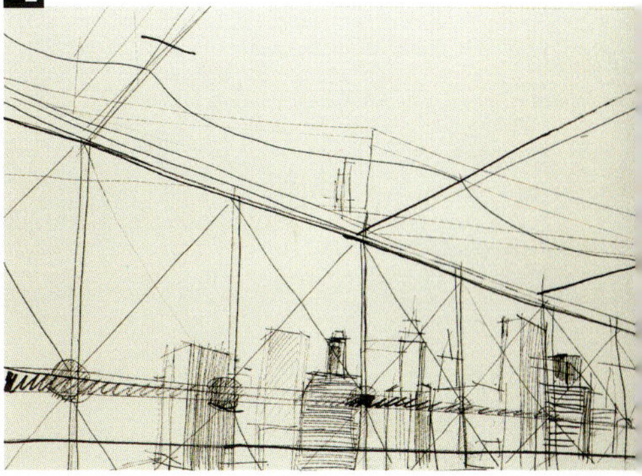

3 In carefully going over the drawing with a damp brush, the ink has been made to run around the lines. This is a characteristic effect of drawings done in ink. In this initial phase many drawings already possess a special charm.

TECHNIQUES USED

◆ Preliminary sketch ◆
◆ Lining with a nib ◆
◆ Coloring with brush and sponge ◆
◆ Wash ◆
◆ Lightening with bleach ◆

3

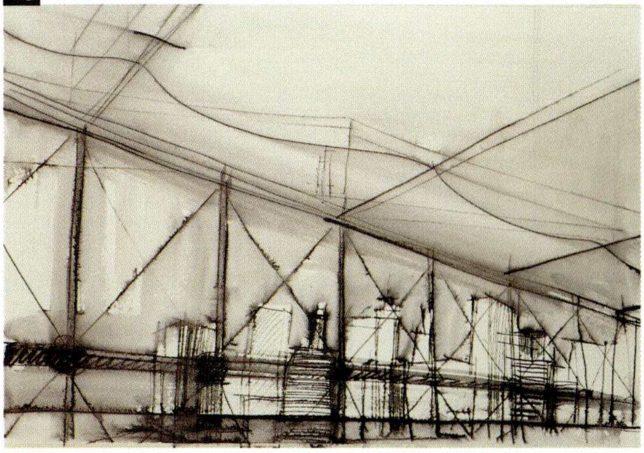

DENSE ATMOSPHERE AND LIGHT

In a city, haze intervenes like an environmental filter that, depending on the degree of pollution, can cancel out the light entirely and produce a dense, thick atmosphere. The pictorial representation of haze is achieved through general velaturas that unify the colors. If these velaturas are not total, but concentrated in the lowest areas of the city or up to a certain height in the sky, the sensation of pollution is heightened. Haze softens the contrasts and neutralizes colors; as a result, it's usual to work in subdued colors when painting urban scenes.

4

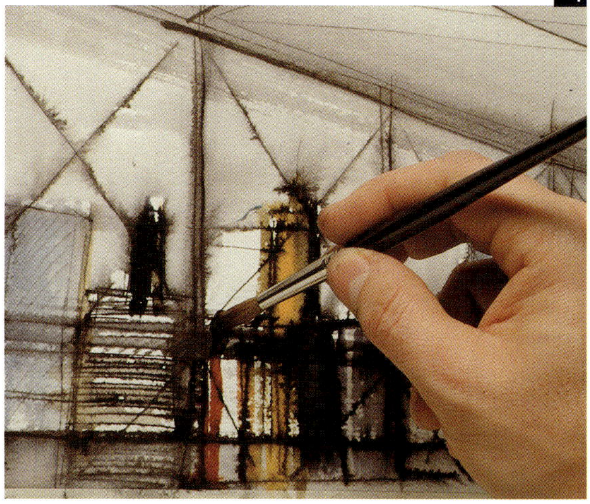

4 The first touches of color in the city buildings are applied with a brush after the ink on the lines is dry, to keep the black from running too much.

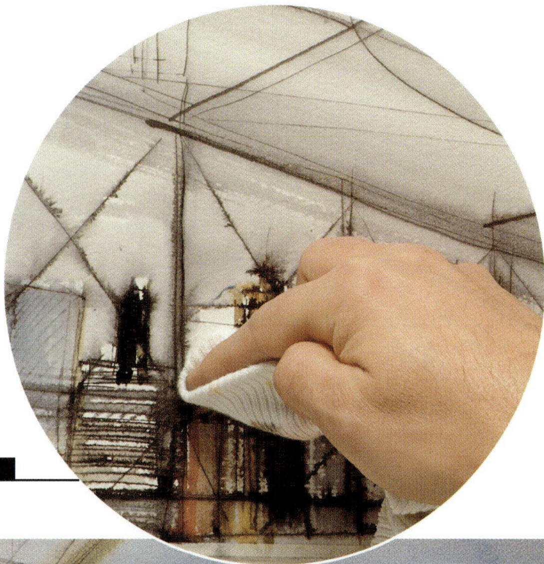

5

6

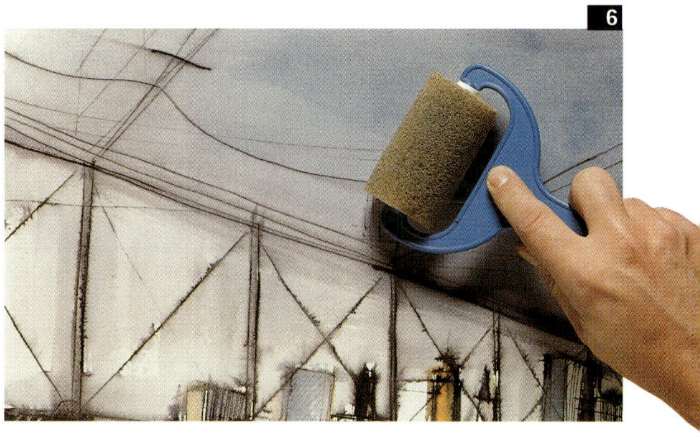

7

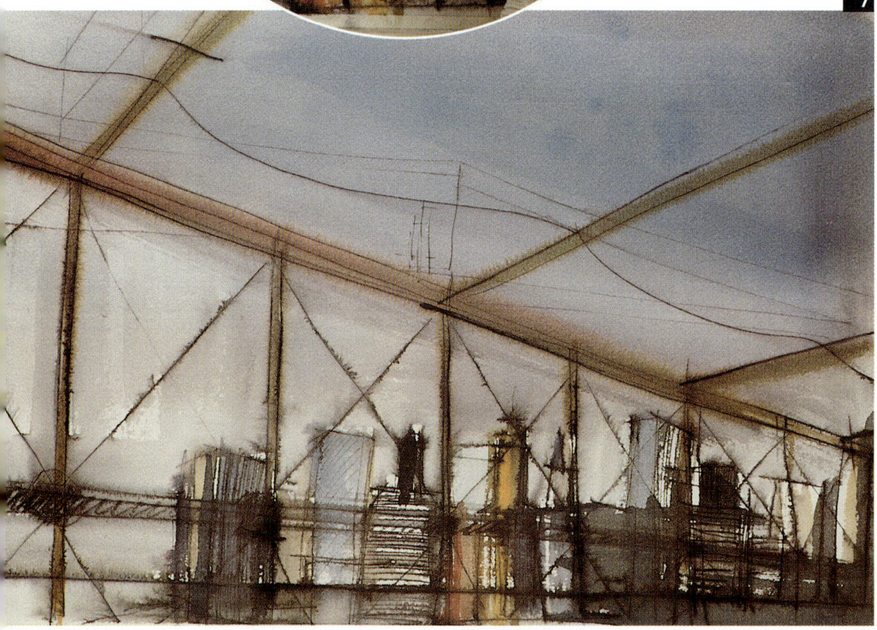

5 When there is too much color in any given area, you can remove part of the ink with a dry rag or paper towel.

6 To fill in large areas with color so that the brushstrokes are not visible, a sponge is used in spreading out the color uniformly.

7 At this point the work is nearly finished. The colors simply need a little more adjustment to create more atmosphere, and a few elements need more detailing.

8

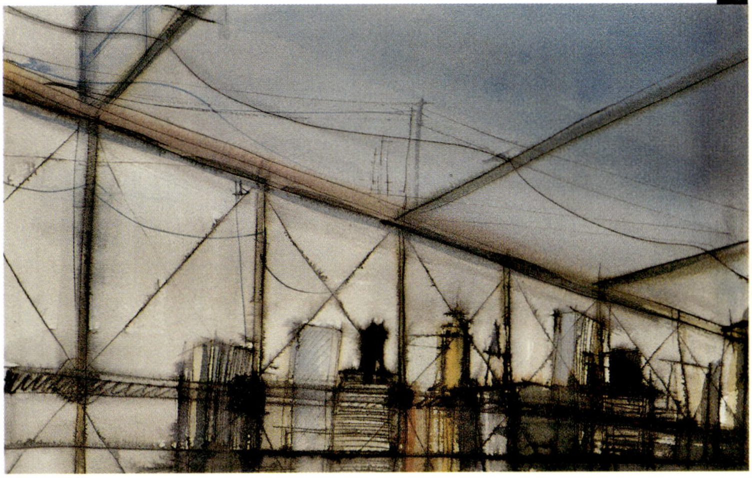

USING BLEACH

The chemical composition of most inks is such that they can be erased by applying bleach. Depending on the concentration of the bleach in the water, the color will either be erased entirely or change shade. Bleach also oxidizes the color of some stylographic inks, but it has no effect at all on India ink.

8 In order to create a heightened sense of atmosphere, the sky and the buildings have been finished off with no areas left white. Since the general chromatic hue is very purple, and everything looks darkened, the bleach will be used to lighten certain areas and create more light.

9

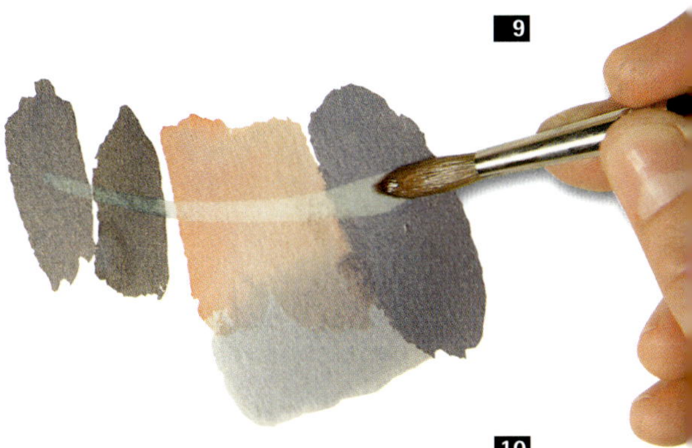

9 Bleach thinned with water lightens the color without removing it.

10 Once the bleach has been applied, the white areas reappear. The blue has also been lightened, and the sky has become more luminous. If bleach is applied over ink colors, light lines appear that suggest interesting reflections.

10

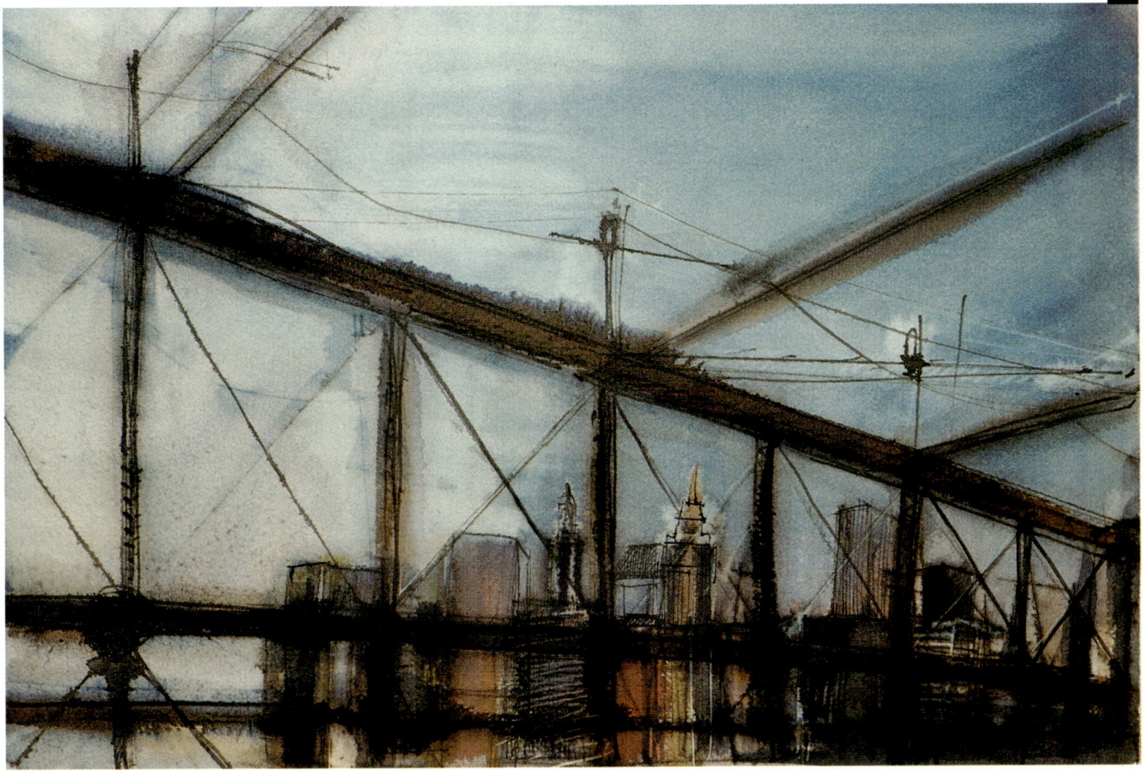

A Triptych Using Mixed Techniques

The last of the projects in this book is done by the author, Josep Asunción; it takes us farther away from the model and involves subjective interpretation of a theme. It consists of a triptych based on a landscape feature such as aquatic flowers. Gardens are considered landscapes even though they are fenced in or limited by their borders and arrangements. When Monet did an interpretation on the theme of water flowers in his pond, similar to the present instance, he worked on the basis of a personal and subjective impression, with no attempt to copy, but rather to re-create pictorially an aesthetic impression. This is the attitude that the artist has attempted to follow, taking inspiration from the great impressionist master.

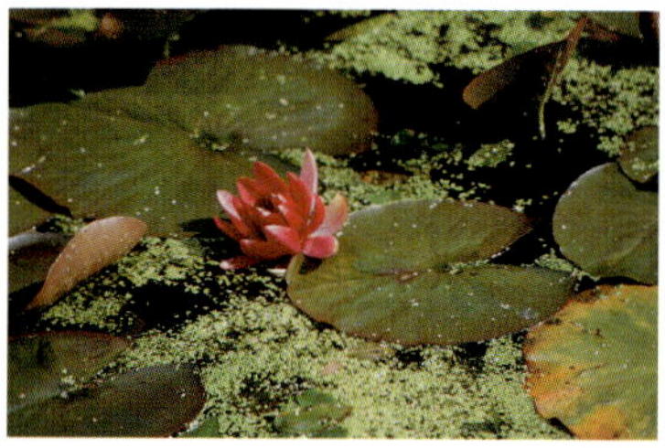

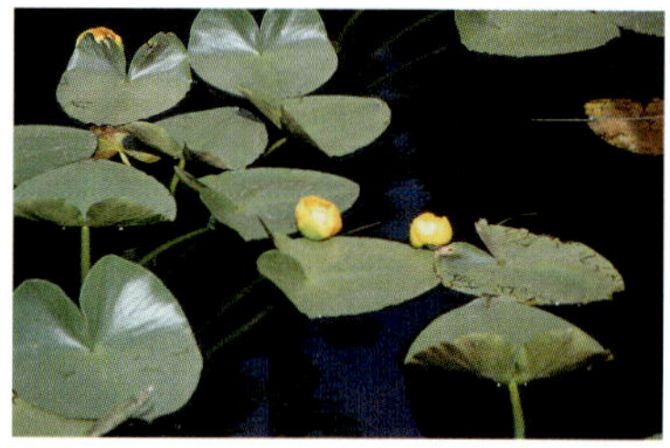

The models that will be used are two different aquatic plants. The first step involves making photocopies so they can be transferred to the support.

TECHNIQUES USED

◆ Transfers of photocopies ◆
◆ Coloring with acrylic washes ◆
◆ Erasing with rags ◆
◆ Brushstrokes in acrylics ◆
◆ Lines done in colored crayons ◆
◆ Spatters and drips ◆

1

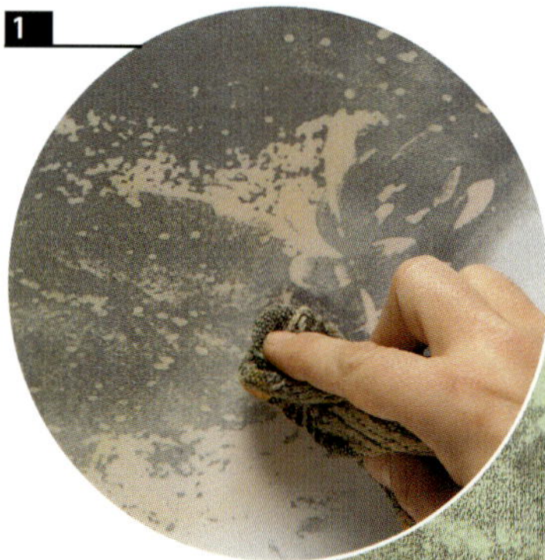

2A

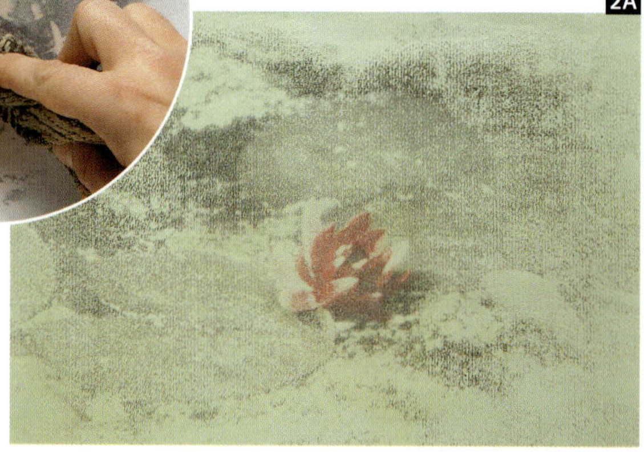

MATERIALS

- Colored card stock
- Photocopies
- Universal solvent
- Acrylic paints
- Assorted artist's brushes
- Rags and sponges
- Colored wax crayons

1 In order to transfer the images photocopied on paper, rub the back of the photocopy with a solvent. In doing this transfer, the direction of the image is reversed, as in a mirror.

2B

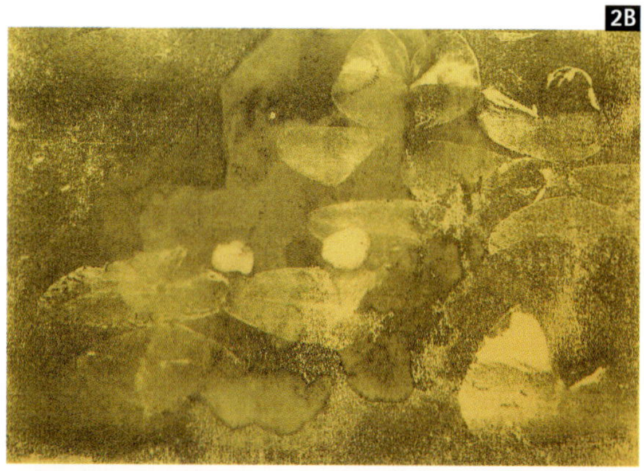

2C

2A The first of the transfers is a color copy on pale green card stock. Color copies are more difficult to transfer than others.

2B The second transfer is done on yellow card stock using a black and white copy.

2C The last transfer is also from a black and white copy, onto a deep orange sheet of card stock. This completes the layout of the three elements of the triptych.

TRANSFERS

Transfers involve the application of images to paper or canvas. You rub the back of the photocopied or printed image from newspapers or magazines using universal solvent or trichloroethylene in such a way that the front adheres to the support beneath it.

3A

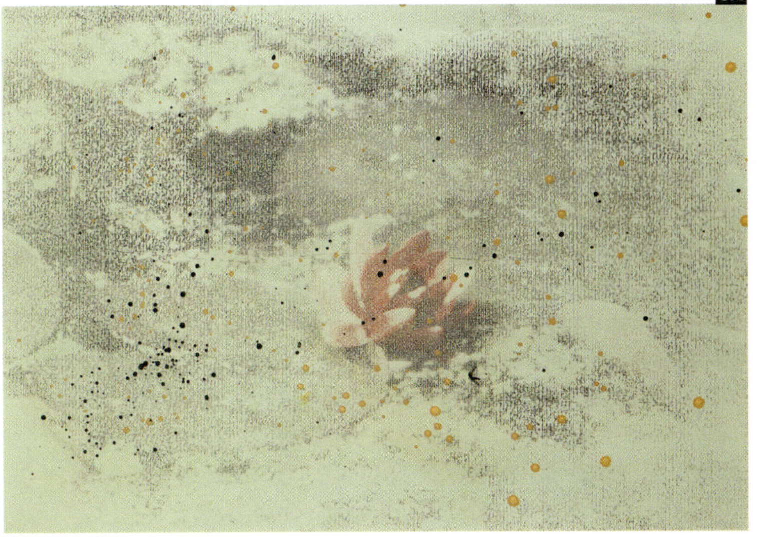

3A In the first of the photos, paint of several colors has been spattered by striking a loaded brush against the handle of another brush held at a certain distance from the support. This dotting increases the liquid sensation of the subject and makes it possible to make random additions.

3B

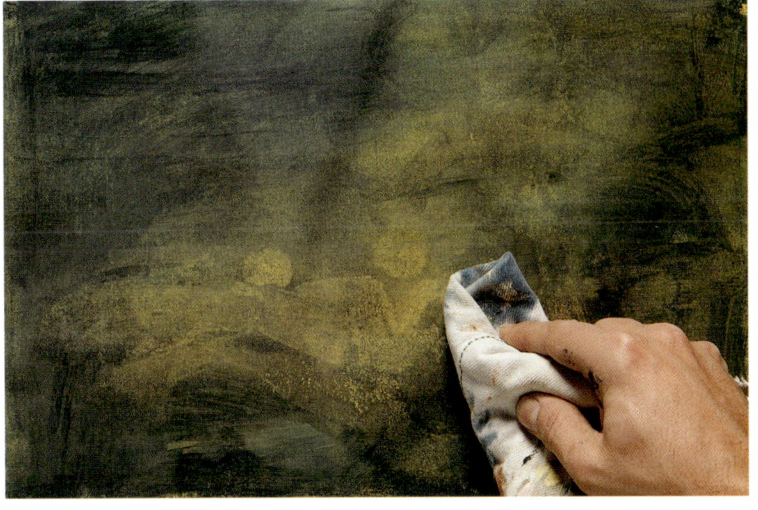

3B A large wash of diluted acrylic in a dark greenish shade is applied to the yellow base, and before it dries some of the green is absorbed with a rag to uncover the yellow. This technique creates a great sense of atmosphere.

3C

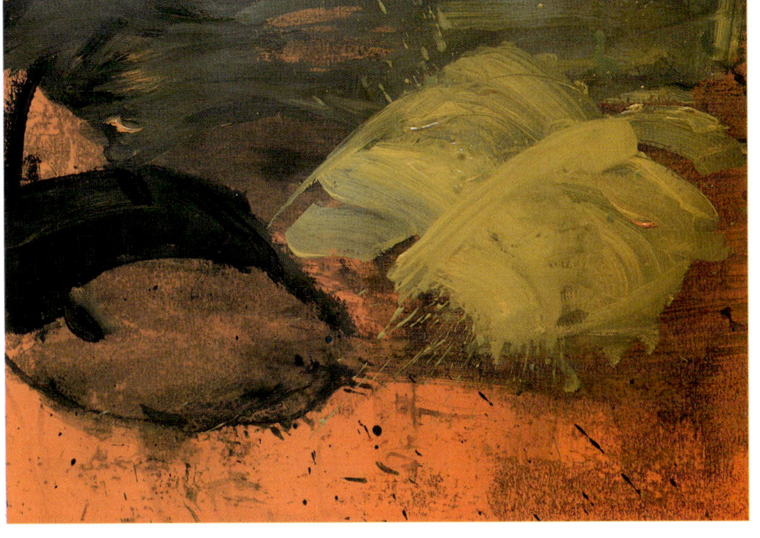

3C The artist has chosen to add to the orange base with quite a lot of paint on a brush to create spatters and fairly viscous impressions.

ERASE, SPATTER, AND PAINT

We have to understand painting as a reversible and ductile process in which erasing is not merely a technique for corrections, but also one more creative tool for the image. There is an analogous case with randomness and chance: spatters, drips, and splashes can be intentionally integrated into this iconographic process with all their sculptural value.

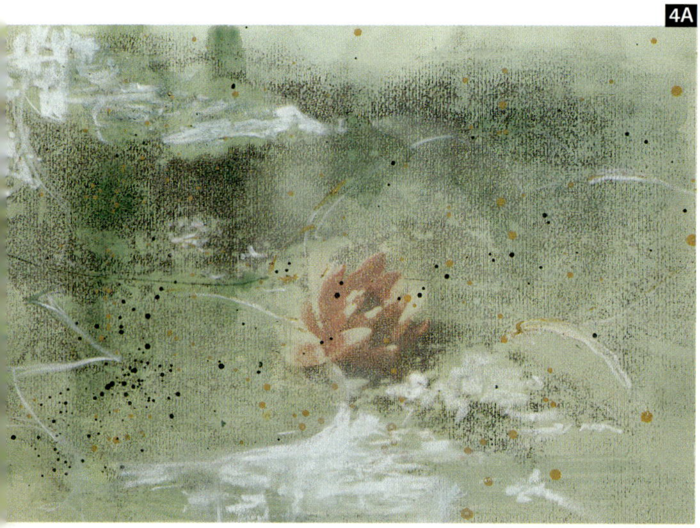

ADVANCING THE THREE PAINTINGS AT THE SAME TIME

A triptych is not an assembly of three pictures, but rather a single picture made up of three combined images (like the frames of a comic strip). Even though each image of the picture is distinct, all three have something in common, a nexus that clearly relates them to one another; this nexus is commonly both thematic and formal at the same time. In painting a triptych, a diptych, or other many-paneled work the painting is done with consideration for each part individually and also with respect to the others, so all parts have to progress at the same pace.

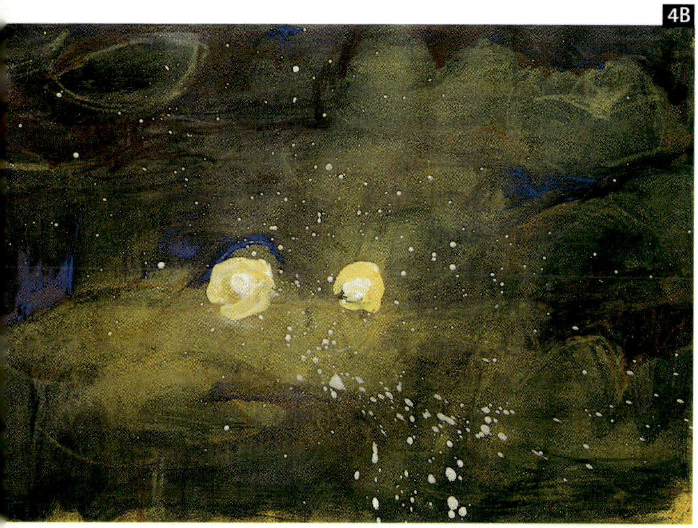

4A Some lines in white done with a wax crayon restore the outline of the leaves on the water and contribute a touch of light. The drawing is not done in clear detail, but rather insinuated.

4B To create great vibrancy on the dark background, the two flowers of the model are reinstated using vigorous brushstrokes and spattering in white and yellow. Suddenly the painting takes on life.

4C In the orange work the flower has been drawn to bring back this basic feature in a very pictorial way in the following step.

THE FLOWER IS THE BORDER

The flower is the most concrete feature of this work. In the interpretation of the scene if the flower is distorted too much or disappears, we lose the only descriptive element that helps us to identify the subject, and we will have crossed the border that divides representation from abstraction. This is the artist's decision. In this case, we have chosen not to cross that border, even though we come close to it.

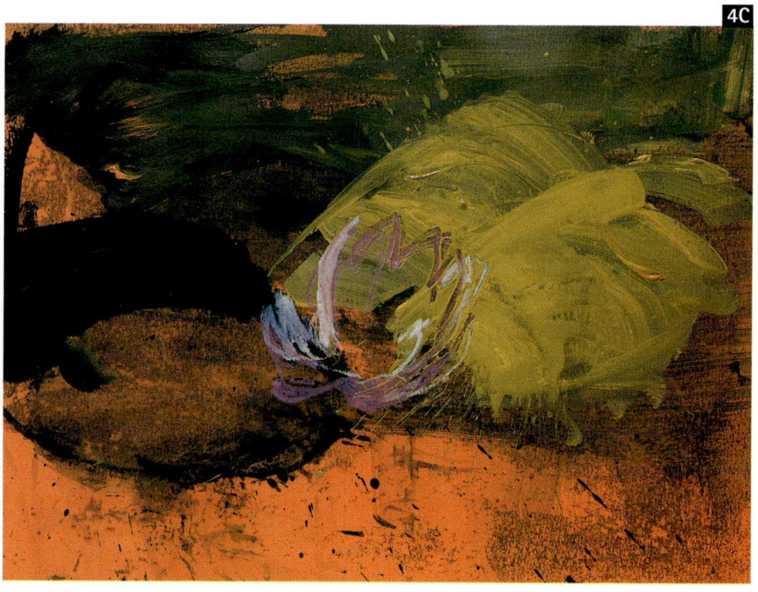

Finding a Personal Interpretation of the Subject

It's not easy to find a personal and unique vision of reality. It's easier to learn to do an accurate representation of visual reality, since that involves only technique, and all techniques can be learned through will and proper methodology. Subjectivity is more complex, and it requires a healthy measure of bravery and liberty to experiment to the point of recognizing the elements you identify with in the results obtained during your search process. In looking at a painting, a certain color palette, type of line, composition, texture, and theme make it possible to associate it clearly with one artist and no other. This is what is popularly known as style. These traits are picked up through years and practice, and especially by following the magical formula that brings together in perfect harmony two decisive attitudes: reflection and daring.

5A

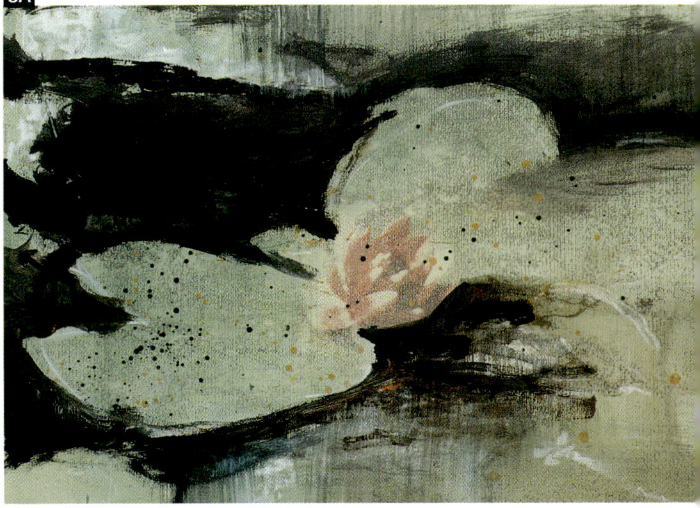

5A In this sequence, we will begin improving the relationship among the images by introducing a common color into each of them: a very dark brown that will provide depth to the water and increase the luminous contrast of the flower. The leaves of the plants will also be detailed further.

5B

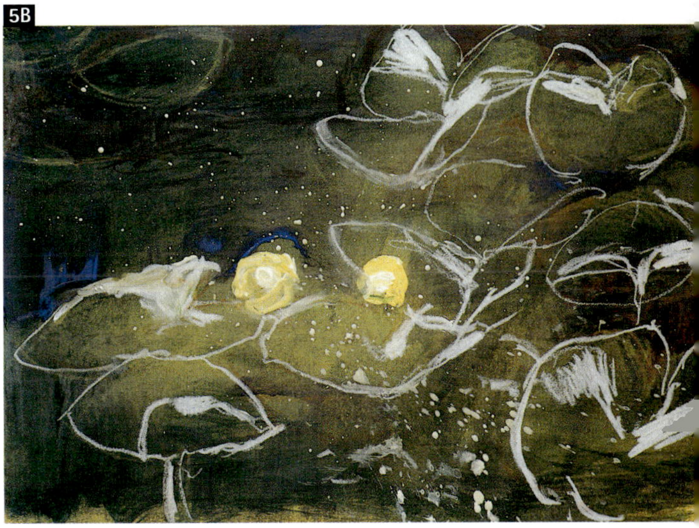

5B In the second image, the leaves are outlined with a white wax crayon, highlighting the expressiveness of the lines. Clearly there are no divisions between drawing and painting, for the image is developed in a global way.

5C

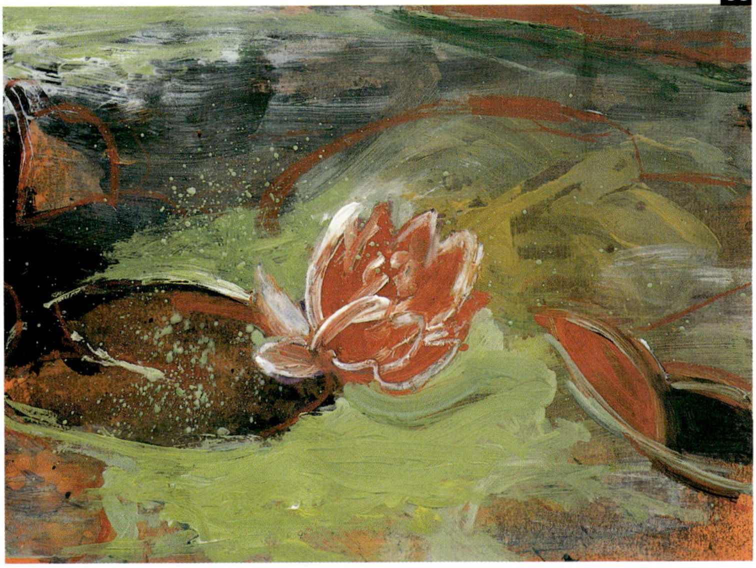

5C A lighter green has been selected for the third image to bring it closer to the first one. The flower is also worked on.

OBJECTIVE AND SUBJECTIVE IMPRESSIONS

Every artist has a different perception of the same reality. Even photographers have a different vision before the same scene, applying different lighting and framing. One might say that there is no such thing as a totally objective vision, and that it is always subjective in one way or another, for people interpret to some degree what they see.

COMBINING RESOURCES

In the end result, the triptych is a perfect summary of combined resources and mixed techniques: transfers, acrylics, and wax crayons used to create an atmosphere, lines, colors, spatters, and impastos. As with languages, the more vocabulary you know the easier communication becomes.

6

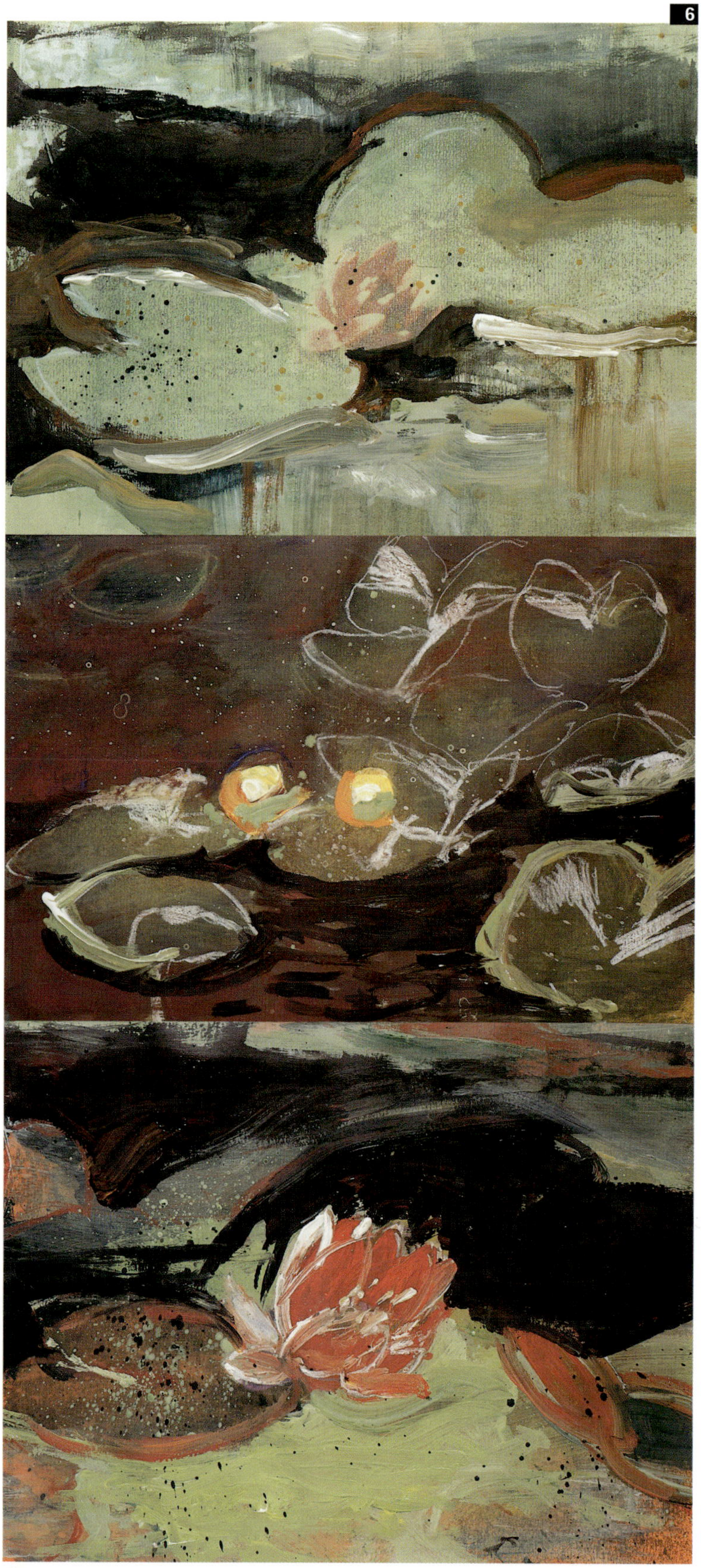

6 Here is the finished triptych. We can see that some colors that are repeated in the three panels of the picture, as well as white touches of light and the compositional structure, help us to perceive unity as well as diversity. This is the basis for the work's rhythm and dynamism.

Other Books from the Publisher on Light and Color

If you want to deepen your knowledge of light and color you will find all kinds of practical applications of the techniques studied in this book in the following titles:

Collections and titles

Art Handbooks:
- *Inks and Washes*
- *Mixing Colors 1. Watercolors*
- *Mixing Colors 2. Oils*

All About Techniques:
- *All About Techniques in Color*
- *All About Techniques in Drawing*

Painter's Corner:
- *The Human Figure*
- *Oils*
- *Watercolor*

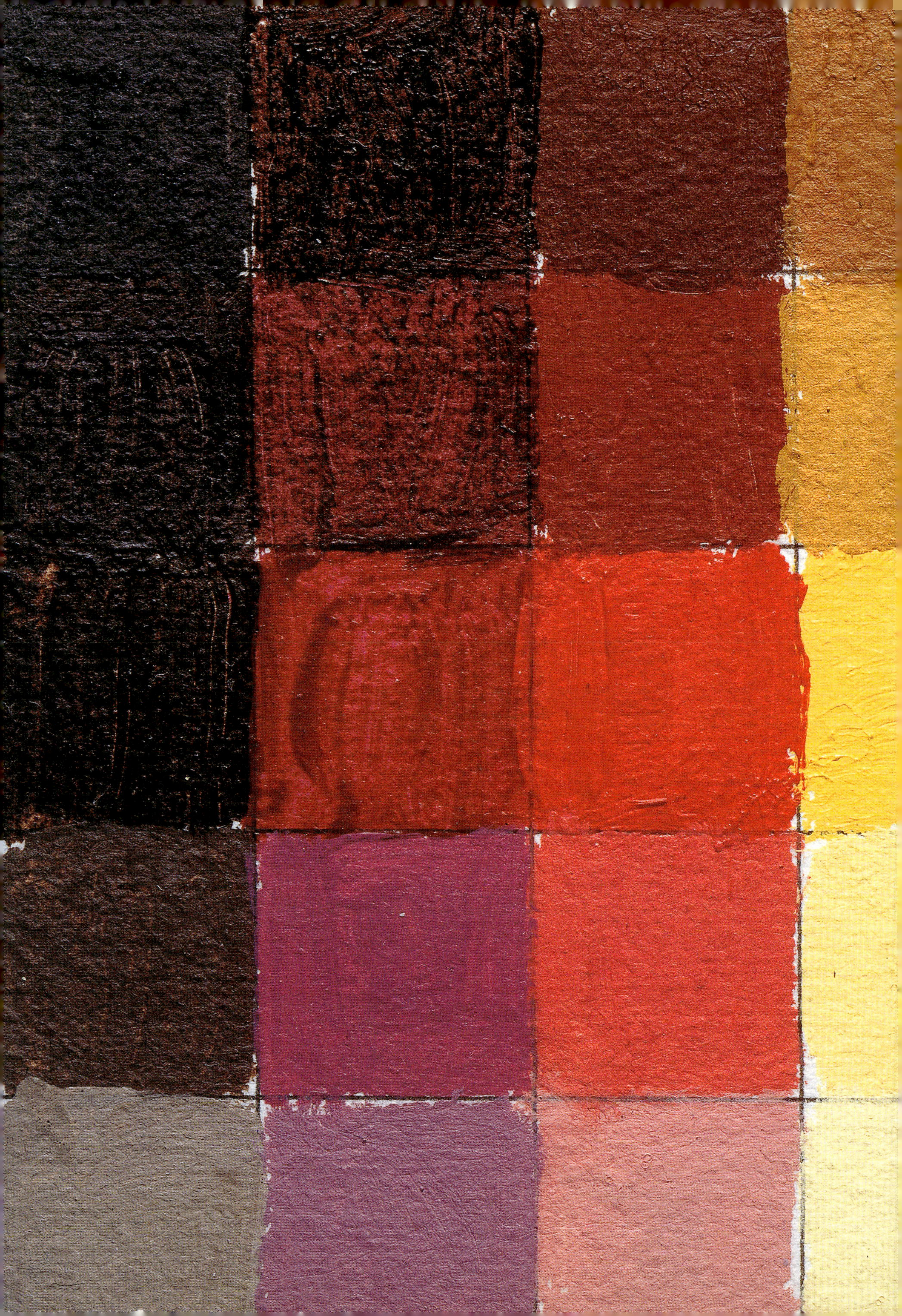